THE CALIFORNIA TRAIL

Yesterday and Today

A Pictorial Journey Along
the California Trail

THE CALIFORNIA TRAIL

YESTERDAY AND TODAY

A PICTORIAL JOURNEY
ALONG THE CALIFORNIA TRAIL

WILLIAM E. HILL

CAXTON PRESS
Caldwell, Idaho
2017

ISBN 978-087004-604-9

Library of Congress Cataloging-in-Publication Data

Names: Hill, William E., author.
Title: The California trail : yesterday and today / William E. Hill.
Description: Caldwell, Idaho : Caxton Press, 2017. | Revised from earlier
   edition published by Tamarack Books in 1993. | Includes bibliographical
   references and index.
Identifiers: LCCN 2016057948 (print) | LCCN 2017000854 (ebook) | ISBN
   9780870046049 (alk. paper) | ISBN 9780870046148
Subjects: LCSH: California National Historic Trail--History. | California
   National Historic Trail--History--Pictorial works. | West
   (U.S.)--Description and travel. | West (U.S.)--Pictorial works. | Overland
   journeys to the Pacific. | Overland journeys to the Pacific--Pictorial
   works. | West (U.S.)--Guidebooks.
Classification: LCC F593 .H55 2017 (print) | LCC F593 (ebook) | DDC
   917.804--dc23
LC record available at https://lccn.loc.gov/2016057948

Lithographed and bound in the United States of America

CAXTON PRESS
Caldwell, Idaho
194642

DEDICATION

To those who have gone before
To those met along the way
and those yet to follow

WILLIAM E. HILL

TABLE OF CONTENTS

FOREWORD

The California Gold rush was an epic event, a sudden and irradiating explosion of energy by the American people. Before 1849 the bold democratic experiment — something unique in the annals of mankind — had been largely confined to lands east of the Mississippi River; the lands west thereof were generally understood to be hostile and uninhabitable. Acquisition of California, after the war with Mexico, caused no stampede. What caused it was the electrifying news of gold at Sutter's Mill, and the resultant gold fever that afflicted over two million Americans.

To reach distant California roughly half of these adventurers went by sea, either around Cape Horn or via land links across Panama or Mexico. The other half traveled by land. There was just one land route that had the virtue of being centrally located and heading straight west — the great Platte River Road that led to South Pass, providential gateway through the Rocky Mountain barrier. While the seafarers also helped to populate California, the overland emigrants with their ox- or mule-powered covered wagons preformed the additional feat of breaking the wilderness barrier, thus making possible the transformation of the United States into a truly transcontinental Union.

William Hill's book is about these landlubbers argonauts and their incredible two thousand mile journey from jumping-off points along the Missouri River, across the dangerous wilderness of prairies, plains, deserts, and mountains to their ultimate destination, California. His book is designed for casual readers who would be content with a bird's-eye view of the overland experience, with samplings from the rich source materials. He has his facts commendably straight and recommends other authoritative books for those inspired to explore the subject in greater depth. Of exceptional interest are selected contemporary maps and the illustrations of three rare and gifted trail artists. The author himself supplies excellent photographs of trail scenes today, taken on field trips to retrace the route to California and relive in imagination the golden odyssey of the Forty-niners.

The California Trail Yesterday and Today is a timely and welcome addition to a rapidly growing body of literature, both popular and scholarly, on a subject of perennial fascination. For all our revolutionary technical advances that compress time and space — so that we might, for example, travel from Missouri to California in three hours instead of the several months it took in 1849 — we still stand in awe of the pioneers who, with nothing but faith, courage, and primitive technology, blazed the trails and laid the foundations of modern America.

Merrill J. Mattes
Littleton, Colorado

PREFACE

California has lured people for more than one hundred seventy five years. For some its appeal has been a place to start a new life and to raise a family, while for others it has afforded a place to make or find a fortune for themselves or to bring back to their families. For me, the lure hasn't been California itself, but the route to California and learning about the problems and dangers that those early dreamers and adventurers faced and experienced as they traveled west.

I can remember, as a boy standing in front of a sign by the road describing the discarded items, the dead animals, and the terrible hardships experienced by those traversing the Forty Mile Desert and wondering how the emigrants ever made it across. Sometime around 1970, on a return trip from California, I came across another sign, probably different from the one I remembered as a boy, but still about the Forty Mile Desert. Reading it helped rekindle my interest in the western trails and in the emigrants that travelled them even more.

I was a history teacher at the time and had a professional interest in learning about the California Trail and the westward movement. But, I also had my personal curiosity, and those two factors became the motivating forces behind my undertaking of many journeys along the various trails since that early trip. I hoped that I could come to understand not only the hardships endured, but also the reasons for their going and the feelings those early emigrants and gold seeking "Argonauts" experienced as they traveled west. I realized that I would have to follow their journey if I really wanted to understand their story. That meant I would have to find and follow their trails.

For almost twenty years before this book was first published I had spent much of my spare time reading the diaries and journals of emigrants and the various guidebooks available to them as the years passed and the trails developed. I had also spent many hours searching for and examining the drawings, sketches, paintings and early photographs made by the emigrants or others who followed the trails and recorded them. Parts of my summers were then spent locating the specific sites that were mentioned or drawn by the emigrants in their diaries or journals. I hoped that by finding, photographing and writing about them I would not only better understand the emigrants and their journey, but I would, in my own way, help to preserve a record of their experiences so they would be available to others in the future. This new edition adds even more information and emigrant illustrations than the former one. Many sites have been newly located and identified. Rarely have so many trail illustrations been included in a single work on the trail.

In recent years two very important movements have occurred that have helped to save our trails west for future generations. First is the formation of new organizations to identify and preserve the trails. One of the more recent organizations is the Oregon-California Trails Association (OCTA), P.O. Box 1019, 524 S. Osage St., Independence, MO 64051-0519. OCTA's major goals are the identification, preservation, marking, and improved interpretation of the emigrant trails and related historic sites. When originally formed in 1982, its focus was on the Oregon and then California trails, but it is now also concerned with the many other emigrant western trails as well. This organization is proving to be an effective and educational organization attracting the attention and participation of both interested laymen and trail scholars alike. Its members have successfully identified and marked large sections of the trails and numerous sites while working with private individuals, businesses, local, state, and federal governments and agencies. It has also helped to protect sections of the trails from being destroyed by new roads, pipelines, mining interests, agricultural expansion and urban encroachment. While not all places can be saved, this organization has worked to minimize the negative impact of these developments on our historic resources. It does so by working with other entities and concerned interests to seek alternatives.

Other earlier groups include Trails West, Inc. and the Nevada Emigrant Trails Marking Committee of the Nevada Historical Society. Both are dedicated to identifying and preserving the old trails, and they have done an outstanding job. Other organizations similar to OCTA exist and are focused on different historic trails, such as the Santa Fe, Old Spanish, Mormon, Lewis and Clark and Pony Express trails and have similar goals in the identification, preservation, and interpretation of those trails. All are worthy organizations and are especially helpful for those interested in traveling the routes.

The other important development has been the renewed interest by the local, state and federal governments in protecting our heritage. Congress has expanded the National Historic Trails System so that it now includes the Oregon, California, Santa Fe, Mormon, Lewis and Clark and Pony Express trails. It has also expanded the designations to include not just the main route, but many of the feeders, cutoffs, and alternates. Thus, the federal government is committed through specific legislation to expand and recognize the importance and preservation of these old highways, as well as the few forts and landmarks already preserved by the Department of the Interior and the National Park Service. In addition to the fine work being done by the National Park Service, the Bureau of Land Management (BLM) and the USDA, the Forest Service has also taken on a more active role in identifying, interpreting and preserving the historic trails on the lands under their jurisdictions.

State governments and local governments are also actively participating in preservation. Even local citizens are working together to protect and promote their local historical sites. The greater Kansas City area can be considered a blueprint for areas and communities wishing to invest in and develop their historic resources. A number of historic trails are associated within the area.

Various local organizations, governmental departments, including those from adjacent areas are working together with the assistance of the state and national agencies to save both their shared and individual history, and to develop them for the economic, educational and recreational benefit of all citizens. Walking, hiking and biking paths are being constructed, and driving tours and guides are being developed. Interpretive signs and displays are being placed along about fifty continuous miles of the trails, and parks are being established as the historic sites are being preserved. It is truly a model of cooperation and coordination.

For future tourists and scholars of the west, these two developments will help preserve for them the way west that our earlier ancestors and countrymen took. Furthermore, in the years ahead it will now be easier for many travelers to understand and experience something of what the trek was like.

This book will introduce you to the California Trail and the emigrant experience. Other books go into much greater detail about specific events and individuals who explored and opened the way, but this one will let you "sample" the trail—to be introduced, to read about, to see and feel the way west was through the eyes and comments of the emigrants. Then you will be better able to hone in on your own particular interests.

In this popular song of the California emigrants and gold rush participants, there can be found quite a realistic description of the trek to California. The song was both humorous and serious, describing both the emigrants themselves and the hardships experienced on their two thousand mile journey to the "El Dorado," or for Betsey and Ike, "Hangtown," as Placerville was often called.

Oh don't you remember Sweet Betsey from Pike,
Who cross'd the big mountains with her lover Ike,
With two yoke of cattle, a large yellow dog,
A tall Shanghai rooster and one spotted hog.

Chorus:
Sing— too- ral- i, oo- ral- i, oo- ral- i- ay
Sing— too- ral- i, oo- ral- i, oo- ral- i- ay

They soon reached the desert, where Betsey gave out,
And down in the sand she lay rolling about:
While Ike, half-distracted, looked on with surprise,
Saying, "Betsey, get up, you'll get sand in your eyes."

Chorus

Their wagon broke down with a terrible crash,
And out on the prairie rolled all kinds of trash:
A few little baby clothes done up with care−
'Twas rather suspicious, though all on the square.

Chorus

The Shanghai ran off, and their cattle all died:
That morning the last piece of bacon was fried;
Poor Ike was discouraged, and Betsey got mad;

The dog drooped his tail and looked wondrously sad.

Chorus

Sweet Betsey got up in a great deal of pain,
Declared she'd go back to Pike County again;
But Ike gave a sigh and they fondly embraced,
And they travelled along with his arm around her waist.

Chorus

They suddenly stopped on a very high hill,
With wonder looked down upon old Placerville;
Ike sighed when he said, and cast his eyes down,
"Sweet Betsey, my darling, we've got to Hangtown."

Chorus

Between 1841 and 1860 about 200,000 emigrants trod the trail to California. They were hardy individuals with a dream of a better life, a spirit of adventure, and a drive for preservation. They were resourceful when they needed to be and thankful when their trek was over.

Their journey west was long and tiresome. The first half was usually the easiest, but the second half proved to be more difficult — there came the mountains, then the deserts, then more mountains, perhaps the snow, and finally, their goal, California! First would come the sun and heat, then the sand and lack of water, and then the rocks and precipitous climbs. For the late-coming emigrants or stragglers, it could also be the lack of sufficient grass or the cold and winter snows. Breakdowns and the loss of materials, either by accident or by necessity to lighten their loads, caused many a hardship. With the exhaustion of food supplies and death of their animals, despair often set in, but if these issues could be weathered and they could overcome "seeing the elephant," their "El Dorado" would still be reached.

This book is a brief history of the early California Trail and a pictorial journey along it through the eyes and pens of the early emigrants along with photographs of the corresponding sites today.

Come join the author and "Betsey and Ike" on a journey west like you've never taken before!

ACKNOWLEDGMENTS

As with any other work, many people have helped by providing encouraging words, suggestions and critical reviews, directions and information on the trail, and by cooperating at various libraries and historical societies. While all are thanked and could easily be noted, recognition must be given to those special few who most deserve it because they best represent all those who assisted.

Over the years I encountered many ranchers and almost all allowed me to walk around or drive through their properties. Many like the Stevensons, the Suns, and the Bucks, however, took not just minutes, but hours and parts of working days to talk about local history, the trail, its location, artifacts, or anything they thought might be either useful or interesting. They even allowed my family to stay or camp on their ranches.

While some libraries and photographic divisions could use better coordination, the staffs of most libraries and historical societies were very cooperative. Looking back over the years their dedication to their work and willingness to assist make all of them invaluable to researchers and authors. There are just too many to list. However, one of the earlier ones of note, Linda Wickert, the Fine Arts Curator at the California Historical Society, was very helpful and went the "extra mile" when she easily could have done otherwise.

Sometimes it takes a chain of referrals to track down an item. Most recently, Martha Grenzeback at the Omaha Public Library and Mary Carpenter at Council Bluffs Public Library were the persons at the end of the chain. Each had their own holdings checked and then took the time to locate an item even though it wasn't in their holdings. Also, many long time park superintendents, such as Wayne Brandt at Rock Creek Station, Duane Durst at the Hollenberg Ranch, Eugene Hunt at Fort Kearny , and Jerry Banta at Scotts Bluff, should be singled out for their pride in their work and cooperation when providing me access and information. Now, all save Eugene, have since retired or taken other positions, but their counterparts have that same caring and dedication.

On a personal level, certain individuals gave me that extra spark of encouragement. Helen Henderson's simple but encouraging words, "Do it!" when I was hesitant and first thinking about writing about the emigrant trails, provided the boost I needed to get started. My parents, brothers, and sisters' constant inquiries about my progress kept me going. My father, Frederick W. Hill, and my son, Will, at times, were my partners while driving along many of the desolate sections of the trails. They provided someone to talk with, to test out ideas, and to help as needed. And, I always say, Will grew up bouncing over tail ruts and even learned to drive on the Black Rock Desert.

Since the book was first published I have been lucky to be able to revisit the old sites, to continue seeing old acquaintances, some of whom have retired, to meet the new generation of individuals who were only kids on some of the ranches when I began, and to meet the new owners, the new park directors, the staff at museums, visitor centers and shops, and the many librarians and archivists, especially those at Yale and more recently, those at McKendree University. Unfortunately, some individuals have moved away and a number have passed away. As before, almost all, old and new, have been very gracious. The Bucks and Rennells always have time, as well as a room for us. Jolene and Rich Kaufman and Arlene Earnst have seen many changes in Scotts Bluff and Douglas, but have always welcomed us and they have always had time to "bend an ear."

A few years ago we returned to a site near Torrington and met the Nichals, the recent owners, and their hospitality matched that of the previous owners. It is also good to see that members of the "younger" generation of ranch families such as the Fitzhughs have the same pride in "holding and caring" for the trail as their parents did. Many of these folks including the Suns have taken time out of their busy schedules and work to welcome us again and to talk about the sites and changes that have occurred. Recently, owners such as the Duncans and the Careys took the time to show us new trail items or sites and invited us back again the next time we come through the area.

With some "old timers" we have even reminisced about my first appearance and how they stopped their work to speak to me. Jokingly, the Lancasters who have since moved, even wondered why they ever stopped their work to show me around, but were glad they did. The pride of the Christensons, owners of a new campground by the old ferry crossing in Glenrock, Wyoming, which has great historical significance, will help ensure that this trail location will remain for future generations to enjoy. These are but a few of the friends met along the trail who have helped us out. My wife, Jan, became a "willing" convert to the trails, and she has been my prime reviewer and trail companion since 1987. My father passed away more than a decade ago. My son, Will is now a grown man with a family. Recently he and his family joined us along part of the California Trail in Nevada and California. Perhaps his children will also be lucky enough to be brought up bouncing over trail ruts, and their children too!

Chapter One

INTRODUCTION

The best analogy to use when thinking of a trail, and especially the California Trail, is to compare its likeness to a rope. It is braided, loosely at times and tighter at others. It is longer than it would be if pulled straight between two points, the Missouri River and the Pacific. It meanders and wiggles and becomes looser over the years. And, it is frayed at both ends and more so as it ages until it finally unravels and falls into disuse and is replaced.

The route to California and the California Trail are not synonymous. The route refers to a more general area or areas that were used. The focus of the discussion in this book will be the main overland wagon trail that developed over the northern route through the area of the Central Plains, South Pass, Great Basin and over the Sierras. It left from various towns along the Missouri River and followed the route up the Platte River.

There were also other routes and ways used by emigrants to get to California. These were the central, southern, and sea routes, and they will be discussed briefly. First, however, let's examine the general route of the main California Trail. The eastern half of the trail coincided with that of what is generally known as the Oregon Trail. Its origins were the various "jumping-off" or embarking places along the Missouri River. Over the years the major embarking areas changed. Beginning in 1841 it was Independence, Missouri, but soon towns such as Weston and St. Joseph, Missouri, Old Fort Kearny/Nebraska City, Nebraska and Kanesville/Council Bluffs, Iowa, became major centers. There were also a number of other minor areas.

The name of a particular route used by the trappers, traders and emigrants was usually derived from the town of origin – such as the

Independence Road, the Council Bluff Road or the St. Joseph Road. Sometimes sections were named for a particular person who developed it or was associated with it, such as Sublette's Trace, the Greenwood or Sublette's Cutoff, or Hudspeth's Cutoff. When an area or route was heavily used by a group it could also be known by the name of the group. The trail from Council Bluffs following the north side of the Platte River is also known as the Mormon Trail or Road. This is true today even though its first use was by trappers, the first emigrants who used it were bound for California, and the majority of those using the Council Bluffs area were non-Mormons. Also, other towns, including Independence, were used by both the Mormons and others.

The trails from all the various jumping-off towns that developed on the Missouri River combined to form one main braid east of Fort Kearny near Grand Island in Nebraska. Here, at the confluence of the routes, the emigrants traveled on both sides of the Platte River. The braid loosens a little at the junction of the North and South Platte rivers, but tightens again along the North Platte heading towards Fort Laramie where the north side travelers crossed to the south side but still followed the North Platte. Soon another route developed which allowed the emigrants to remain on the north side and closely follow the river. West of present day Casper, Wyoming the rope's strands tightens along the Sweetwater River as it approaches the South Pass. Now the rope loosens more and more over the years as it passes through western Wyoming, northern Utah and southeastern Idaho into Nevada. By the time it reaches the Humboldt the strands tighten again as it crosses the Great Basin, but then slowly over the years become frayed as it crosses the Sierra Nevada as the travelers headed towards their individual destinations in many of the newly discovered goldfields.

Many emigrants used other routes besides those described above. Some, using the main trail to Salt Lake City, turned southward from there. In 1849 a southern route from Salt Lake City was developed. It followed the roads down the Mormon Corridor to where it intercepted the Old Spanish Trail near Cedar City in southwestern Utah. The Old Spanish Trail had originated in Santa Fe as a commercial route to connect with Los Angeles. It made a loop to the north or northwest before turning southwest towards that city. The Old Spanish Trail was originally a pack trail. Emigrants to California needed a wagon route, and improvements were made to accommodate them or parallel trails developed. William Henry Jackson, who is mentioned later in this book, took this route to Los Angeles, California and returned over it in 1867. Some emigrants tried a new cutoff from the Salt Lake-Los Angeles Road and went through an area that came to be called "Death Valley," so named because of all the suffering that faced the travelers there. Another route that took emigrants to California emerged later. It was over what has been called the Central Route. It will be mentioned again briefly in the history chapter. This route was developed in the late 1850s by Captain James H. Simpson of the Topographical Engineers. He had been ordered to survey a wagon road across the Great Basin between Camp Floyd and Genoa, Nevada. He completed it in 1859 and emigrants began using it almost immediately. It was soon used by the Overland Stage and also by the short-lived Pony Express. Like the other California routes this too changed a little over time.

Some emigrants took the Santa Fe Trail out of Independence and continued on after it was joined by the Cherokee Trail which had come from Salina, Oklahoma. When the Cherokee Trail turned off in Colorado some wagon companies followed it and then crossed southern Wyoming until it met the main trail in the Green River area. Others starting on the Santa Fe Trail went all the way to Santa Fe and then continued west on the Gila River route and entered into Southern California. Still others started their journeys to California over what are now called the Southern Routes. Many left from Arkansas and Texas and places such as Fort Smith and Galveston. Only in recent years have these routes been getting the scholarly attention that they deserve. As more is known about them the emigration statistics may be affected.

The statistics on the following page were taken from John Unruh's *The Plains Across*, University of Illinois Press, show the number of emigrants by year that came to California by the overland route.

Based on these statistics, it seems that about two hundred thousand emigrants went overland to California. Another one hundred thousand went to Oregon and Utah during this twenty year period.

In addition to the overland routes, there were still other ways of traveling to California, which during some years proved to be more popular with the emigrants and Argonauts. These were the sea routes. By booking passage on a sailing ship or steamer one of several routes

California Emigrants by Year

Year	Count	Year	Count
1841	34	1851	1,100
1842	0	1852	50,000
1843	38	1853	20,000
1844	53	1854	12,000
1845	260	1855	1,500
1846	1,500	1856	8,000
1847	450	1857	4,000
1848	400	1858	6,000
1849	25,000	1859	17,000
1850	44,000	1860	9,000

could be used. The most popular was the all-water route around Cape Horn. The distance was about thirteen thousand nautical miles. The others went by water, but with land crossings of Panama, Nicaragua, or Mexico.

Of these, the longest but quickest, the Panama route, had been used by the Spanish merchants and navy since colonial days to travel to California. The relatively short Isthmus of Panama land crossing has been considered the most hazardous when compared to the Mexican & Nicaraguan routes.(Ball:5) However, it was the U.S. interest in California, and then the discovery of gold that brought about the fuller development of these routes, especially the Panama route. Even though the Panama route was the fastest, the route around the Horn was the most popular in 1849. The customhouse recorded that 15,597 people arrived in San Francisco via the Horn while 6,489 people came via the Isthmus crossing of Panama. (Jackson, D: 94)

Because of the popularity of the sea routes with many of the California Argonauts during the gold rush era, a brief examination and comparison of them with the overland routes with their some of their respective problems will be reviewed.

The emigrants who used the sea routes as compared to those who used the overland route tended to come from different areas and socio-economic groups. Generally sea passage expenses were significantly higher than those associated with overland travel. The cost per passenger started at about $150.00 per person, but averaged about $300 or more for the trip around Cape Horn.(Johnson,W.: 53) The total cost for a trip by way of Panama was about $455.00. (Street: 53) During the gold rush tickets were frequently sold by "scalpers" for three times as much or more, and they were readily purchased. Tickets for steerage that may have started at $100.00 and cabins that sold for $200.00 and $250.00 were sold for four times as much or more. (Jackson, D.:113) The cost included not only the passage, but also the food during the voyage. Since the cost was significantly higher, the sea route tended to be used by wealthier people such as doctors, lawyers, businessmen, and other professionals. The passengers also tended to come from the coastal and urban areas, especially the northeast with New York City as the main port. For the average rural family, the total cost was prohibitive, yet, occasionally a single person might use it.

The overland route was generally taken by the interior or rural inhabitants. The cost per capita tended to be lower. The many single men who went overland during the gold rush frequently signed with a wagon company and paid from $50.00 to $150.00 depending on the work arrangements made with the leader. The typical farm family averaged between four to six people and traveled by wagon. Many had their own wagons.

It is a little more difficult to figure costs for the overland route, but by using various guidebooks, a good basis can be found. Depending on the specific type and number of draft animals used—oxen, mules, or horses — approximate total costs can be determined. Ware's 1849 guidebook figured the total cost of an outfit - wagon, teams, equipment and supplies at $600.00 for a four yoke ox team and $670.78 for a 3 span mule team. (Ware: 12-13) Street's 1851 guidebook listed the estimated total expenses at $522.16 for an outfit of five yoke of oxen, wagon, equipment and supplies and about $300.00 additional for a six mule team outfit. (Street: 55) Marcy's 1859 guidebook listed $200.00 for an eight-ox team and $600.00 for a six mule team plus supplies. (Marcy: 28) Horse outfits cost even more.

The wagon itself was a small farm or spring wagon, not those large Conestoga often seen in movies today. It cost from $80.00 to $85.00, and with cover or canvas might cost almost $100.00 (Street: 12).Thus, by using the average number per family and the cost of the wagon and team outfit, the approximate cost of transport was between $100.00 and $200.00 per person. However, since many of the early emigrants were farmers, they already possessed the wagons and draft animals which decreased their costs even further. Those emigrants who still had some stock and their wagon when they arrived in California could reduce their net cost in half or even more if their wagon and stock could be sold.

Each year as more and more improvements were made along the trail miscellaneous expenses tended to increase. More ferries and bridges were constructed. In some places a toll might even be charged for a particular stretch of the trail that was improved. Typical charges for ferries and bridges averaged from $3.00 to $6.00 per wagon. For some small bridges the charge was only twenty-five cents per wagon, while the most expensive was recorded at $16.00 at one Green River ferry in Wyoming. One emigrant put his extra expenses at $75.00, but suggested a family bring $150.00 to be sure.

There were perhaps three major advantages for traveling by ship. First, they could leave at just about any time of the year as long as voyages were scheduled. The most difficult part of the passage was usually rounding the Horn, and it could be especially difficult if the trip occurred during the Southern Hemisphere's winter months of July and August. The overland emigrants were severely restricted for travel timewise. They could only leave in late spring when there was sufficient grass on the plains to support their livestock. If they left too early the prairie grasses might not have grown sufficiently to feed the animals. If they left too late, the grass might already have been overgrazed by the earlier departing companies. Also, if they left too late or traveled too slowly they chanced getting caught in the snows in the Sierra Nevada as the Donner party did. Therefore, most wagon companies left within four to six weeks of each other from April to May. As a result they were rarely out of contact or sight of another wagon company, especially during the years of high emigration.

The second advantage of going by sea was that the emigrants could carry more supplies and equipment if they desired and wished to pay for its passage. It was the only way to get the large and heavy mining equipment to the Pacific west coast. It could not be hauled over the mountains.

The equipment overland emigrants could take was limited by the size of their wagon and the number of people sharing it. The average number of people per wagon was four, depending on the year of emigration. Most of the early emigrants brought only one wagon and were very lucky if they still had it when they arrived in California. Once it was clearly established that wagons could safely get over the mountains, emigrant families in the early to mid-1850s often took a second or perhaps third vehicle. Other factors that also played significant roles were the preplanning, the strength and health of their draft animals, and their ability to last the journey. Many an emigrant was forced to jettison some or all of their belongings before their trip was over. A reporter from a St. Louis newspaper at Fort Kearny wrote that "soon it was found that the loading was too great for the teams, and now overboard goes everything. The road is lined with various articles—even gold vases and gold washers." Farther west along the North Platte near Courthouse Rock Wilkins noted,

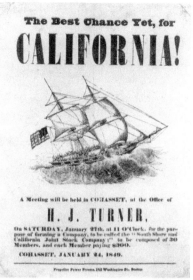

The Best Chance Yet, for

CALIFORNIA!

A Meeting will be held in COHASSET, at the Office of

H. J. TURNER,

On SATURDAY, January 27th, at 11 O'clock, for the purpose of forming a Company, to be called the "South Shore and California Joint Stock Company," to be composed of 30 Members, and each Member paying $300.

COHASSET, JANUARY 24, 1849.

Courtesy of the Bostonian Society
This is one of the posters extolling the virtues of both the ship and the voyage by sea to California and the gold fields.

"The road all along is strewed with old clothing boots provisions, particularly beans, I notice are left, and the wreck of wagons, as tho' a conquered army had passed over it." (Wilkins: 45) At Fort Laramie he wrote that "a great many parties abandoning their wagons at this point and take to mule packing…" (Wilkins: 47) Those who packed could carry even less than those with wagons. For those emigrants who kept their wagons, many would finally be abandoned on the deserts when their animals gave out.

There was a third advantage for those emigrants who decided to cross the Isthmus of Panama, and that was time. The trip at its fastest could take between one and two months, depending on the year the journey was made. In Street's guidebook of 1851, he listed the total approximate time as forty-five days by steamer. (Street: 53) It was the completion of the railroad across Panama by Wills Aspenwall in 1855 that drastically reduced the crossing time from days to a few hours. The record for the route by way of Panama was twenty-one days in 1855.

This chart shows the 1849 voyage of the ship *Apollo* which lasted about nine months. The voyage was about 1300 nautical miles. Each day's position was noted on the chart, and its progress or lack of it can be seen. The trip "around the Horn" was very popular with the forty-niners.

The 13,000 nautical mile trip around the Horn usually took a little less time than the overland journey. During the earlier years, the voyage ranged from four to eight months.(Johnson,W.:64) A few ships, like the *Apollo,* took as long as nine months while the earlier overland journeys took between six and ten months. The sailing record in 1849 was made by the *Greyhound,* one of the new clipper-type ships, which made the voyage in 112 days. The *Flying Cloud's* record trip was eighty-nine days from New York to San Francisco in 1851. (Jackson, J:162) In 1853 the *Northern Light* returned to New York from San Francisco in only seventy-six days. These were more the exception than the rule. By the early 1850s the average time for a clipper ship was about 132 days or a little over four months. (Ball: 30) In 1851 over 15,000 sea-going Argonauts took passage by way of the Isthmus. Few went around the Horn or used the other sea routes.

(Jackson, D.: 315) Yet, as improvements were made on the overland trails, travel became faster and faster. In a little more than a decade the time was nearly cut in half, and the sea routes lost some of their advantage.

However, there were many problems that faced the oceangoing argonauts. Some were similar to those experienced by the overland emigrants, but others were different.

Disease was one of the major problems that faced both the overland emigrants and those that went by sea. Cholera was the major killer on the California trail during the years, 1849, 1850, and 1852, taking an estimated two thousand lives each year. On June 10, 1849 a few days west of Fort Kearny, Wilkins wrote," A man from a small company of 4 wagons ...stated that three of his company had died that morn^g of Cholera, that they had previously buried four, and that he was the only well man left in the camp." (Wilkins: 42) On June 19, Wilkins noted, "Past a great many newly made graves to day, and find a great deal of sickness amongst the emigrants, almost in every company we pass. Diarrhea running into Cholera are the prevailing complaints." (Wilkins: 44)

Cholera was also contracted by those who traveled by ship. In 1849 people in Panama City were afflicted with it; it had come in with the gold seekers who then carried it to San Francisco. On his return voyage in July, 1852, Byron McKinstry noted thirteen deaths due to cholera occurred during the nine day trip from Panama to New York. (McKinstry: 380) The healthy people aboard could not keep separated from those with the disease nor avoid possibly contaminated stores or leave the ship while at sea. In 1855 one ship with 650 passengers lost 113 to cholera. Nevertheless, the disease never came close to killing the number of people aboard ship that it did on the overland route during the cholera outbreak's worst years. In fact, one estimate put the total deaths at around fifty for all the voyages for 1849, making it the safest way to California. (Jackson, D: 107) Many more may have died in the cities, such as Panama City, however.

Smallpox, a contagious disease, was feared as it was a killer of emigrants on both land and sea. On the *Grecian* the first death due to smallpox occurred during the second week out, and twelve recorded cases the next week, but after that there were no more recorded deaths. (Ball: 30-1) Fortunately, many people had been vaccinated at the time.

Courtesy, New York Historical Society

The map above shows the crossing of the Isthmus of Panama drawn by George Clark in 1850. The route involved boat travel up the Charges River and then overland by mule through the jungle to the Pacific and then to another ship. Before the completion of the railroad the difficult crossing took about five days.

Other diseases, such as yellow fever and malaria, were dangerous for those crossing the Isthmus of Panama. This was especially true before the completion of Aspenwald's railroad in 1855 which reduced the amount of time people were exposed to the dangers of the jungle. In 1851 J.D. Borthwick crossed Panama. Writing about the conditions in Panama City he recorded that, "There was here at this time a great deal of sickness, and absolute misery, among the Americans. Diarrhea and fever were the prevalent diseases. The deaths were very numerous…" (Borthwick: 30)

One unique malady of the seagoing emigrants was sea sickness, and it was the most common illness of all. It struck most passengers, usually at the outset of their journey. Borthwick noted, "The greater part of the passengers, being from the interior ... had never seen the ocean before, and a gale of wind….Those who were not too sick… were frightened out of their senses, and imaged that all manner of dreadful things were going to happen to the ship."(Borthwick: 4) In 1852 Charles Harvey's first diary entry stated that the ship sailed from New York with "loud Cheers" and "booming of cannons." The very next day, March 3, he noted that he "felt poorly eat very little…good many passengers sick." For March 4, "lay in my berth all day sick, eat nothing. Sea quite rough" Similar entries continued until finally on March 8 he wrote, "felt little better, eat little grewel for breakfast" (Ball:38) Even John Beach, son of the owner of the Ship *Apollo* suffered from it when only four days out of New York. (Johnson, W: 61) John Angell, sailing on the *Pacific,* was sick for twenty-seven consecutive days. (Jackson, D: 97). Isaac Baker noted during his voyage that some of the lady passengers who had become sick went on deck and sat behind a saw horse rigged with reins pretended they were riding in a horse drawn carriage. (Johnson, W.:59) The stench inside near their berths must have been terrible during the initial days or weeks, or during terrible storms. Although sea sickness was a major problem, it was not a cause of death. Fortunately, most people finally got accustomed to the normal rolling and pitching of the ship, and some even likened it to the rolling of a wagon on the open prairie.

For the emigrants traveling overland, perhaps the most similar situation was the stench emanating from the dead and decaying animals along the roadside. This situation tended not to occur at the beginning of their journey, but in later half when they entered the drier areas and deserts or were near alkali water. Many emigrants commented about the dead animals and the foul odor as noted later in the text.

Travelers either by land or by sea had additional concerns. Weather was a problem for all emigrants. On the sea, storms could increase the amount and severity of seasickness, but they could also be more troublesome. In 1852 the *Comet* was battered by a hurricane, and the *Grecian* lost her mizzen mast and fore topmast in another gale. In 1849, three weeks out of New York, the *Henry Lee* was severely damaged by a storm. Two of her masts were split and much of her canvas and rigging destroyed. It took twelve days to repair her masts and rigging. (Jackson, D: 94)

The storms at the Horn could cause delays. While a lucky ship might make the passage in a week, most ships took a month or more. (Jackson, D:103) This was the worst part of the journey. The *Henry Lee* took forty days to round it. Passengers on the *Pacific* often resorted to lashing themselves to their berths during bad weather. They were constantly soaked and hot food of any kind was impossible.(Jackson, D: 102) J.D. Borthwick said that during one gale that "boxes and chests of all sizes, besides casks of provisions and other ship's stores, which had got adrift, were cruising about promiscuously.... In the morning we found the cook's galley had fetched away, and the store rendered useless." (Borthwick:.5) Most overland emigrants threw out some of their supplies or belongings when they realized they had too much or later when their animals gave out. While similar events were rare on the sea, the captain of the *Osceola* was forced to jettison some of the passengers' cargo that had been stored on the deck. (Jackson, D.: 96)   That wasn't the only problem with winds and storms. Sometimes ships, such as the *Union* and *John A. Sutter,* ran aground. The occurrences could be worse still. In 1857 the ship *Central American* sank and about 400 passengers were lost. However, in 1849, none of the more than five hundred sailing vessels that left the East coast sank, all arrived in California. (Jackson, D: 94)

At other times ships were forced to wait for a "fair wind." Charles Harvey's entry for one day was, "Dead calm." (Ball: 41) And, on another, he wrote, "Quite warm. The wind died away this morning and we are becalmed again water is getting short provisions poor and a hot sun which makes it very unpleasant and discouraging." (Ball: 82) The *Elizabeth* was becalmed in the extreme cold of Patagonia for nearly three weeks, and the *Apollo* waited almost two weeks west of San Francisco for a fair wind to take her into port. (Johnson, W: 61)

For the overland emigrants the unpredictable prairie storms could bring torrential rain and hail in minutes, which could flood river crossings for days, make the trail muddy, aka, heavy, or even flood them out. In 1850 George Keller reached the Ham's Fork but "found impossible to ford, on account of its swollen state." It took three days before they finally crossed and three attempts to construct a ferry strong enough to take the wagons and the violent currents. On the evening of June 12, 1853, James Woodworth had camped in a hollow for the evening. He wrote, "The wind ... bleu with great violence At the same time a terrible storm of rain accompanied with hard thunder came on ... [the hollow]it soon filled to a depth of six Inches with water and all the bedclothes were swimming in it We of course were obliged to evacuate the tent without ceremony and pass the night as best we could..." (Woodworth: 14)

Just as the overland emigrants had problems with provisions, passengers aboard ships frequently complained both about the quantity and quality of food and the foul-tasting water from the ship's casks. One steamer passenger complained, "The pork is rusty, the beef rotten, the duff half-cooked and the beans contained two bugs to a bean." (Jackson, J: 158) By the end of a voyage provisions were frequently down to salt meat, beans, and hardtack. (Johnson, W: 64) Mores Cogswell, a passenger bound for California on the *Sweden,* wrote that "the beans are 3 to a quart of hot water, with a small piece of rusty pork." (Jackson, D: 97) In 1860 Henry Huston on the steamer *Sonora* commented that some of the food was "'old enough to vote,' then 'roast beef' with a brown crust and all inside raw and bloody." The fish "all well rotted; Bread, Fruit and other solids come in about the same shape; Butter is here a liquid; tea and coffee are both nicknames, as those liquids very seldom have a taste of those vegetables, for which they are named." Water was often rationed, and passengers on the *Grecian* complained about the rationing of water by the cupful.

On the overland trail food supplies were down to a minimum by the time the emigrants reached the Humboldt and Carson sinks. James Wilkins wrote of the Pioneer Line, the first commercial wagon train to cross the plains, that "they like us had nothing left but bread and bacon." (Wilkins:72) Finding freshwater supplies was also a problem because springs and streams were frequently contaminated by human and animal wastes and dead carcasses. Furthermore, on certain parts of the trail, such as the Sublette Cutoff, Salt Lake Desert, Black Rock Desert and Forty-Mile Desert, good water was located from forty to eighty miles away.

Scurvy was one disease usually associated with sea voyages. While records do indicate that some died, they do not indicate that the problem was as severe as many first feared. It was, however, another problem that hit the overland emigrants. Wilkins wrote on September 12, 1849, "Mr James was expected to die with the scurvy." (Wilkins: 72) He died three days later. One week later on September 19, he recorded "we are most of us taking the scurvey, myself amongst the rest, the gums bleed, and the skin is becoming discoloured in patches." (Wilkinis: 73) D.T. McCollum, another emigrant on the trail, noted that "nearly half the passengers in the Pioneer Line…have had the Scurvy, and four have died with it." These accounts were expressed late in the journey near the Humboldt and Carson sinks. In 1850, however, George Keller did state that people were suffering from scurvy at Fort Laramie, which was back much farther east on the trail.

The success of the journey of sea passengers and overlanders depended on very different circumstances. Those who sailed placed their trust in the hands of the ship's captain and his crew for a successful journey. It was their responsibility and skill in sailing and dealing with conditions that largely determined the outcome. They were responsible for the daily functioning of the ship and upkeep. The captain had the ultimate authority. The passengers did not function as sailors. Their role was usually minimal, and they were free from the work of sailing the ship. They also had little impact on the decisions made by the captains. Once on board, passengers were there for the duration of the sea voyage. If disenchanted passengers disembarked the ship while at a port, there was little likelihood that they would easily find passage on another ship. Short of a major mutiny they were compelled to remain under the control of the captain and his ship.

While the earliest wagon companies had guides, most later companies were organized by emigrants traveling together without a guide. They selected or elected their own leader or captain. A large percentage of those companies changed in both membership and leadership during the course of their journey. Individuals or families often decided to leave one company and join another traveling nearby. For the overlanders the success of the journey was dependent first on their own preparations and then, once the journey was begun on their own daily hard work and cooperation. Every emigrant, man, woman and child, had responsibilities or chores that had to be done every day. All were important to their success. The work began before sunrise and continued throughout the day and sometimes into the night. In addition, emigrants, unless sick, did not ride in the wagons, they walked. The physical work was extensive. They were responsible for overcoming any problems they faced. Exhaustion was a daily fact of life.

As for the seafarers, once the voyage had begun and they had developed their sea-legs, they soon realized that they had to contend with boredom. The daily scenery did not change and there was not much in the way of sightseeing. Yet, a few well-organized groups were prepared. One party sailing from New York on the *George Emory* brought along cards, chess, backgammon, four musical instruments and a 150-volume library to read on their voyage. (Johnson, W.: 65) There probably wasn't much left of the books once they arrived in San Francisco. On another ship Charles Harvey recorded that he passed much of his time by reading, playing euchre, jackstraws, hunting lice, and carving canes and rings. While some ships, such as the *Sweden*, sailed without stopping, most made one or two stops. On the Atlantic the ports could be Rio De Janeiro or Santa Catarina, and on the Pacific, Talcahuano or Valparaiso. Brief as the stops were, the passengers made

Smithsonian Institution Photo # 38416-C

Here is the San Francisco harbor literally jammed with vessels. Many of them were abandoned and left to rot while the crews took off for the gold diggings.

the most of them. On the other hand, overland travelers frequently commented on the changing landscape and many took time or walked one to four miles to "sightsee" by looking at a gorge, or strange mound or rock formation, or climbing rocks and carving their names on them. They often lamented about not having enough time to enjoy them once they got there. Exhaustion not boredom was a major problem for the overland emigrants.

While emigrants on the overland route often had trouble finding campgrounds with sufficient grass and water, they at least could sleep in the "wide open spaces." Passengers on ship were often overcrowded. In 1849 the average size of the typical bark sailing ship going around the Horn carried forty-eight Argonauts, plus the crew and was ninety-three feet long and about twenty-four feet abeam. (Jackson, D: 95) This did not leave much room for the passengers to roam. By the 1850s, the new larger clipper ships could carry about 300 passengers, but space was still tight. The *Crecian*, built in 1851, was considered a "medium" clipper ship and could normally hold over 330 passengers, plus crew. It had two decks, three masts, was 182 ½ feet long and 36 ½ feet abeam and 18 ¼ feet in depth. (Ball: 35-6) Even though it was much larger than the earlier ships, it still provided very little room in which people could move around. Larger ships were built later, but they might also take more passengers.

The early steamers could carry about 200 passengers, while by the late 1850s and early 1860s some could carry 700, but still space was tight. In 1849, the first steamer to leave from Panama City for San Francisco was the *California*. By this time word of gold in California had spread. The ship was built for 210 passengers, but the captain was forced to take on board over 365. The overflow had to sleep on the deck. (Jackson, D: 81) Even on regular voyages sleeping quarters were crowded. Sleeping berths were often tiered—three abreast two feet apart one on top of the other. (Johnson, W.: 64) Passengers on the *Alexander Von Humboldt* were nine to a compartment—a six foot square. (Jackson, D: 115) One could only imagine what the aroma must have been like after months at sea or during stormy weather.

One last problem for oceangoing vessels and emigrants was the event of fire and explosions on steamers. Although fire was a rare occurrence, the ship *Independence* burned in 1853, and 125 out of 300 passengers died. For the overland emigrants their major problem with fire was finding enough wood, sage, or buffalo chips for their cooking fires. Often they would make use of a discarded wagon as a fuel supply. One has often heard of great prairie fires the emigrants faced, and some did exist, but there just aren't many records to substantiate them as a common problem. By the time they were traveling during the drier months of summer, they were in deserts or drier areas of the trail where there was less vegetation to burn.

These then were some of the difficult realities facing the oceangoing emigrants and their overland counterparts. Despite the problems, traveling by sea proved to be extremely popular after gold was discovered in 1848. San Francisco had welcomed only a handful of U.S. ships in 1848, but in 1849 over 775 ships brought the Argonauts. In 1849 more people came by ship than came by wagon. Of the estimated 90,000 people who came to California, an estimated number of 40,000 came by sea. Another 15,000 came through Mexico and another 10,000 through other trails and routes. (Watkins: 88) On the California Trail about 6,200 wagons brought between 19,000 and 23,000 emigrants to California (Stewart:231-2). In the years that followed, both sea and land routes continued to be popular and the population of California grew rapidly. By the end of 1852 its population was estimated to be nearly one quarter million people.

Chapter Two

EARLY HISTORY OF THE TRAIL

1810-21 The Mexican war for independence from Spain was instigated by Father Miguel Hidalgo y Costilla on September 15, 1810. Formal independence for Mexico was finally granted and signed in 1821.

1819 The Adams-Onis Treaty was signed with Spain. This set the northern boundary of the Mexican Territory as the forty-second parallel to the Continental Divide. The area directly north of it was the Oregon Territory and was claimed by the United States, Great Britain, and Russia. Russia still had an outpost in California, Fort Ross, which it had established and dedicated on September 10, 1812. They would later sell the fort to John Sutter.

1821 After Mexican Independence, U.S. interests in California begin to increase. At first there were merchant ventures that shipped cattle hides and sea otter skins back east. Later, Americans came to California in hopes of starting a new life or finding gold.

1824 The South Pass was traversed by trappers including Jedediah Smith, Jim Bridger, Thomas Fitzpatrick, and James Clyman. Within a few decades, nearly all of the traffic heading west for Oregon, California, and Utah was funneled through the broad flat pass.

Tom Fitzpatrick and other trappers are said to have camped at Independence Rock and celebrated the Fourth of July there. Some sources also credit Fitzpatrick with naming the rock. Other sources assert that William Sublette and his trappers gave the rock its name while celebrating Independence Day there in 1830. The large granite rock would become a major landmark on the overland trails to California and Oregon. Father DeSmet later called this rock the "Great Register of the Desert" because of all the names written and carved on it by those who visited it — both trapper and emigrant alike.

1826 Joseph Robidoux set up a trading post near the banks of the Missouri in the Blacksnake Hills. The site was to become the city of St. Joseph, Missouri.

Jedediah Smith, the well-known mountain man, led a party of trappers to California and the San Gabriel Mission. He was looking for new beaver grounds and also hoping to find the mythical San Buenaventura River, which would open the Rocky Mountains to oceangoing ships. By entering Mexican California he broke the law, was put in jail, and then released on the promise that he would leave California by the same route he entered. He started his return trip, but decided to hunt and set up a stockade on the Stanislaus River. While some of his men remained, he left for the Rendezvous at Bear Lake and returned to California when it was over. He was jailed and then released again on his promise to leave and not return. This time he headed north to the Oregon Territory. Other trappers, such as Sylvester Pattie had similar problems with Mexican officials.

The route Smith used to enter California was not well documented, and there is little evidence that it was used by later emigrants. However, a river where they camped while going north to Oregon did come to be known as the "American River", and this does become important in California's history.

1827 William Sublette and Moses "Black" Harris, returning from the Salt Lake Valley, left the Platte River near Grand Island and cut southeast towards Kansas and the Little Blue, then east of the Big Blue to the Kaw and then down the valley. This route, called "Sublette's Trace," was used by trappers. The route with minor changes became the later route of the Oregon-California Trail.

Cantonment (Fort) Leavenworth was established by the military on the west bank of the Missouri River. It provided protection for the

Santa Fe Trail. During the years of the early gold rush in California it served as another of the jumping-off centers for the emigrants.

The town of Independence, Missouri, was founded. By 1832 it became the jumping-off place for the Santa Fe Trail, replacing New Franklin and then Fort Osage. Later it would serve the same purpose for the California and Oregon trails. The first wagon company left for California from Independence in 1841. Independence Square and the courthouse marked the beginning of the trails. It was the springs in the area that made Independence a natural location for both the town and the trails.

1828 Hiram Scott, a trapper, was left by his companions and disappeared. The following year William Sublette found a skeleton that was believed to have been Scott's. The bluffs along that section of the Platte River were named for him. Over the years different stories developed about who Hiram Scott was and how he came to die. As early as 1830, the first written record of the legend was recorded by the young mountain man named Warren Ferris.

1828-36 Andrew Jackson was elected President of the United States, and he soon began negotiations with Mexico to purchase California and New Mexico. After six years the negotiations broke off. Successive presidents continued to try to obtain California.

William Sublette and others left for the West from St. Louis in 1829. For a time they followed the Santa Fe Trail west out of Independence and then turned northwest to cross the Kansas and joined his earlier trace. This route used by many of the trappers and traders became the established route for the later emigrants.

1833 John C. McCoy founded the town of Westport a few miles west of Independence and inland from the Missouri River. Westport Landing, near the mouth of the Kansas on the Missouri River, was established for steamboats. It was located a few miles upriver from the Independence landing and would also become a jumping-off site. By the mid-1840s the area had been developed more, and it finally grew to become Kansas City, Missouri.

Joseph Redderford Walker was possibly the most famous and successful of the mountain mem. Walker helped Benjamin Bonneville in the 1830s and John Fremont in the 1840s. He was the first to really explore the Great Basin, even more than Jedediah Smith did. He opened up much of what became some of the western portions of the California Trail, discovered the Walker Pass and was the first white man in Yosemite Valley. In 1837, he was a guide for Sir William Drummond Stewart's famous hunting expedition to the Rockies. He helped to guide many of the early emigrants to California. Most historians believe this portrait by Alfred J. Miller is Walker, however, some question it.

Painting Joseph R Walker – Courtesy, Joslyn Art Museum, Omaha, Nebraska

1833-34 Joseph Walker, another famous trapper and mountain man, traveled from the Salt Lake region down the Mary's or Humboldt River. He crossed the Sierra Nevada range down near its southern end at a pass that now bears his name, Walker Pass. While his whole route was not used by the emigrants many traveled on certain parts of it. In 1869 the transcontinental railroad also used part of it.

1834 Some believe that Kit Carson and other trappers were the pathfinders for the route up the Raft River Valley from the Snake to Goose Creek and over to Bishop's Creek, headwaters of the Mary's or Humboldt River. Carson explored part of the valley down the Humboldt River along the general route used earlier by Walker and then returned. Trappers now used this route to trap beavers in the upper Mary's River region. It later became the main branch of the California Trail from Fort Hall.

Fort William (Laramie) founded May 31, was constructed near the mouth of the Laramie River on the North Platte by Robert Campbell, William Sublette's co-partner. This fort was visited by Alfred J. Miller, painter for Sir William Drummond Stewart, in 1837, while he was on a "tour" of the American West. Miller's paintings of the fort are the only ones known to exist and are readily recognized today. The fort changed owners during the next few years, and a new adobe fort replaced it in 1841. This, coincidently, was just in time for the development of the California-Oregon trails.

Nathaniel J. Wyeth contracted to sell supplies at the Rendezvous, but by the time he arrived there were others already selling supplies to the mountain men. In mid-July Wyeth decided to construct a trading post on the Snake River and called it Fort Hall [after one of his benefactors.] In 1837 it was sold to the Hudson's Bay Company, which enlarged it from its original size to about eighty by one hundred and twenty feet. In 1856 the fort was abandoned, and by 1862 it had succumbed to the flooding by the Snake. The fort served as the last major resupply area for the California-bound emigrants who did not take the many cut-offs that had developed earlier along the trail.

1836 The first California revolution for Independence was led by native-born Californios, Juan Bautista Alvarado and Jose Castro. Alvarado's proclamation of independence on November 7, 1836, was supported by thirty U.S. and British frontiersmen. However, when the Mexican government appointed Alvarado the legitimate governor of California, he ended the rebellion. In 1846 Castro was planning another rebellion against Mexico, but the Americans supported Bear Flag Revolt swept by him.

John Marsh arrived in California. He was an adventurer, trapper, storekeeper, former Indian agent, and finally major landowner in California. He left Missouri for California when threatened with arrest for selling guns illegally to the Indians. Once in California he set up a practice as a physician. Shortly thereafter he obtained a large ranch of about fifty thousand acres on San Francisco Bay. His ranch became one of the goals for many of the later California emigrants. He also actively encouraged Americans to come to California.

1837 John Moore founded the Missouri River town of Weston. For a few years in the 1850s it rivaled Independence and St. Joseph as a jumping-off place. James Wilkins disembarked here in 1849. By 1860 Weston's boom period was over.

1839 John Sutter arrived in California. He originally left Switzerland to escape a jail sentence and came to the United States. He traveled to Oregon in 1838 with a party of missionaries. He went to California by way of Hawaii and Alaska. He was another adventurer like

John Sutter's dream was to create his own empire. He was well on his way to accomplishing this until the discovery of gold and the takeover of California by the United States. Both of these events caused Sutter more problems than benefits. Sutter's fate was like that of John McLoughlin's of Oregon—both men helped the early emigrants and both men lost their empires and never recovered.

Sutter's Fort State Historic Park

Marsh, and soon he became another large landowner. He persuaded Governor Alvarado to grant him eleven square miles of land, about forty-seven thousand acres, and finally obtained two more large land grants. He promised the governor he would set up a colony of Swiss to serve as a buffer between the American, British, Russians, and the Mexicans. His colony of "New Helvetia" was at the junction of the American and Sacramento rivers. There he built his fort which became the headquarters of this empire of the future—Sutter's Fort; it became the desired destination for many of the Americans who came over the California Trail. Today, Sutter's Fort has been restored and reconstructed and is open to the public.

The two ranchos of John Marsh and John Sutter soon developed into the end of the trail for pre-gold rush emigrants. They served as resupply depots for the emigrants who succeeded in arriving in California and needed materials and supplies to start their new lives. Many even found temporary employment with Sutter. For the early years of the trail they also served as a base station for rescue missions for emigrants needing help back on the trail. The parties that finally rescued the survivors of the Donner party left from Sutter's Fort. Thus, for the California emigrants, these two ranches played a role similar to that played by the Lee and Whitman missions and Fort Vancouver for the Oregon emigrants.

John Bidwell, a member of the Western Emigration Society, tried to get people interested in traveling to California. His work, plus that of others, such as John Marsh and the old trapper Robidoux, had stimulated the interests of many people in Missouri, Arkansas, Illinois, and Kentucky. By the winter of 1840, plans were made by many of them to meet in Independence by May 9, 1841 to start their journey to California.

1840 British and Americans at home and in California increased their agitation for a takeover of the Mexican state of California.

1841 The old wooden Fort William stockade was abandoned and replaced by another structure made of adobe called Fort John. Most emigrants along the trail called it Fort Laramie as they had the earlier Fort William. Laramie Peak is the prominent geographical feature in that area and served as a landmark for travelers. The new fort measured about 123 feet by 168 feet. Francis Parkman, a young adventurer and writer stayed there in 1846 and gives one of the best descriptions of the fort itself. He states, "The little fort is built of bricks dried in the sun, and externally is of an oblong form, with bastions of clay, in the form of ordinary blockhouses, at two of the corner. The walls are about fifteen feet high…The roof of the apartments within, which are built close against the walls, serve the purpose of a banquette. Within the fort is divided by a partition; on one side is the square area surrounded by storerooms, offices, and apartments of the inmates; on the other is the corral, a narrow place…The main entrances has two gates with an arched passage intervening." (Parkman:89-90) This was a major resting place for emigrants and it signified the completion of the prairie portion of their journey.

The Russians voluntarily left Fort Ross and with it their interests in California. They had agreed in 1824 not to expand their interests below fifty-four degrees, forty minutes north. John Sutter purchased the fort from the Russians and their role in California's history was over. Fort Ross has been restored and reconstructed and can be visited today.

This was the year the U.S. emigrants began to arrive in California over what ultimately developed into the California Trail. There were three groups—one from Oregon, including women and children, another from New Mexico, following the caravan trails to Los Angeles, and the third, the Bidwell party. This last group was comprised of the first emigrants to travel across the Sierra Nevada to John Marsh's ranch and then to Sutter's Fort along the general northern route that came to be known as the California Trail.

The party of emigrants met in May in Independence, Missouri, as they had previously decided. The party consisted of sixty-nine people. The company was known as the Bartleson-Bidwell party. Luckily, they were able to join a party of missionaries, including the well-known Father DeSmet who was being guided by two mountain men, Thomas Fitzpatrick and Joseph Meek. They followed Sublette's Trace and the route which was now becoming known as the Oregon-California trail. West of Soda Springs, the company divided. Thirty-four emigrants continued with the missionaries on the Oregon Trail to Fort Hall and then to Oregon. Thirty-five emigrants turned south to break open a new route to California. While much of the route they took was not followed by later emigrants, parts of it were to be used. Nancy Kelsey and her baby, Ann, were the first white women and child on the California Trail. In Utah, they called one of their camping places Rabbit Springs, and it is still known by that name today. They faced great hardships crossing the Great Salt Lake Desert and finally after moving southwest found a pass, Harrison Pass, in the Ruby Mountains and crossed over to the Mary's or Humboldt River. They followed the river but were forced to abandon their wagons before crossing the Sierra Nevada. They continued by foot and pack animals. They followed the Walker River and crossed the Sierra Nevada at or near the Sonora Pass. They were the first emigrants, but because they left their wagons, the first successful trip by a wagon company would not occur for a few more years. The Sonora Pass that they probably used was not traversed again by other emigrants until 1852.

1842 John Fremont, guided by Kit Carson, headed out from Westport to South Pass and the Rocky Mountains. He and his cartographer, Charles Preuss, mapped the trail and recorded information which became very useful to emigrants who used the route. A few years later they completed the route all the way to Oregon and published their reports, which were widely read and used in the late 1840s.

No emigrant wagon companies left for California, but companies left for Oregon and, thus, the first half of the California Trail developed. About twelve of the men who went west to California in 1841 returned to the States, trying to find a better route while also using parts of their 1841 trail. They were led by Chiles and Hopper. Many of the members of this party became important to the history of California and the trail. Creeks, rivers, towns, lakes, mountains, and forts were named after these hardy emigrants. Many also became guides for later emigrant companies and helped to open new routes and will be noted later in this book.

President Tyler tried again to negotiate with Mexico to obtain California. However, his efforts failed when a brash Commodore Jones "captured" Monterey on October 19, thinking war with Mexico had broken out. As a result the Mexicans became even more suspicious of the United States.

1842-43 Jim Bridger and Louis Vasquez built a trading post near the Black's Fork of the Green River. It was on the bluffs, but was shortly moved to the bottomland. This trading post became a major stopping and resupply area for the early emigrants and for the later ones who used the Salt Lake Road or cutoff to California. For those emigrants who took any of the later developed various cutoffs, such as the Greenwood or Sublette, Dempsey, Kinney, Slate Creek, Baker-Davis, or Lander Road, the fort was bypassed. Brigham Young purchased the fort or post in 1855, but it was abandoned and burned in 1857 during the Mormon War. The U.S. Army took over the site and began the construction of a new fort on the old location almost immediately. Today parts of the old military fort have been restored and a replica of Bridger's old post has been built near its original location. The fort is a state historic site and is open to the public as a living museum.

1843 St. Joseph, Missouri was laid out in the area of Robidoux's old trading post. It soon developed into another of the major embarking areas for the westward journey. The following year a route from St. Joseph connected the area near present-day Marysville to the trail out of Independence. In 1860-61 St. Joseph also served as the eastern terminus of the Pony Express.

Joseph Chiles organized a wagon company to return with him to California. Even though he had not succeeded with wagons in 1841, he decided to try once again. The company included about eight wagons and thirty people—many were relatives and friends, including women and children of people already in California. His wagon company traveled behind the "great Migration" of emigrants to Oregon and also behind John Fremont who was on another trip of exploration to Oregon. His return to the States from Oregon would bring Fremont through California. Chiles' party followed the already defined route of the Oregon Trail as it was then called, all the way to Fort Hall. There he decided to divide the company. Joseph Walker led the largest group with the women and children and the wagons, while Chiles took some of the men with pack animals and hoped to find a different route farther to the west. Walker turned off the Oregon Trail at Calder Creek, cut over to the Raft River, then to the City of Rocks, over the mountains to Goose Creek and down to the Humboldt to the Sink. The plan was to meet Chiles there. Then they would find a new route over the Sierra Nevada and complete the journey together. However, Chiles was not there, so Walker headed south along the route he had used in back in 1834. As for Chiles, his route continued on the Oregon Trail until west of Fort Boise where he cut southwest. He finally picked up the Sacramento River and more or less followed it to Sutter's Fort. His route was as poor as the previous one. Walker's party had again been forced to abandon their wagons near Owens Lake, and thus, it would take another year before wagons would successfully make it all the way over the Sierra Nevada and into California.

1844 This year Fremont completed his exploration and mapping of the route to Oregon that he had begun in 1842. Fremont decided to return to the United States by heading south into California. By February he made it to Sutter's Fort. This venture into Mexican territory by members of the U.S. Army made Mexico nervous. Fremont claimed he needed fresh horses for his journey to cross the Sierra Nevada. He then returned to the United States mapping his route all the way. While his route was not used by the emigrants, his maps showed that the land between the Rockies and Sierra Nevada formed a "Great Basin." He would return again to California in 1845, giving names to a number of places and changing that of the Mary's River, named earlier by Peter Skene Ogden of the Hudson's Bay Company, to the Humboldt. The Carson River was named for his scout, Kit Carson, and the entrance to San Francisco was later named "the Golden Gate."

Elisha Stephens was another mountain man and guide. In 1844, he led the first successful wagon train over the Sierra Nevada into California over the Truckee route through the area of what is commonly called Donner Pass. This is the only known photograph of Stephens. It was taken twenty years after he led the emigrants over the mountains.

Clyde Arbuckle Collection, San Jose, CA

Peter Lassen, a Dane, obtained a land grant from the Mexican government about one hundred miles north of Sutter's Fort on the Sacramento River. Lassen had come to California by way of Oregon in 1839-40. He had hoped to create an empire like Sutter's and to get rich off the new emigrants. His chance would come in a few years.

This was the year that the first wagon company made it over the Sierra Nevada, establishing, at last, a useable wagon route. It was led by Elisha Stephens who served as captain. The Stephens-Townsend-Murphy party, as it is often called, set off from Council Bluffs, Iowa, in March 1844. It was comprised of twenty-three men, eight women and fifteen children. Caleb Greenwood and his sons acted as pilots or guides for the first half of the trail. It followed the north side of the Platte River and crossed at Fort Laramie and took the established Oregon Trail as far as South Pass. (This route on the north side of the river later became known as the Mormon Trail.) Shortly thereafter they decided to try a new cutoff. Isaac "Old Man" Hitchcock suggested that they cut west instead of heading southwest to Fort Bridger and thereby save some time. It seemed that Hitchcock had a general idea of the route and that it may have been used by Bonneville in 1832, but not since then. The company discussed it and voted to try it. While the route proved to be longer and drier than they originally thought, all made it safely across. In fact, some men returned back over the route to the Big Sandy to look for cattle that had been lost. The men returned successfully to the Green. This route came to be called the Greenwood Cutoff, and later the Sublette Cutoff.

After crossing the Bear Mountains, they headed north towards Fort Hall. Shortly after leaving Fort Hall, they cut across and followed Walker's route all the way down the Humboldt. At the Humboldt Sink and the "Forty-Mile Desert," as it was later called, they came in contact with an Indian called "Truckee." He told them of a stream and a passage west across the desert. They crossed over to it and followed the stream up into the mountains. Today the river still bears the name given it by the thankful emigrants as does a meadow area, respectively, the Truckee River and Truckee Meadows, the present site of Reno, Nevada. From there the emigrants continued up the Truckee and crossed the Sierras at an area later known as Donner Pass. However, recently identified physical evidence and research has led some historians to place the actual pass and crossing a little to the north of that area. That site of the original Truckee Pass is now called Stephens Pass. While the emigrants were forced to temporarily leave their wagons at various places along the trail and some of the emigrants were even forced to spend part of the winter in cabins they built at Truckee (Donner) Lake, they all arrived safely by the spring of 1845. In addition to the first emigrant use of the Greenwood cutoff and the bringing of the first wagons to California, two children were born along the way: Ellen Independence Miller near Independence Rock and Elizabeth Yuba Murphy near Yuba Creek.

Lansford Hastings left California by sea for the East, hoping to encourage emigration to California and to publish a guidebook. His guidebook would contain the infamous Hastings Cutoff, the route taken by the ill-fated Donner party in 1846, but only vaguely described and never traveled by Hastings. He had originally gone to Oregon in 1842 and then left after not finding what he had hoped for and decided that California was the better place to make his fortune.

1845 James K Polk became president and pledged himself to obtain California for the United States. His plan was three-pronged. First, he hoped to obtain it by direct negotiations and purchase. Second, he encouraged independence movements in California by pledging to protect any Americans seeking to make California part of the United States. As a result, Secretary of State Buchanan instructed Consul Larkin to "arouse in their bosoms that love of liberty and independence so natural to the American continent," and that "if the

People should desire to unite their destiny with ours, they would be received as brethren." Polk's third prong was war, if all else failed.

More emigrants and wagon companies headed west, but most were still bound for Oregon. St. Joseph was the major embarking area. Caleb Greenwood and his sons returned from Sutter's Fort back over the California Trail to meet the Oregon bound emigrants. They were to encourage them to head for California instead of Oregon. At this they proved to be immensely successful. Over fifty wagons and more than 250 emigrants, including women and children, turned away from Oregon near the raft River and headed for California. This was five times as many people and wagons than that which had made the first successful journey in 1844. William B. Ide and his family were one of the families that traveled to California. He, along with other emigrants of 1845, would play a major role in the 1846 Bear Flag Revolt for independence.

Lansford Hastings headed for California, but he traveled by horse, not wagon.

A more unfortunate first is recorded this year—the first death of an emigrant caused by an Indian. A man called Pierce was killed on the Truckee River. It should be noted that perhaps part of the blame could be placed on the actions of John Greenwood, one of Caleb's sons, and Sam Kinney who in 1844 had earlier instigated trouble with the Indians along the Humboldt. From that year on hostile encounters with the Paiute and Shoshoni, or "Diggers," as they were generally called, became more of a problem. However, the major issues facing the emigrants still remained time, distance, food, deserts, and winter snows.

1845-46 John C. Fremont left on his third official journey of exploration. He explored and traveled through much of the territory along the California trail, but most of it was not related to the trail and would have little impact on the emigrants' route. He would, however, play a larger role in the California revolt, and this would ultimately impact his career. Walker and Carson acted as his guides during the journey.

1846 This was a major year for the history of both the California Trail and California because of the revolt and its impact, the continued emigration, and the events surrounding some of the wagon companies. By December 1845, Fremont was back in California with a larger and stronger military and scientific force than he had had previously in 1844. Having narrowly avoided conflict with the Mexicans, he left for Oregon. However, in May he was overtaken by a Marine Corps courier Lieutenant Archibald Gillespie, and after discussions he returned to California in time for the California Revolt. Even today there is still much speculation about what exactly transpired during their meeting, and what instructions, if any, Fremont received from Gillespie. Events began to unfold rapidly, but it must be noted that communications were not as rapid as today's. On April 25, Mexican troops had opened fire on General Zachary Taylor's forces at the Rio Grande, and on May 11, President Polk sent a War Message to Congress. Back in California the Americans continued their agitation and William B. Ide, a former school teacher, proclaimed California an independent republic, the Bear Flag Republic, on June 14, 1846, at Sonoma. Fremont came to the aid of the Americans, Commodore Sloat landed in Monterey on July 7, and the Bear Flag Republic was dissolved and the California fighters joined the U.S. Army as the California Volunteers under Fremont. On July 9, Captain John Montgomery landed in San Francisco and the American flag was raised. While fighting still continued in places, the Mexican forces capitulated, and the campaign was over on January 13, 1847, when Fremont and Andies Pico signed an agreement. The formal treaty came in 1848.

A large company of Mormons, 238 emigrants, arrived from New York by ship with Sam Brannan as their leader on July 31, 1846. There had been discussions earlier among the Mormons about making California their "Promised Land." However, by the time they arrived, Brigham Young had already decided on the Great Salt Lake Valley. Yet, Sam Brannan and these Mormons, and some from the Mormon Battalion who arrived much later, would still play an important role in the development of California and the California Trail.

Levi Scott and Jesse Applegate opened the Applegate Trail to Oregon. The route was actually blazed eastward from Oregon to the main trail along the Humboldt River. Political events, both in Oregon and in California, caused many people to think that a southern route to Oregon was needed and that was part of what inspired Scott and Applegate to develop the new route. Those wishing to take the Applegate Trail to Oregon left the old Oregon Trail at the Raft River and followed the California Trail down the Humboldt. Where the river turned south the Applegate portion continued west and then northwest to cross the Black Rock Desert and then west entering Oregon from the south. The cutoff from the Humboldt was later incorporated into the Lassen route to California in 1848 and played a major role in the migrations of 1849.

Roller Pass was opened over the Sierras. The trail split off from the established Truckee route near Truckee (Donner) Lake. Within a few years it becomes the major route for those traveling on the Truckee route. While the political status of California was being resolved, another great crisis was occurring that has come to be almost synonymous with the California Trail and the hardships faced by the emigrants — the Donner disaster.

The Donner party had been one of the last parties to leave Independence. Almost from the beginning they seemed to be haunted by delays and problems. At Alcove Spring in Kansas, which was named while they were camped, the party experienced the death of James Reed's Grandma Sarah Keyes. This death, however, was not to be the last. Today a marker can be found near where they camped, but it is a recent one. The actual grave site is still open to debate. Some believed it to be under the county road near the entrance to the old parking lot, while others place it by the trail ruts in the field. At the spring, the stone carved by James Reed with his initials and last name and date can be seen. Also carved in a rock which had originally formed part of the ledge are the words "Alcove Spring." It was named by Edwin Bryant and carved by George McKinstry, also members traveling together at that time. (See photo section.)

The Donner party had heard of the Hastings' Cutoff and was planning on taking it. However, long before getting to Fort Bridger where they would leave the main established trail they were warned by James Clyman, another famous mountain man and friend of James Reed, that there was no trail there and that they should not try it, but should instead continue on to Fort Hall. However, once at Fort Bridger, Jim Bridger seemed to indicate that the route was possible. Yet, in reality, it had never been tried. Even the route to Salt Lake

31

Courtesy of California State of Parks. Image 090-P48957

James and Margaret Reed and family were emigrants associated with the Donner disaster of 1846. Near Iron Point, an argument broke out between Reed and another member of the party as their wagons were climbing a hill. In the fight that ensued Reed killed the man. Reed was evicted from the wagon company. His family, however, was allowed to continue with the rest of the party. Although forced to travel by himself, Reed made it to California and waited for the arrival of his family. Once it was realized that they were stranded along with the rest of the party, arrangements to rescue them were undertaken. However, it was not until the spring that rescuers were able to reach the survivors.

had not been traversed with wagons. However, Hastings had already started with other wagons to try his new route and was reportedly ready to help guide the Donners if they could catch up. The Donners and some others decided to try it while the rest decided to follow the established route to Fort Hall. Those who took the established route made it safely to California without any major problems. The Donners, however, were never able to catch up. They did send Reed ahead to find Hastings. He did, but Hastings would only "point out" a different and supposedly better route which would take only a few days. The new route bypassed the rugged Weber Canyon that the earlier wagon company had taken, and instead, crossed the Wasatch Mountains. As the Donners soon found out there was no trail over the mountains, and they had to cut one. This further delayed their passage. Most of the route they cut became the main route to Salt Lake that the Mormons and others emigrants took in 1847. Once the Donners got to the Salt Lake Valley they encountered more problems. Hastings reported that the desert crossing was only about forty miles across, but in reality it was more like eighty miles to Pilot Peak. Again the Donner party lost more time and equipment.

It now seemed that hardships and delays were a constant companion of the Donners. When they finally were able to find a route and pass around the Ruby Mountains and rejoin the main California Trail they determined it had not really saved them time or mileage. Farther down the trail along the Humboldt near Iron Point Reed got into a fight with John Snyder, another member, and killed him. Reed escaped executed but was banished from the company and forced to leave. His wife and family remained with the company. Reed, and another who volunteered to join him, finally made it to California. Reed was later one of the people to lead rescue parties to help the starving and stranded survivors that winter.

By the time the Donner party reached the Truckee, winter was fast approaching. They reached Truckee Lake and the pass, but decided to rest before the final climb. Snow was already on the ground and another storm hit and it continued for days. The pass was blocked, and then they faced more snow. They were forced to remain on the eastern side of the mountains. Some stayed in the old 1844 cabin, while others built shelters for protection while hoping and waiting for a break in the weather. It never came. Some tried to get over the pass on foot, but they were forced back. Hunting in the deep snow was almost impossible and there was nothing to hunt. Most of the animal were either hibernating or had already moved to lower elevations. They soon ran out of food, Starving and desperate with some members dead and others dying, they turned to the only food supply they thought available—the bodies of those members who had already died. The rest is history.

Earlier, while still on the desert, two members of the party were sent ahead to Sutter's Fort to obtain additional supplies. There they learned that Reed had successfully made it to California, and they relayed the problems and delays that the party had experienced. Later, when the Donners had not shown up they realized that they were stranded in the mountains. However, the California revolt had already started, and men and supplies were needed for the revolt. This delayed rescue attempts. By the spring of 1847 all those still alive were brought over the mountain to California. Reed, himself, brought back members of his own family. Of the Donner party, forty members died and forty-seven survived. It had been the worst disaster on the California Trail. Today names such as Donner Pass, Donner Lake, and Donner Creek all commemorate the tragedy. Hastings was discredited and would never recover his honor, and the Hastings Cutoff had seen its day. There are many books written on the subject for those interested in the complete history and story of their ordeal.

1847 This was the year of the major Mormon migration from Winter Quarters to the Great Salt Lake Valley under the leadership of Brigham Young and the establishment of Salt Lake City. The Mormons traveled on the north side of the Platte River finally crossing it by Fort Laramie. They continued west along the established trails to Fort Bridger and then followed the route cut by the Donner party the previous year. Even though this route coincided with the Oregon and California trails, the route has become known as the Mormon Trail. Over the years, the Mormons made improvements and opened ferries to facilitate river crossings along the trail which benefitted all the travelers.

The small California port town of Yerba Buena took a new name, San Francisco.

Only ninety wagons headed for California, and none of them took the Hastings Cutoff. Charles Hopper led the first company of twenty wagons over the route that broke off from the main Oregon Trail farther along the Snake at the Raft River. Hopper had been with the Bidwell-Bartleson party in 1841 and Chiles in 1842. Other wagons used the route cutting off at the Raft River, and this became the main route used from that time on.

1848 This year was a major turning point in the history of California and the California Trail. Many events would occur that would change the course of history, most notably the discovery of gold and the formal takeover of California by the United States.

On January 24, 1848 James Marshall discovered gold in the tailrace in a newly constructed mill on the American River. John Sutter, owner of the mill, wanted to keep it a secret until he could figure out just what to do about it. However, it was a secret that could not be kept. Stories were soon being told and finally on May 8, 1848, Sam Brannan reportedly shouted, "Gold! Gold! Gold on the American River!" on Montgomery Street in San Francisco, and the word spread like wildfire. Walter Colton, Alcalde of Monterey, wrote, "The blacksmith dropped his hammer, the carpenter his plane, the mason his trowel, the farmer his sickle, the baker his loafs, and the tapster his bottle. All were off to the mines, some on horses, some on carts, some on crutches, and one went in a litter." The gold rush had begun!

On February 2, the formal Treaty of Guadalupe Hildago ended the Mexican War. The states we know of as California, Arizona, New Mexico, Nevada, and Utah were ceded to the United States.

California State Library, Sacramento
James Marshall was the man credited with discovering gold on January 24, 1848 at Sutter's Mill. California was never the same again.

This same year also saw many changes in the trail itself. Military forts were being constructed and started to replace the fur company posts. Another route was opened around the Great Salt Lake and two new routes were opened across the Sierra Nevada to California.

The construction of a new fort near Grand Island on the Platte River showed the government's concern about the safety of the emigrants on their westward trek. At first it was called Fort Childs, but it was soon changed to Fort Kearny and replaced the old Fort Kearny back east on the Missouri at present-day Nebraska City. The new fort was built right on the trail near the junction of the trails coming from the east and those from the southeast. Lieutenant Woodbury was in charge of the construction and he had cottonwood trees planted around the square. Today all of those trees are dead. The last one fell only a few years ago. They are being replaced by new ones. The fort was finally abandoned in 1871. Today there is a partial reconstruction and a very good visitor center.

Captain Samuel Hensley, who was with Chiles in 1843, was to lead a pack train west from Salt Lake. However, terrible hardships on the salt flats forced him to return to Salt Lake City. Then he decided to follow a new route north to Fort Hall that had been opened by Hazen

Kimball. Hensley decided to follow it north for about eighty miles and then to head west to meet the established California Trail. In crossing this section, they encountered a creek, which still bears the name given it — Deep Creek. The route came to be called the Salt Lake Road, the Salt Lake Cutoff, or the Deep Creek Cutoff. This route north out of Salt Lake became the dominant route used by emigrants who went by way of Salt Lake through the 1850s. The Hastings' route west out of Salt Lake was not used.

A group of Mormons led by Samuel Thompson had been called by Brigham Young to return to Salt Lake City from California. They had been told that the Truckee River route was very hard and too dangerous to travel, so they decided to blaze a new route following old Indian trading routes. They left near present-day Placerville on July 17. Their company included seventeen wagons, forty-five men and one woman. The route they pioneered has come to be called the Carson route. Tragedy Spring was one of their camping grounds where three of their scouts were killed, and it retains the name today. Farther along the route Hope Valley was also named by them. They picked up a branch of the Carson River and followed it down the eastern side of the Sierra Nevada, and then turned north over to the Truckee route near the Forty Mile Desert. They then continued east over the established trail exchanging information about their route with westward traveling emigrants. When they arrived at Steeple Rock (Twin Sisters) near City of Rocks, they turned east to follow Hensley's new route. They had met him on the trail and exchanged information about their respective routes. They arrived in Salt Lake City on September 20, 1848.

Joseph Chiles' company of forty-eight wagons was the largest of the California-bound emigrant companies. It had followed the trail to Fort Hall and then down the Raft and Humboldt rivers. There the emigrants also met the Mormons and were told of the new route. When Chiles came to the Humboldt Sink, he turned south along the western side of the Carson Sink over the desert to the Carson River and followed it until it met the route blazed by the east-bound Mormons. This new sixty mile section of Chiles' soon became a major portion of the Carson route. Two other companies led by Clyman and Cornwall also used the new Carson route.

Peter Lassen headed east hoping to bring emigrants back over a route that would end near his ranch. He planned to leave the existing

California Trail at what is now Lassen Meadows and then follow the Applegate Trail towards Oregon. He hoped he would find a route that would take him west towards his ranch, but he ran into problems. He returned with a wagon company and they turned off the Applegate Trail as planned, but could not discover the route he had hoped to find. He traveled farther along the Applegate Trail and they finally turned off south near Goose Lake. Within a couple of weeks they were in trouble and at one time members of the company even threatened to hang him. Fortunately, two wagon companies from Oregon found the tracks where he turned off the Applegate Trail, and followed them. One company was led by land hungry Peter Burnett. They caught up with Lassen and with their added strength they were able to cut a new route to Lassen's ranch.

The Lassen Route as it was now called was the third major route into California. However it was 200 miles longer than the Truckee or Carson routes, given Sacramento as the most common destination. Forty-niners who used this new route were misled about claims that it was a short cut.

1849

Benoni Hudspeth's first trip to California was in 1843. In 1849 he served as captain for one of the larger wagon companies going to California. It was comprised of seventy wagons and over two hundred fifty people. They had followed the main trail to just west of Soda Springs. Instead of turning north to Fort Hall, he decided to lead them directly west to meet the California Trail coming down from Fort Hall, hoping to cut off miles and thus saving precious time. Other wagon companies behind him followed his wagon tracks. The Hudspeth Cutoff was born. In reality, the twisting and turning cutoff resulted in little savings of either mileage or time.

This was the year of the gold rush and the forty-niners, also known as Argonauts. The California Trail was over-flowing with people in wagon companies and pack trains. The trail and natural resources would have to accommodate about fifty times the number of people and animals that it had in the previous year. In this year the makeup of the emigrants also changed. Almost all the emigrants were males off to the diggings or for adventure. This was also true for the oceangoing Argonauts. It was also the first year for a commercial venture to take emigrants to California. Messrs. Allen and Turner had their Pioneer Line. The charge was two hundred dollars. They would take about one hundred twenty people west. Poor planning caused problems and hardships which faced them all the way. However, this did not stop commercial ventures, and in the following years others were organized.

Joseph Ware's guidebook, *The Emigrants' Guide to California*, was published and became popular with many of the forty-niners. Ware had never been over the trail, but completed it based on reports of others—including Fremont and Sublette. He changed

Idaho State Historical Society, Photo 58-130

Benoni Hudspeth

the name of the Greenwood Cutoff to the Sublette Cutoff and also recorded the wrong mileage for the desert crossing section, making it shorter than it really was. He made other errors when describing the conditions along the Humboldt Valley and sink, calling these areas "rich and beautifully clothed with blue grass." (See a small section of *The Emigrants' Guide to California* in the section on guidebooks.)

On July 19, Benoni M. Hudspeth and John H. Myers broke off from the main trail to Fort Hall just west of Soda Springs near Sheep Rock where the Bartleson-Bidwell party had gone in 1841. However, instead of turning south with the Bear River, they headed directly west to meet the California Trail on the western side of its loop north. By doing so they hoped to save both time and the mileage it would have taken to go to Fort Hall. On July 24, they arrived back on the main trail from Fort Hall. Many of the wagons following behind them saw the wagon tracks turn off the main road to Fort Hall and followed them—almost like "the blind following the blind." Elijah Farnham noted on July 20 that the cutoff "now looks like an old road of a great deal of travel." The road to Fort Hall was used less and less by the California emigrants. J. Goldsborough Bruff, captain of the Washington City and California Mining Association wagon company, followed the Fort Hall road and felt that the cutoff actually saved little or no time or mileage.

The pattern of usage of the various routes shifted in 1849. West of the South Pass the route selected by the early emigrants was the Salt Lake Road by way of Fort Bridger. Most of the emigrants that came during the middle of the period chose the Sublette Cutoff, and those near the end decided to go by way of Fort Bridger. Part of the reason for this may have been due to the great volume of the emigration and its negative impact on the natural resources. Perhaps word of this had been passed back along the trail.

Out in the Great Basin a similar pattern developed. The Carson Route was selected by most of the early emigrants, while the Truckee route was taken by those traveling during the middle of the emigration period. Then on August 11, Milton McGee led his wagon company off the main trail at Lassen's Meadow and headed up the Applegate or Lassen route. Again, those behind started to follow, possibly thinking it was the main route. Even Myers and Hudspeth followed. By the time they discovered what they had done it was too late and too difficult to turn back. On September 19, even Bruff followed. The last emigrants arrived at Lassen's ranch on November 26. Perhaps these shifts were beneficial. If all the migration had tried to take the same route the grass and game would have been depleted even more and the hardships and suffering that did exist would have been made much worse.

A new route south out of Salt Lake City developed. It was known as the Salt Lake – Los Angeles Road. It followed the southwesterly development by the Mormons down what has been called the Mormon corridor. The route joined the Old Spanish Trail, a commercial pack train trail that originated out of Santa Fe, at Cedar City and then continued along it. The use of wagons by emigrants and traders on this old pack trail necessitated changes in it. It became a second route out of Salt Lake City, another alternative route for California bound emigrants. It was on this road in 1857 that the Mountain Meadows Massacre of an Arkansas wagon train occurred.

1850 In this year travel along the California Trail doubled that of 1849 with nearly 45,000 emigrants taking the trail. Horses, as draft animals, were becoming more popular with the emigrants. Perhaps this was because they were faster than oxen or mules. Few emigrants would take the Truckee route or the Lassen route, which was sometimes called the "Greenhorn Cutoff." Most emigrants used the Carson Route. Another route was opened in June back in Wyoming. Up until then the emigrants who traveled on the north side of the Platte were advised and crossed to the south side trail at Fort Laramie. With the ferry out and not willing to ford, some emigrants decided to remain on the north side and continue on successfully. Others followed. The route was described in Andrew Child's 1852 guidebook and later became known as Child's Route. Emigrants faced even greater hardships than the previous year. Cholera was commonplace again and took as high a toll as it had in 1849, and weather conditions were worse. The increase in usage of the trail took its toll on the natural resources which were having a more difficult time recovering. This only exacerbated the emigrants' suffering along the trail.

A trading post, in the area sometimes referred to as "Ragtown," was set up on the Carson Route where the trail met the Carson River after crossing the desert. Farther west along the route Mormon Station was constructed, and in 1851 it was relocated about a mile south. Both these trading posts had the effect of easing the difficulties of the trek. Some supplies were available, although the prices charged were certainly not very modest as many emigrants complained.

Along the trail improvements were being made and noted by the emigrants. This trend would increase with each year, as new ferries, new bridges, blacksmith shops and small seasonal trading posts sprouted up here and there along the trail. Each year the physical condition of the trail improved.

California entered the Union as a free state on September 9. Its entrance was made possible by the Compromise of 1850 which balanced the interests of the proslavery groups with those of the antislavery groups. In return for California's entrance, the Fugitive Slave Act was passed, and Utah and New Mexico territories were organized with the slavery issue to be decided by the residents at a later time.

1851 Fewer people used the California Trail this year, but authorities differ on the number. Historian Merrill Mattes, for example, estimated the numbers only as high as 5,000 – 10,000, while Stewart thought it could be as low as 1,000. By this time some of the glitter had faded from the gold rush. Striking it rich was not very common,

Jim Beckwourth was the son of a slave and a southern planter. He became a mountain man and later a guide for the emigrants. He discovered the Beckwourth Pass across the Sierra Nevada and opened the trail named after him.

Colorado History

and emigrants heard of cholera and the terrible hardships on the trail encountered the previous year. Besides, there was Oregon where land was easier to obtain, and it seemed that the trail there was easier. People still went to California, but by sea. An estimated 15,000 went by way of the Isthmus of Panama while only a trickle sailed around the Horn.

A short, but new route was opened in Scotts Bluff through Mitchell Pass. Prior to this development the emigrants bypassed the area by going through Robidoux Pass. Today the Oregon Trail Museum is located in Mitchell Pass, and you can walk along the route used by the emigrants and their wagons on their way west.

Another branch of the trail was opened by Jim Beckwourth. It split off the Truckee route near the Truckee Meadows, by present-day Reno, crossed the Sierra Nevada to the north through Beckwourth Pass and continued west to Bidwell Bar, another gold mining area.

In September, the Treaty of Horse Creek, or what has sometimes been called the First Fort Laramie Treaty, was signed with many of the Indian tribes of the Great Plains. The territory was divided into specific tribal grounds, and the U.S. government agreed to provide the Indians with supplies for the next fifty years; the Indians were to then allow the emigrants to pass through their lands unharmed. The peace that this was to be ensured did not last very long. Almost immediately some people wanted it changed, and Congress reduced the number of years the Indians received allotments.

1852 This was a banner year for trail travel to California. The numbers were even higher than in 1850. It is estimated that over 50,000 emigrants including families again traveled over the trails with large herds of cattle and sheep totaling about one hundred thousand. The improvements along the trail were now having their impact. Whereas in 1846 the trip had taken 136 days by oxen, this year the fastest ox-train completed it in 85 days and one with mules did it in 72 days. Unfortunately, cholera was also back on the trail as much as it had been in 1849 and 1850. The incidence of death from this disease was high.

On the St. Joe Road Marshall's Trading Post and Ferry was opened at the crossing of the Big Blue in present-day Marysville. It saved time especially during periods of high water when fording was difficult.

Nobles' Road was opened. William H. Nobles took the Lassen Route to the Black Rock Desert. Instead of following the Applegate route northwest across it as Lassen did, he headed west along its edge and along the Smoke Creek Desert. He then crossed the mountains and headed for Shasta City. This is what Lassen had hoped to establish earlier. The first wagon company consisted of twenty-six people. This route would later become popular with those emigrants going to northern California.

Another split in the trail developed on the Carson Route, the Johnson's Cutoff. It headed off west to the south shore of Lake Bigler now known as Tahoe and then on to Placerville. This section replaced part of the route pioneered by the Mormons. It became the main route for the next decade. Today U.S. Highway 50 follows the general route.

The Sonora Road was opened. It was another of the splinter routes that broke off the Carson route. It continued south on the Walker River and then followed it up and over the mountains to Sonora. This was similar to the route taken by the Bidwell-Bartleson party in 1841. In 1853 the route was heavily used.

Back along the trail just west of South Pass some small cutoffs were also being developed off the route to Fort Bridger. These cutoffs turned off but connected with the Sublette Cutoff. They were the Kinney and Slate Creek cutoffs. They were soon joined by another, the Baker-Davis Road. These became more popular because they cut out the long dry desert crossing on Sublette's Flat.

1853 This year emigration west dropped again. However, it was still about twenty thousand emigrants with one hundred fifty head of cattle and sheep.

Another splinter developed off the Applegate trail near Clear Lake by the Oregon border. This was the Yreka Road which also took emigrants to northern California and the town of Yreka.

1854 The Kansas-Nebraska Act was finally enacted. It provided for the establishment of the territories of Kansas and Nebraska. It formally opened many of the former Indian treaty lands to settlement and the establishment of towns. As a result, towns were officially platted at some of the jumping-off sites, and others were established along the trails over the ensuing years.

Conflicts between the Indians and emigrants increased along the eastern half of the trail in the Platte River Valley. The incident that precipitated it involved a lame cow and an emigrant. Accounts vary but most hold that a cow wandered off into a Brule village. Instead of attempting to get it back, the emigrant continued on to Fort Laramie to get help from the U.S. Army. Lieutenant John Grattan with cannon and twenty-nine men under his command returned to retrieve the cow. By the time they arrived the Indians had already killed and eaten most of the cow. Grattan wanted the Indian responsible for killing the cow. The Indians were willing to give the emigrant a horse to replace the cow, but they were not willing to turn over the individual. Grattan fired the cannon at the village and fighting ensued. When the fighting was over, the Brule Chief Bear was dead along with some other Indians. Lieutenant Grattan and all of his command, save one soldier who escaped to tell of the "massacre" were dead. The soldier died two days later of his wounds. Indians, emigrants, and the army were now at odds, and raiding increased for the next couple of years.

1855 Travel along the California trail continued to drop off. This year it was back to the pre-gold rush level and not until 1859 would it approach the 1849 level.

1856 Another splinter route developed near the end of the trail. The Big Trees route was opened. It split from the Carson Route east of the Carson Pass and headed towards Stockton. It was devised by the businessmen of Stockton to divert the emigrant traffic for their own benefit. Improvements were built into the route and the worst crossings were eliminated by eight bridges with the main bridge being fourteen feet wide and seventy-five feet long. The town even sent out representatives to tell the emigrants of the new road with all of its improvements and of all the troubles encountered on the old road.

1857 While the California Trail remained in use traffic was still light. Improvements and additional new routes were being developed. Some used parts of the older routes and others bypassed sections altogether.

The U.S. government was being pressured to act. Congress appropriated $300,000 for improvements on what was officially referred to as the "Fort Kearny, South Pass, Honey Lake Wagon Road," but still commonly called the California Trail at least as far as the Lassen Cutoff. Besides improving the grades and crossings, they built reservoirs at places such as Rabbit Hole Spring and Antelope Spring in Nevada, which greatly reduced the hardships there.

1858 Demand for improved communications between California and the eastern portion of the U.S. was increasing. The Butterfield Stage Line opened. Stage service started at Tipton, Missouri, and then followed the southern route through Texas, New Mexico, Arizona, and then into California. It was sometimes referred to as the Oxbow route.

Fort Bridger was rebuilt by the U.S. Army. It served as a military post until 1890. Emigrants continued to stop there. By that time nothing was left of Jim Bridger's trading post and the remnants of the old stone Mormon fort were removed. Today many of the surviving military structures have been restored, and it is a living history museum and state historic site.

Fort Caspar was established at Louis Guinard's trading post and bridge. It was called the Platte Bridge Station and was named Fort Caspar in 1865 after Lieutenant Caspar Collins who was killed in the Battle of Red Buttes near there. Troops were withdrawn in 1859, but returned in 1862.The reconstructed fort and the museum are open to the public.

Captain Simpson of the topographical engineers began the exploration for a new wagon road route across central Nevada. It went south out of Salt Lake City to Camp Floyd, which had been constructed after the "Mormon War," and then west across into Nevada to connect with the Carson route at Genoa, Nevada. He did some initial exploration in the fall but had to return because of the weather conditions.

1859 In April Simpson left on his expedition to survey a new wagon road to Genoa. He completed it and returned. The new road was immediately used by some emigrants and became more popular in the 1860s as it became known. In 1860 this central route was used by the Overland Stage and the Pony Express. Travelers going through Salt Lake City now had a choice of three routes to California.

The Lander Road was opened. This was part of the government improvement plan authorized by Congress in1857. Frederick Lander started surveying the region near the South Pass for a better route. The one he developed turned off east of South Pass just before the last crossing of the Sweetwater and followed its bend northward. The route was aimed for Fort Hall, thus bypassing the long dip to Fort Bridger and the desert crossing on the Sublette. Work had started on it in 1858, and it opened in1859. It soon became very popular. One estimate for its first year put the number of emigrants at thirteen thousand.

1860s By the 1860s the population of California had grown and spread out. Towns were popping up all over and roads were beginning to crisscross the state.

The Pony Express was established in 1860. It existed for only about nineteen months. Its route incorporated parts of the old trail and many of its recent cutoffs. It started at St. Joseph, Missouri, one of the jumping-off towns and ended in Sacramento, the city that grew up at Sutter's Fort and then to San Francisco, the harbor town that welcomed so many of the oceangoing Argonauts. The Pony Express generally followed the St. Joseph Road until it joined the old main trail and followed it or a variant all the way to Salt Lake. There it followed Simpson's central route across Nevada and then back on one or more sections of the Carson route. With the completion of the cross country telegraph in 1861, the Pony Express came to an end.

The Pony Express only operated about nineteen months.

The 1860s saw increasing conflicts between the Indians and settlers. Not only did they increase in California and farther east all along the trail, but also on the trails to Santa Fe and Oregon. Fort Churchill was constructed on the Carson River to protect the settlers, the emigrants and the Pony Express. Today the remains of the fort is a Nevada State Park.

In one sense, the most significant event of the 60s that had the greatest impact was the building and completion of the transcontinental railroad in 1869. It is often thought to represent the end of the trail emigration era. In some respects that was true, but for many a poor person or family the wagon and the trail west were still the cheapest and only way available for them. The trail, however, was now very different. Only twenty years before, when once having crossed the Missouri, the early emigrants actually had to open the trails and cut wagon roads across the plains, through the deserts, over the mountains and through the forests.

Later emigrants were able to follow one of many of the routes available or take roads specifically constructed to take them to a particular location. Guides were a necessity, but soon they were replaced by guidebooks and well established trails.

The early emigrants had to cut the banks and cross the streams, or, if necessary, wait until the rivers receded or construct their own ferries or ford them and endure the dangerous currents. Soon more and more of larger rivers had established ferries and bridges available for the emigrants. Even many of the smaller ones were bridged.

The earliest emigrants could look forward to less than a handful of trading posts and forts to replenish their supplies. These early ones had been established by fur companies primarily to trade with the Indians. Now many of the posts and stores were created mostly to serve the needs of the emigrant trade. The military also built forts or took over fur posts which provided places for both trade and security. Seasonal entrepreneurs increasingly had set up posts in even the most dangerous areas, and soon towns and cities were established on the trail with all the trappings of civilization. These provided the later emigrants with all sorts of opportunities for trade, rest and safety. Stagecoach stops, and for a short time Pony Express stations, could be found every fifteen to twenty miles along portions of the trails. The time required for the journey was reduced by weeks, and sometimes even months.

During the early years men were the dominant travelers on the trail. Women and children were in the minority, but in the later years women and children were the majority. By the 1860s the trails that led west had become two-way roads and were no longer seasonal. The trails blazed for the emigrants were later not only used by individuals and families going west, but heavily by the military and commercial interests. The military provided protection by sending solders along the trails and into the areas, while traders and freighters supplied the constant flow of goods to the forts and growing communities, as the lands from the plains to the coast were settled. However, even those emigrants who took the "iron horse," were following in the footsteps of the early emigrants and Argonauts. Much of the bed of the railroad followed one or more of the portions of the trail that had developed over the years. Today, even a large portion of the route of Interstate 80 and other highways generally follow the route of many portions of the trail and its variants.

FINDING THE WAY

For the emigrants going west knowledge about the geography, the weather, food and water resources, vegetation, the inhabitants, the route, available trails, and their destination was critical. The more knowledge and the more specific it was, the better their chances for success. Each year's migration added to the base. As the number of emigrants grew, more people were available as sources for knowledge.

Information was available from a wide variety of sources. Trappers and traders, missionaries, military expeditions and related reports, letters to friends, family or newspapers back east, published emigrant journals or books, newspaper articles, guides and guidebooks, and maps. And, as the emigrants moved along the trail they questioned all they met for the most up to date advice and read the signs sometimes posted by earlier travelers.

The next few sections are related to this base of knowledge. Information about some of the guides and guidebooks, maps, and diaries will be described and examined.

Chapter Three

GUIDEBOOKS

B y the end of the 1840s and the early 1850s, the emigrants had a much better idea of where they were going and stood a much better chance of getting there. The earliest emigrants had no guidebooks and knew only vaguely where they were. They largely depended on the use of guides or pilots who were usually mountain men, such as Joseph Walker, Tom Fitzpatrick, Andrew Sublette, "Black" Harris, Caleb Greenwood, James Beckwourth, and Jim Bridger. The knowledge of the area that these men had was important, but so were their skills at survival because they had to lead emigrants to lands they themselves might never had explored.

By the mid-1840s, there were enough emigrants themselves who had been over the trails that they began to act as guides, publish their journals, or write guidebooks based on their journals. Large sections of the trails were now easier to identify because they had become well-worn. This was especially true of the section where the Oregon and California trails coincided.

Guidebooks were developed through a type of evolution. The earliest, such as Hastings', didn't tell much about the specifics of the route but provided more psychological support and encouragement. Later ones soon became more specific concerning the routes, and by the time of Ware's 1849 guidebook, they frequently included an overall map of the trail. By the early 1850s, the better guidebooks, such as Horn's used a milepost approach that had been perfected earlier by William Clayton in his guide for the Mormons. Also, most of the new guidebooks now included one or more of the new cutoffs that had been developed, such as the Sublette, Hudspeth, or Salt Lake which,

Lansford Hastings

Lansford Hastings was another of the California emigrants who dreamed of creating his own empire. He first traveled west in 1842. Then, Oregon was his goal, not California. After a short stay in Oregon, he decided California was the place to make his fortune. However, he is most remembered for his guidebook, the infamous Hastings Cutoff, and its association with the Donners.

Courtesy of the Bancroft Library #Graff 1954

respectively, bypassed Fort Bridger, the Great Salt Lake Desert, or Fort Hall. Some included the new routes to the different gold fields.

There were a number of guidebooks that had a significant impact on the westward movement of the emigrants to California. Some of the better-known ones today were written by Hastings, Ware, Clayton, Horn, Child, and Marcy. Not so well-known today, but popular among the forty-niners was the small handwritten Willis's guide. Portions of some of the above guides will be examined and discussed briefly, and the small Willis handbook is included in typeset in its entirety.

Probably the best known early guide is Lansford Hastings's *The Emigrants' Guide to Oregon and California*. It was written in 1844 and printed in 1845. Hastings had gone to Oregon in 1842, moved down to California, and finally returned to the States to encourage more emigrants to go to California. His guide was one of the few available for the early emigrants, and it is the one associated with the Donner disaster of 1846. The guide was comprised of fifteen chapters with just over 150 pages. It had, however, only one chapter (nine pages long) devoted to all the routes to California from Canada to the Horn, including a new proposed cutoff, which became known as the Hastings Cutoff. (See the included TH Jefferson map.) Most of the guide described what was to be found in Oregon and California. One chapter was devoted to preparations and what to bring. This was probably the most useful of all.

The following quotations are from Chapter 14, which was concerned with the different available routes to travel to California and Oregon. First, Hastings described the Oregon "Trail" west from Fort Hall:

"From this fort, those who go to Oregon, continue down Lewis' river, fifteen days, to Fort Wallawalla; and thence down the Columbia, ten days, to the lower settlements in Oregon.

"From Fort Hall to the Pacific, by the Oregon Route, a distance of about eight hundred miles, there is but one continued succession of high mountains, stupendous cliffs, and deep, frightful caverns, with an occasional limited valley.

"This portion of the Oregon route, from Fort Hall to the Pacific, has always been considered, wholly impassable for wagons, or any other vehicles; yet, it is said, that the emigrants of 1843 succeeded in getting their wagons entirely down to the Willamette settlement. This they may have done, but I am confident, from my own experience, that each wagon must have cost the owner of it more time and labor, than five wagons are worth, even in Oregon."

Certainly this was not an encouraging description. Then he described the accepted or old route to California:

"Those who go to California, traveled from Fort Hall west southwest about fifteen days, to the northern pass, in the California mountains; thence, three days to Sacramento; and, thence, seven days, down the Sacramento; to the Bay of St. Francisco, in California."

Sounds pretty easy, doesn't it?

Finally, he described the geography of both the old and newly proposed routes:

"The California route, from Ft. Hall to the Sacramento River, lies through alternate plains, prairies and valleys, and over hills amid lofty mountains, thence down the great valley of Sacramento, to the bay of St. Francisco, a distance from Ft. Hall, of nine hundred miles. The Indians are, in many places, very numerous; yet, they are extremely timid, and entirely inoffensive. Wagons can be as readily taken from Ft. Hall to the bay of St. Francisco, as they can, from the States to Ft. Hall; and, in fact, the latter part of the route, is found much more eligible for a wagon than the former. The most direct route, for the California emigrants, would be to leave the Oregon route, about two hundred miles east from Ft. Hall; thence bearing southwest, to Salt

Lake; and thence continuing down to the bay of St. Francisco, by the route just described."

It is easy to see how people reading this would head for California. It seemed like only a few easy weeks away by wagon from either Fort Bridger on the new cutoff, or from Fort Hall on the old route. Hastings even implied that the trip was easier once past the forts. For those emigrants who believed him, they soon learned that he was mistaken. It seemed he was wrong about almost everything, from the Indians to the timing and the ease of travel over the "lofty mountains." For members of the Donner party they learned too late. Virginia Reed, one of the young survivors, learned her lesson well and put it best, "Never take no cut offs and hury along as fast as you can."

Joseph Ware's *The Emigrants Guide to California* was available to the forty-niners and was a fairly popular one, but while better than Hastings's, it was still fairly general for the section of the trail that was exclusively the California section, as can be seen in the following:

"in its course from the Raft river, the road takes a southwest direction, and follows the trail across the dividing ridge to the head of the Humboldt or Mary's river, distant one hundred and seventy miles. For two days you travel along the Raft river; camps good. The road over this distance resembles the country west of the South Pass in the Rocky Mountains for the same distance. There are places in which great care is required, and some difficulty may be experienced in consequence of the unevenness of the road in passing over the dividing ridges of the mountains. On the RATTLESNAKE RIVER you can find good camps, there are plenty of good springs also. The prevailing plant is wild sage, which, in some places, will continue to be your dependence for fuel, though there is some good timber.

"We would earnestly advise you to oppose experiments in your party, in leaving the regular route of travel to try roads said to be shorter. You will get to California in good season if you keep straight ahead. If not, you may lose a month or so of time, and experience the fate of the Donner's party. BY trying a new road they lost nearly sixty days, and were overtaken by snow, and spent the winter in the mountains, where nearly forty of them perished. Lose no time foolishly on the road, that can be spent with profit to yourself and teams. You strike the HUMBOLDT RIVER at its head. From thence your course is down its valley for three hundred miles. It is the principal river of the great basin."

There were two guidebooks written by Mormons. Ira Willis'[Willes'] *Best Guide to the Gold Mines 816 Miles* was hand-written. He had gone to California with the Mormon Battalion in 1846 during the Mexican War and was nearby when gold was discovered at Sutter's Mill, and even worked at the mill. Returning to Salt Lake with the Mormons that pioneered the Carson Route in 1848, they also took the new cutoff back to Salt Lake, which had been pioneered by Hensley earlier that year. This route was the one described in his guide. It was the only guide readily available to forty-niners that really described a solid and traveled route to California. It seems that both James Wilkins and J. Goldsborough Bruff had copies, which they used.

The other Mormon guide, *The Latter-Day Saints' Emigrants' Guide*, by William Clayton was published in 1848. His guide was much more specific and accurate. It used a milepost approach and included detailed information about water, crossing, landmarks, obstacles and camping sites. It became a model for the later guidebooks of the 1850s. Clayton's guide covered the route from Council Bluffs to Salt Lake City, and Willis's covered the route from Salt Lake to California. Compared to Clayton's guide, the Willis guide was a Spartan edition, but it was better than anything else and was well received. The

Best Guide
to the
GOLD MINES
816 miles
by
IRA J. WILLIS
G. S. L. City

(2)
Thence to the Old Road near .
   the Steeple Rocks,   6.
" to Goose Creek over a hill   10.
          191.
Several camping places from the
Steeple Rocks to Goose Creek.
" up Goose Creek, good camping. 22.
" to the Hot Spring Valley 13.
" " " 2nd Spring (good camp[)] 5.
" through the Valley 32.
Found good camping places,
none of them are more than 10 miles apart
" to a Branch of Mary's River
  good camping 8.
" through a kanyon crossing
the Branch 9 times, camping 8.
" to Mary's River good camping
all along 19.
      299.
" to Martins Fork of Mary's River
good camping all along 60.
      359.

Way Bill of distances, camping place, rivers, hot springs etc on the Route from G. S. L. to the GOLD MINES	Miles
To Bear River, crossing the Weber 4 miles this side of Capt Brown's Roadometer Measure	84.
(Good camping at short distances[)]	
Thence to Malad or Mud Creek	3.
" " the 1st Warm Spring	6.
" " " 2nd do camping	14.
" " " Spring in the Mts. good camping	11.
" down deep Creek cross at the Bend	6.
" " " " good camping	6.
" to Springs in the plains poor "	10.
" " Cajiers [or Cajius] Creek good camping at several places in sight on left	16.
" up Cajiers [or Cajius] Creek, good camping	9.
	176.

(3) Thence over a hill through a kanyon to where you strike Mary's River again (good camping & good in the kanyon.[)]	20.
Then to a pass in the hills where you cross the River twice good camping 'all along	72.
" " the next crossing of Mary's River good camping all along	46.
" over a drive without grass or water	14.
" to the lower crossing of Mary's River (good camping[)]	14.
" to the lower camping place on the River, grass-scarce	26.
" to a Slough, poor camping grass scarce	15.
" " the Sink of Mary's River . grass & wood scarce	20.
The best water here is in a slough that passes through a bend & a narrow Bluff. Here also you may find	566

(4) a new track on your left that Childs intended to make last fall which ..ly be nearer & a less distance to do without grass & water.	
By the Battalion route from the Sink to the hot Springs, no grass, poor water	20.
Thence to Truckie River, good camp.	25.
	611.
[Should be 631]	
The road forks here. You will take the left hand road to Salmon Trout river good camp	25.
(Childs road if made comes in at this or the next camping place[)]	
Then turn to the right and cross a bend, good camping	15.
" up the River good camp	8.
" cross a hill to the river good "	12.
" to Pass Creek Kanyon, good camping every few miles	42.
" through Pass Creek Kanyon	5.
	738.

(5) Then to Red Lake or the foot of the dividing Ridge. Calif. Mts	11.
	749.
good camping, nigh by.	
Then to Lake Valley, good camping	6.
" over the highest Ridge to Rock Valley, good camping	10.
" to Leek Springs, good camping & good by by [sic] the way	13.
" " Camp Creek, poor camping	10.
" down the ridge and then you arrive into a valley two miles, on your left grass plenty	16.
" to Pleasant Valley Gold Mines	12.
	816.
" " Sutters	55.
	861.
[Should be 871]	
Truckie & Salmon Trout are not the same river but Mary, Ogden & Humboldt are.	

originals were handwritten and one is currently in the possession of the National Park Service, Yosemite National Park, California, who graciously allowed the reproduction from pages of the type set version.

It seemed that every year new guidebooks were being prepared, and generally they were getting better. Six pages, covering about one hundred sixty miles, from *Horn's Overland Guide* (1852) are included courtesy of the Everett D Graff Collection, The Newberry Library, Chicago, Illinois. Horn's guide included the Hudspeth Cutoff on the California Trail. In order to compare it with Hastings' and Ware's start at "West Branch, Raft River." This is where the Hudspeth Cutoff joined the main trail coming down from Fort Hall and the Snake River. Follow it through "Pyramid Circle" (City of Rocks) where the Salt Lake Road joined the main California through "Thousands Springs Valley" and finally to the Humboldt or Mary's River. For a comparison, the equivalent section in the Willis guide is from Steeple Rock through Hot Spring Valley to Mary's River. This same section was also covered in the Hastings' and Ware's excerpts, but as can be seen, they were so general that they were of little help for the emigrants. Additionally, both the Willis and Horn guides used the same general Carson route to cross the Sierra Nevada into California. However, by Horn's time the Carson route had changed somewhat. His guidebook provided added detail, and emigrants felt much more confident with something like this in their hands.

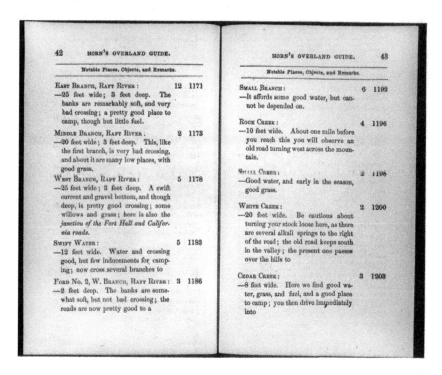

Notable Places, Objects, and Remarks.

PYRAMID CIRCLE:* 5 1208
—And pass through it.

JUNCTION GREAT SALT LAKE AND CALI-
FORNIA ROADS: 1 1209
—This is just at the west end of Pyramid Circle, and affords some grass and
fuel, but no water.

SMALL CREEK: 3 1212
—This is the second creek from the
junction; good water, and some fuel
and grass; flat roads.

FLINT SPRINGS AND BRANCH: 4 1216
—In reaching this place you cross a
small creek, about two miles from it;
at this spring and branch you have
good water, and advantages for camping.

* Pyramid Circle is a delightful place. It is 5 miles long, and about
3 miles wide, level within the walls around, and studded throughout
with numerous tall white and green stones, from 60 to 150 feet high,
and 10 to 20 feet in diameter at the foot—some of them running
almost to a point at the top. It is surrounded by mountains which
are covered with pine and cedar trees, and is altogether a beautiful
and picturesque scene. Upon these stones are written, painted, and
engraved, the names of many visitors, with the dates. This circle is
entirely surrounded by the mountains, except an inlet at the east
end of about 50 yards, and an outlet at the west end of about 20
yards.

Notable Places, Objects, and Remarks.

STEEP CREEK: 2 1218
—Just before reaching it you have some
hills and a rough road; down the hill
to the right of the road is some grass
and timber, and a good place to
camp.

OLD ROAD: 3 1221
—Here on a hill an old road leads to
the right; the road is now hilly and
very rough to

BRANCH OF GOOSE CREEK: 1 1222
—10 feet wide. Some grass and fuel,
and good water.

GOOSE CREEK: 3 1225
—25 feet wide; 3 feet deep. The valley of this creek furnishes many good
camping places, and much good grass.

SMALL CREEK: 6 1231
—It is not wide, but very deep, with
soft banks.

RECORD BLUFF, to the left: 10 1241
—It is a sandstone, upon which is written the names of thousands of travelers; Good Creek is just to the right;
good camping.

Notable Places, Objects, and Remarks.

CAÑON, east end: 4 1245
—The road is quite rough up this *cañon*
along a branch of Goose Creek, to a

STONY HILL: 5 1250
—This hill, though rough and rocky, is
easily ascended.

THOUSAND SPRINGS VALLEY: 9 1259
—Here we find several small streams of
warm water, and some mineral water,
but little that is good to use.

SMALL CREEK: 13 1272
—10 feet wide; 2 feet deep. A good
place to camp; wild sage for fuel,
and tolerable good water, while you
find the best of grass.

HOPE SPRINGS: 24 1296
—You will find considerable branch
water all along before you come to
this spring, but it contains the very
best of water; you will now go south
to the mouth of a

CAÑON: 1 1297
—Where you will find some grass, and
a good place to camp.

Notable Places, Objects, and Remarks.

CAÑON CREEK: 9 1306
—6 feet wide. Good water, but no
grass; you will pass over a rough
road for some distance to

DECEPTION VALLEY: 18 1324
—This valley from the surrounding hills
has the appearance of a beautiful
meadow, but it is all weeds.

DEEP FORK (of Humboldt): 5 1329
—12 feet wide; 4 feet deep. The water is clear, and current swift; some
grass and fuel, and a fair place to
camp.

HUMBOLDT RIVER: 6 1335
—3 rods wide; 5 feet deep. It is very
bad crossing, and within one mile you
cross two other branches of it, which
are also bad; the roads are then good
down the river to

WEST BRANCH, HUMBOLDT RIVER: 23 1358
—4 rods wide; 4 feet deep. A solid
gravel bottom, and good crossing; no
grass.

Chapter Four

DIARIES

E migrant diaries came in all sizes and shapes. Each emigrant had their own style and purpose. Some like J Goldsborough Bruff's (1849) were extremely detailed, illustrated, and were contained in a number of journal books. Others, like William Baker's (1852) had only a line or two for each day in a single journal. Some emigrants wrote regularly and other infrequently.

Merrill Mattes, the eminent historian and authority, suggested that about one of 250 emigrants kept some form of written record of their journey. For historians these diaries are the major source of information and insight into the trail's history and the emigrants themselves. Yet, no single diary can be considered the definitive one. Conditions on the trail could change in a few days, not to mention from one year to another. One year it could be hot and dry, the next wet and mild. The physical location of the route changed and new cutoffs were developed while others fell into disuse. Wagon companies often made small improvements to the trail as they went, thus making it easier for the next company. Even the government made physical improvements over the years.

Different sections of the trail had different characteristic and demands. The type of draft animals selected — oxen, mules or horses, impacted their travel. The planning, organization, and leadership of wagon companies were critical but varied widely. Well-run companies and poorly-run ones could share the trail at the same time and place. Some companies ran out of supplies early while others still had some to discard or to sell or share. For some companies it seemed that things were always going wrong, while others had no serious problems. Some people left one company to join another or sometimes to continue on their own. During some years disease seemed rampant on the trails, while in other years it was nearly non-existent. Some wagon companies were predominantly comprised of families looking for a new home, while other could be comprised of only men on their way to the gold fields to seek riches and then return home. Even the character of the particular emigrant had its impact. Each wrote from his/her own perspective, age, interest, and expectations. Men and women saw things differently. All these factors combined to give each emigrant their own experience and special relationship to the trail. Therefore, the accounts written by these diarist varied greatly and could relay a very different impression of the trek west. This is not to say that they did not have similar experiences. However, only by examining a variety of diaries can one fully understand the emigrant experience.

Some emigrants were keeping their diary planning to have it published and available for later emigrants. That fact alone caused them to approach keeping their journal differently. Edwin Bryant went to California in 1846. In "The Preface" to his *What I Saw in California* he writes that "He has carefully avoided such embellishment as would tend to impress the reader with a false or incorrect idea of what he saw and describes. He has invented nothing....His design has been to furnish a volume, entertaining and instructive to the traveler and emigrant to the Pacific." His journal was about four hundred fifty pages in length and was full of information about every imaginable subject. Another book written by two emigrants was Overton Johnson and William Winter's *Route Across the Rocky Mountains*. They were part of the 1843 Great Migration to Oregon. Their book was one of the first to include a summary "Bill of the Route" or general mile post description of the route to Oregon. They also went to California before they returned to the States. Their volume, around one hundred fifty pages, also included some information about California and the route back to Fort Hall. It was published in 1846. Both these two volumes were available, sought, and read by later emigrants for guidance.

The following diary excerpts are from those of three emigrants: James Wilkins (1849), The Henry E. Huntington Library and Art Gallery; Wakeman Bryarly (1849), Yale University Library; and Eleazar Ingalls (1850), The Newberry Library. The three diaries varied, but are "typical" in that their daily entries are not too long, nor too short. They provide the reader with insight into what it was like to be on one major section of the trail. The impact of the different factors and conditions that combined to give each his own personal experience comes through clearly to the reader.

By the time the emigrants had reached the Mary's or Humboldt River they had come about sixteen hundred miles, depending on where they began. Yet, the worst part of the California Trail still lay before them—crossing the desert and then the climb over the Sierra Nevada. If the emigrants hadn't seen it already, this is where they got close up to the "elephant," — the symbol for the extreme hardships and the despair they caused. Come join our three diarists as they leave the Humboldt Sink and dike and head off to cross the Forty-Mile Desert for either the Truckee or the Carson rivers and then climb the Sierra Nevada. Emigrants traveling on the Applegate-Lassen route had already turned off at the Meadows. They had to contend with the Black Rock Desert and then the mountains. Their experiences were similar to those on the Forty-Mile Desert in the following passages. Bryarly would follow the Truckee, while Wilkins and Ingalls, the Carson Route.

Notice their comments concerning earlier expectations, the problems experienced their wagon company and others, the climatic and physical conditions found and endured on the desert and then the climb over the mountains, and the general impact of these factors on their own feelings and future expectations. Remember also, the account of Betsey and Ike in the song noted at the beginning of this book.

Read along in the emigrants' own words and relive their journeys as they describe their trek along the two most dangerous portions of the trail — the desert crossing and the climb over the mountains. See also the pictorial section for corresponding original illustrations and recent photos of these sections.

WAKEMAN BRYARLY, 1849

Bryarly left St. Joseph, Missouri, on May 10, 1849, and took the Sublette Cutoff. He then went by way of Fort Hall because the Hudspeth Cutoff was not yet opened when he passed. He was part of a mule team train. He reached the sink on August 11 and the Truckee River on the thirteenth. The ascent up the Truckee took the emigrants to Donner Lake. On August 22, Bryarly made the final ascent not up Donner Pass, but nearby Roller Pass. On September 1, 1849, he arrived at Johnson's ranch.

Since Saturday at 2 o"clock, we traveled 65 miles without *wood* or *water* to last evening (Monday) at 6 o'clock.

Saturday, August 11th.

The morning was fair, beautiful, & pleasant. Early, everything & everybody was in active preparation for a start In the evening. Grass was bundled & packed & stowed in the wagons. Loose mules were packed also, & everyone riding an animal had his fodder behind him. Casks & kegs, gum bags & bottles & gun covers, coffee pots and tea kettles, canteens, jugs & bottles, *everything* was filled with water & at 1 o'clock the order to gear up was given & at 2 we bid farewell to the marsh & our numerous friends. The road goes direct across to strike the old road some 5 miles. It was a new one, & made through the sage brush & of course was not very good, but the old road was as smooth as a table & hard as a rock. It passed over what is in high water part of the sink & consequently there was no vegetation save a few sage bushes, which were upon mounds several feet above the level. Stock of all sorts, horses, mules, oxen & cows were scattered along, having corralled themselves in the arms of fatigue & death. Here for the second time upon our journey we saw the mirage upon the immense white basins. It was a poor example, however, but was very deceiving to those who had never seen anything of the kind before.

Twelve miles upon the old road brought us to the *Sink*, the disideratum of long hoped for weeks. "How far to the Sink?" has been a question *often* asked & *often* answered, *often* heard in the last month. The Sink extends over several miles & is generally grown up with rushes & grass. There is immense basins however on all sides, which, in high water, receive the back water. The road keeps in these basins, which extend *miles & miles* without a vestige of vegetation, but so white & dazzling in the sun as scarcely to be looked at. We rolled by this, the water of which cannot be used by man or beast, 4 miles, & came to some sulfur springs or rather wells. Here we camped for the night. These wells were dug in a slough, & the water was very like many of our sulphur springs at home. The animals drank it freely & it seemed to do them no harm. In this slough just below the spring were a great number of cattle & mules, which had become mired & were not able to get out & were left. Some of them were still alive. The most obnoxious, hideous gases perfumed our camp all night, arising from the many dead animals around. In the morning some were found laying immediately by us & in the vicinity 30 were adding their scents to the nauseous atmosphere. Our animals were turned to the grass we brought already dried, & they seemed relish it much.

We were *past the Sink*. This is glory enough for one day. I would ask the learned & descriptive Mr. Fremont & the elegant & imaginative Mr. Bryant, where was the beautiful valley, the surpassing lovely valley of the Humboldt? Where was the country presenting the most splendid "agricultural features?" Where the splendid grazing, the cottonwood lining the banks of their *beautiful meandering stream*, & everything presenting the most interesting & picturesque appearance of any place they ever saw?

Perhaps Mr. Bryant was speaking ironically of all these most captivating things that he saw, or perhaps he thought it was "too far out" for anyone else but himself to see. If not, I have only to say, "Oh shame where is thy blush."

We have travelled along it several hundred miles, from its commencement from a little pool that you could drink up is thirsty, to its termination in the sink. It is so very crooked in its whole course that I believe it impossible for one to make a *chalk mark* as much so. Frequently I have stood & fished on each side of me in two different parts of the river, the distance around being a half a mile or more. It is a *dirty, muddy, sluggish, indolent stream*, with but little grass at the best of times, & as for cottonwood, there is not a switch of it from one end to the other. A friend of mine remarked, it was fit for nothing else but to sink to the "Lower Regions," & the quicker it done the better. He much preferred calling it the "Hellbodlt River.

Distance, 23 miles

Sunday, August 12th

We rolled out at daybreak. The road was firm, hard, level, & smooth. In four miles we came to the forks of the road. Here we found many placards, the most of which advised their friends to take the right. The left was but little travelled in comparison to the right & we took it [right]. We rolled through the same kind of basin as yesterday and 10 miles we stopped to breakfast, which was cooked with some pieces of wagons we picked up on the road. We layed by until 2 o'clock having given grass & water to our stock, & again rolled. The road continued the same for several miles, when we left the basin forever, the road then being upon a ridge with a few sage bushes & rocks. We rolled thus 15 miles, which brought us to the Hot Springs.

Seventy dead animals were counted in the last 25 miles. Pieces of wagons also, the irons in particular—the wood part having been burnt—were also strewn along. An ox-yoke, wheel & a dead ox; a dead ox, yoke, & wheel; a wheel, dead ox & a yoke, was the order of the day, every hundred or two yards.

These Hot Springs are one of *The* things upon this earth. The pool is some 25 or 30 yds. In circumference & around it are a great number of springs, some placid & luke warm, others sending off considerable steam & hot water, & others again, bubbling & boiling furiously & scalding. The water when cooled was drinkable, but sulphurish & very salt. There was a great number of kegs & casks, boxes & wagonbeds here, which had been used to cool the water by others. These were filled & after some hours our stock drank it. A piece of meat, held in one the boiling springs, boiled in 20 minutes, perfectly done. By putting the water in your coffee-pot & holding the pot over the bubbling, it would boil in a few minutes. In this way many of us cooked our suppers.

Thousands of dollars worth of property thrown away by the emigration was laying here. Wagons & property of every kind & description, not saying anything of the dead animals & those left to die. The machinery of a turning machine that must have cost $6[00] or $700. A steam engine & machinery for coining that could not have cost less than $2[000] or $3000, were also laying here, all sacrificed upon this Jornado. These things they say belonged to the notorious Mr. Finley [?] who also lost 55 cattle of 80.

Distance, 25 miles.

Monday, August 13th.

We started this morning 2 ½ o'clock. The road was again in a basin & was level, hard, & smooth. Soon after daylight our animals showed evident signs of fagging. Four miles from Hot Springs we came to some sulfur springs. They were very salty & not good, but had been used by others. The sun was most powerful, & the reflection made the shinning dirt made it most oppressive. We rolled 12 miles, & having come to where we strike the sand which we had been dreading all the time, we stopped to breakfast. Some of our teams did not get in for some time after the others, they having fagged so much as to fall in the rear.

Here we fed the last of our grass & gave the last of our water. Several wagons were here, the animals having given out & were taken to the river ahead to recruit, which we learned was but 8 miles, but deep sand all the way. Several of us started soon after eating & came on to the river & luxuriated ourselves & horse with delicious water. The teams started at 1 o'clock but finding they would in all probability give out or at least be a dead strain all the way, they determined to double teams & bring half over & recruit the mules & bring the remainder today. This was accordingly done & seven wagons arrived safe & our animals watered & turned to good grass. Some remained behind with the wagons & water was packed back to them.

This Salmon Trout [Truckee] River. It is a beautiful clear, swift stream, & the water is delicious. Large cottonwood trees skirt the banks, which gives everything around an air of comfort once more. In approaching it the trees are seen a mile off, & to the parched, famished, & wearied man & beast they are truly "a green spot in the desert." We are safely over *the desert*, however, without losing a single animal, although many are very far gone; but a day or two recruiting, which we think of giving them here, will put them again all right. The water of the Hot Spring which was used freely by both the men & animals affected them most singularly. Two or three hours after drinking, it produced violent strangling to both. The men in particular were very much annoyed also by the most violent pain in the urinary organs. It was truly laughable to see their contortions & twistings after urinating, which they desired to do every hour. The mules also seemed to suffer much, but their symptoms lasted only 10 or 12 hours. Upon examining an old canteen that had had this water in it, with a grasshopper, I discovered the evident fumes of nitre, & upon examination found it contain much, & no doubt these unpleasant symptoms were caused by it. The dead animals were not so numerous today although there was yet sufficient to be very annoying from their perfumes. On the other (Carson) Road I am told they are much thicker, more than half of the head migration having taken that road.

Distance, 20 miles.

Tuesday, August 14th.

All night the teams, with loose mules & oxen, were rolling in, causing a general buzz all night. We layed in camp until noon, our mules being in excellent grass. They were then brought up & taken back for our remaining teams, which arrived in camp at 12 o'clock at night. They report many more dead animals upon the road yesterday. Every train that has arrived has lost one or two upon this last stretch. The weather today was most oppressively hot & we congratulated ourselves were not on the parched desert.

There is two roads here, one to the left on the same side of the river with a stretch through the sand of 25 miles to water and grass, the other crosses the river & keeps up the river through a kanyon 16 miles & crossing the river many times. From all we have been able to gather, we determined to cross the river, taking the right hand road. We had today a general inspection of our provisions & find we heave only sufficient to last us ten days. This was alarming & our Quartermaster was ordered to look out for more.

Wednesday, August 15th

All night the starved & famished mules & cattle were rushing through our camp, very much to the annoyance & risk of injury to those sleeping upon the ground. Many teams arrived last night, with the same proportionate loss as those before them. Everyone, without a dissenting vote, cursed the desert, and yet thank God they are over it with their little loss.

The morning was again very hot & we almost dreaded the idea of exposing ourselves to the hot rays of the sun upon the road. Our mules were brought up at 11 o'clock & we again hooked up. We crossed the river & rolled two miles when we came to a sand bluff which was very hard pulling. We passed upon this one mile & a half & nooned, turning our mules across the river to grass, it being the only grass in several miles. Our Quartermaster having made arrangements to obtain some flour & pork from a train behind, the sick wagon was left to bring it when it should arrive. One mile from noon we got off the sand & crossed the river & was soon in the kanyon proper. We passed along this, crossing the river four times in 5 miles. Here night overtook us, & not being able (to) proceed farther, & finding Capt. Smith awaiting us, we pulled out on the side of the road & tied our mules to the wheels, feeding them upon willows & cotton bushes.

Owing to the scarcity of the grass, the Captain determined to keep a camp ahead (of us), & leave one behind at each place to point out the grazing spots, & I to remain behind to take charge of the train. Our herders have been reduced to the ranks, each teamster taking care of his own extra mules, & the other extra ones rode by the men.

A fellow statesman & friend, Mr. Long, having overtaken us today, invited Mr. Washington to accompany him through, he being upon pack mules & expecting to arrive a week before us. I tendered to him the use of my "Walking Squaw" & he determined to accept & started off an hour before us. By the way, the Hot Spring water acted very singularly upon the "Squaw." Soon after arriving at breakfasting on the morning of the 13th at the beginning of the sand, she was taken with violent pain, as though she had the cholic, & very much to the astonishment of all, she was *confined* & brought forth. This abortion no doubt was caused by the water. We know not her history & consequently cannot tell the pedigree of the little one, or whether she herself had been *imprudent & slipt her foot*, but who knows but in this, was lost the race of as fine stock as ever the world saw. "Squaw," with her nation's peculiarity, was as much herself again in half an hour as though nothing had happened, & was hitched to the sick wagon & dragged it through the sand to the river. (The power of endurance of some of these ponies is most astonishing.)

Distance, 8 miles.

Thursday, August 16th.

We had a most unpleasant camp last night, & at daylight we were again upon the road. Yesterday evening it clouded up with heavy black clouds, with rolling, rumbling thunder, accompanied with vivid flashes of lightening. In the course of half an hour we were blessed with a hail storm, with a fine shower of rain. This is the first for 7 weeks & we hailed it with delight. Last night it was cloudy & very dark, with distant thunder, & being the very narrow place in which we were, with high mountains upon each side, and only able to see the sky looking straight up, gave it a most dismal and sepulchral appearance, & daylight was most welcomed. We rolled 3 miles & coming to some grass upon a flat we stopped to breakfast. Here we remained 2 hours & again rolled 5 miles, when we came to better grass & corralled for the day for the purpose of waiting for our provision train, as well as to feed our mules.

We crossed the river today 7 times, making 12 times in all. Some of them were deep & very rocky, with a swift current, so much so as to take some of our mules off their feet. It was amusing to see many of our men riding their mules across. They would do it most cautiously, picking out their way in every step, but in spite of all this, they would frequently fall, sometimes rolling over their sides & corralling them most beautifully in the water. Our friend Locke, in particular, was riding "a very high mule" whose legs were "twisted out "—& which landed him most beautifully in Salmon Trout. The current is so strong that a man can but with difficulty walk across, & consequently it is very dangerous to be thrown in. As yet everything has passed in safely & we hope, with care, it will continue to be so.

Distance, 8 miles.

Friday, August 17th.

It rained again last night & a very heavy dew also fell. We started at 6 o'clock & crossed, & recrossed the stream. Eight miles we nooned, crossing in this distance 8 times. Here we had tolerable grass, our Captain having picked it, & left one to point it out to me. We remained here until 2 when we again rolled. In the evening, we rolled 7 miles, crossing the river 4 times, making in all 22. [24.]

The road between the crossings was sandy in some places, rocky in others, & very steep both going up & coming down in others. After 7 miles we emerged in a beautiful, green, velvety valley, which, upon first coming in view, presented a most cheering appearance. We here crossed a slough, the crossing of which was fixed & bridged by our Captain & party ahead. Before this was done, it is said it was almost impassible, each having to be cordelled across. We passed over in safety & encamped in this lovely valley, with blue grass to the horses' knees. We passed two graves; one had drowned several days before, the other had died today. We came within sight for the first time of the Sierra Nevada mountains, or rather of the chain. During the day it has been cloudy, with constant rumbling of thunder in the distance. In the morning we had a very nice shower, & several times during the day it gave us. a pleasant sprinkle.

Distance, 15 miles.

Saturday, August 18th.

It was our determination to lay here until the provisions train should arrive, consequently we endulged in an uncommon knap after sunrise. Grass was fine, wood plenty, & water delicious, with a beautiful camp, & we all enjoyed it very much. Grass was mowed & packed, & in the evening we hooked up & moved up the valley 3 miles so as to be neared the stretch of 15 miles for which we prepared the grass. Two men were left here to conduct the [provision] wagon over the slough & bring them up to us.

Distance, 3 miles.

Sunday, August 19th.

The provisions did not arrive last night, very much to our disappointment, but today about 9 o'clock it came in sight, when immediately we hooked up & rolled. We soon left the valley, the road being very rocky with large round stones. In six miles we struck the river, where we nooned, giving some of our grass to them the animals.

Upon a proposition, the flour & bacon was divided between the different messes, on account of the scarcity of the provisions & thinking that they would be more economical in using them.

We rolled out at 2 o'clock. The road was rough in the extreme & very hilly. We crossed the river 4 times making 26 [28] times altogether. Ten miles we came to the river again. Before striking it we came to large trees of pine, cypress, & lignum vitae. The banks of the river & the sides of the mountain are also covered with them. The valley where we strike the river is narrow, but had excellent grass upon it, but by some person or persons unknown, (it) was burned off & part of it was still burning. We tied up to the wheels & fed the remainder of the grass we had provided ourselves with yesterday.

Distance, 16 miles.

Monday, August 20th.

The scenery around us last night would put at defiance the artist's pencil. It was one of the most majestic ones that ever falls to the lot of man to witness. Immediately upon the opposite side of the river, the mountain commenced its ascent, covered with large timber of fir, pines of all sorts, & arbor vitae. They were not thick but presented rather, the appearance of a grove with good verdure & no underwood. The valley was narrow but was visible for a mile or more. In a thousand different places, both on the side of the mountain and along the valley, the trees & grass had been set on fire. It was a dark night, the clouds having gathered over very threateningly at sundown, & the bright blazing fires up the mountain and down the valley, the roaring & splashing of the river over the rocks, accompanied with the occasional fall of a tree that had burned through, with the howling of wolves (one word illegible) in their round, all presented a scene to be wearied & silent beholder not soon to be forgotten.

We started at daybreak & crossed the river. The road turned immediately to the right in a north direction & continued for one mile, when it went in a northwest direction, ascending a spur of mountain, one of the chain of the California mountains. We ascended this, it being in some places very steep, & then again coming upon a little table of land upon which had been good grass, & upon one with a cool but small spring. After rolling there 5 miles, we opened upon a beautiful little valley with a very steep hill to descend to it. We went down in the valley & nooned. This valley is oval in shaped & had plenty of good grass & water in it.

We rolled again at 2 P.M. The road here took a south direction, having travelled northwest this morning. We passed along through the woods, which was very large timber of the same description as before described. Occasionally we struck a little valley with good grazing & water. Four miles we encamped I one of these valleys. At our noon today we learned from a gentleman, that the Indians had killed one of his mules with an arrow last night. They were about starting in search of them.

Distance, 9 miles.

Tuesday, August 21st.

It was very cold last night & many of us that had not prepared for it suffered much from it. The grass was covered with a white hoary frost, which crackled under our feet. The water in our buckets was frozen to considerable thickness. We started early & rolled over the same kind of road as yesterday evening, through woods, valleys, & up & down hill, but none very steep. Three miles brought us to a larger valley than usual, with a stream of water coming from the mountains on our right. This is one of the tributaries of Truckee or Salmon Trout. We rolled 6 miles over the same sort of country with high mountains upon each side of us & came to another large valley with a larger stream running through it—another tributary to Salmon Trout. Here we nooned.

Around our camp last night the awful & distressing cries of a panther was heard, first in one place, then soon after in another. The guard came in one after another to double arm themselves for this formidable enemy, but he did not return too near. Today, one was seen only a short distance from camp, in the road. He stopped & turned to take a survey of those behind, & then trotted, slowly away. They had no rifle & consequently did not pursue.

We rolled in the evening at 2 P.M. The road still the same, except a little rougher. Four miles, the road turned left. Here, upon our left distant some hundred yards from the road was the Truckee in all its glory again, splashing & dashing over the rocks. Here we met one of our advance who informed us we were but five miles from the base of the great *bugaboo*, that which has caused many a sleepless night, with disturbed dreams to the discouraged emigrant, *"The Sierra Nevada" Mountains*. We were much inspired & equally rejoiced, as we had no idea we were so far on our way. We were informed there was no grass at the base, or near it, & consequently we rolled a mile or so farther & camped.

We were informed that the cabins of the "Lamentable Donner Party" were also on our road, as well as also the [Donner] lake but one mile from the present trail. I immediately started off to look for these mournful monuments of human suffering. One was only 150 yds. from our camp upon the left of the trail. This (cabin) was still standing. It was two in one, there being a separation of longs between. The timbers were from 8 inches to a foot in diameter, about 8 or 9 ft. high & covered over with logs upon which had been placed branches & limbs of Trees, dirt & c. The logs were fitted very nicely together, there being scarcely a crevice between. There was one door to each, entering from the north and from the road.

There were piles of bones around but mostly of cattle, although I did find some half dozen human ones of different parts. Just to the left of these was a few old black burnt logs, which evidently had been one of those (cabin) which had been burnt. Here was nearly the whole skeleton. Several small stockings were found which still contained the bones of the leg & foot. Remnants of old clothes, with pieces of boxes, stockings, & bones in particular, was all that was left to mark that it had once been inhabited.

In the centre of each was a hole dug which either served as a fireplace or to bury their dead. The trees around were cut off 10 ft. rom the ground, showing the immense depth the snow must have been. After examining this I passed on one mile where the road went to the left in a more southerly direction. The old trail went on straight down the valley to the Lake which was distant one mile. I went on to the lake & was fully repaid for my trouble, for it was one of the most beautiful ones on record. It was beautiful, fresh, pure, clear water, with a gravelly bottom, with a sandy beach. It was about 2 miles long, three-quarters wide & confined between three mountains on three sides, which arose immediately from its edge. On the other was the valley by which I had approached it through which a little stream was passing off from it. I here took a delightful bath & felt renovated.

In returning I came to another of the cabins, but which has been burned by order of Gen'l Kearney. Here also I found human bones. The skulls had been sawed open for the purpose, no doubt, of getting out the brains, & the bones had all been sawed open & broken to obtain the last particle of nutriment.

Bryant has given a most satisfactory account of the suffering of the unfortunate emigrants of Donner's party & the many trials, deprivations & sufferings, with loss of life runneth not in the knowledge of man. To look upon these sad monuments harrows up every sympathy of the heart & soul, & you almost hold your breath to listen for some mournful sound from these blackened, dismal, funeral piles, telling you of their many sufferings & calling upon you for bread, bread.

There seems to be a sad, melancholy stillness hanging around these places, which serves to make a gloom around you, which draws you closer & closer in your sympathies with those whom hunger compelled to eat their own children, & finally to be eaten by others themselves, & their bones now kicked perhaps under any one's feet. There was also another cabin upon the opposite side of the road, but I did not visit it.

Accompanying the Pittsburgh [Company] was a man by the name of Graves, who was one of the survivors of this party. I conversed with him several times about the road when meeting with him upon trip, but he avoided & alluded any conversation about his misfortune. I was told by a member of his Company, that the night before they came to this place, Graves started off without saying anything to them, & did not join them until after they had passed. He preferred viewing the place of his unprecedented suffering alone, not wishing that the eye of the unsympathising man should be a witness to his harrowing feelings.

A meeting of our company was called today & our QuarterMaster was appointed to select two other gentlemen to go ahead of us, to obtain provisions necessary for us upon our arrival, & also to find out all the important information necessary for us to commence operations in the mines. They accordingly, this afternoon, left us, having their provender tied on behind them.

Distance, 14 miles.

Wednesday, August 22nd.

It was very cold last night, & it occurred to us forcibly that if it was cold here in August, what it must be in January. Early everything was in motion. In one mile we crossed a little stream to the left, which runs from the Lake. Here we stopped,& cut sufficient grass for feed. After rolling one mile farther we struck the foot of the mountain. The Road was very rough & in many places steep both going up & coming down. Every now & then there was a little table upon which was a little grass. We rolled thus 2 miles when we nooned (or rather rested, not taking our mules out) upon one of these tables. We stopped 2 hours, when we ascended a steep & very rocky road with many short turns around the large rocks & trees. One mile brought us to the foot of the "Elephant" itself. Here we "faced the music" & no Mistake. The "Wohaughs" could be heard for miles, hollowing & bawling at their poor cattle who scarcely drag themselves up the steep acclivity.

We immediately double teamed, & after considerable screaming & whipping, thus arrived safe at the top. They then returned & took up the remainder with like success. We were but four hours ascending, & we were much disappointed, but agreably so, in not finding it much worse. Certainly this must be a great improvement upon the old road where the wagons had to be taken to pieces and packed across. We rolled down the mountain 4 miles, the road being rough & steep half way & then striking a valley, where it was good. We passed through a grove of woods & then emerged into a valley & encamped.

We were all in the most joyous & elated spirits this evening. We have crossed the only part of the road that we feared, & that without any breakage, loss or detention. I had but the one & only bottle of "cognac" that was in our camp, & which I had managed to keep since leaving the Old Dominion. This I invited my mess to join me in, & which invitation was most cordially accepted. When lo & behold, upon bringing it out, it was empty–yes positively empty. The cork was bad & with numerous joltings, it had gradually disappeared. This was a disappointment many of us will not soon forget.

Distance, 8 ½ miles.

JAMES WILKINS, 1849

Wilkins left Weston on May 8, 1849. He traveled with an ox train. He went by way of Fort Bridger and the Sublette Cutoff. On September 9, he arrived at the Sink and the Carson River by September 10. The next two weeks were spent recruiting, ie., resting their stock and themselves, and then continuing up the Carson River. On September 23 the climb up the mountain commenced. And, on October 16, Wilkins arrived at Sutter's Fort.

Sunday Sepr 9th

Came only about 18 miles since our last encampment to this place, where we have been laying two days, cutting hay. we are now about 15 miles from the sink, and as we have found unexpectedly good grass, we think it better to lay in our supply here for the desert, and recruit our cattle, than to risk going further, for all is uncertainty and rumour about the road in advance. This is the last good water we shall have for 70 miles they say, and we are filling every vessel that will hold it. The great object of dispute amongst us now is which of the two roads we shall take, that we are informed branch off from the sink over the desert. The old road or what is called Child's [Chile's]) road, the reports about them are so contradictory, that we do not know what to do. Provissions are getting very scarce along the road among the emigrants generally. we have as much hard bread and bacon left as is necessary, but our sugar flour vinegar beans dried apples in fact everything else is gone, and we must see hard times before we reach California. The late barren country we have passed thro' has told hard upon out cattle—and others too. If we may judge by the number of dead cattle we passed the last 18 miles. We expect to leave here some time to night, and go down to the sink by daybreak so avoid the midday sun, as the reflection from it on the sand makes it intensely hot in the middle of the day, and distresses our cattle very much. Scurvey is becoming very prevalent among the emigrants. we have heard of several deaths with it—

(This entry opened with five and a half lines which Wilkins later struck out: I wish California had sunk in to the ocean before I had ever heard of it. here I am alone, having crossed the desert it is true, and got to some good water, but have nothing to eat all day; my companions scattered, our wagons left behind. that desert has played h—l with us.")

We arrived at the sink late in the night [Sunday, September 9], having it 25 miles instead of 15, the water poisonous, and not a spear of grass. we pushed on near 3 miles further to where some holes had been dug in the ground, and water strongly impregnated with sulphur had been found. but few of our cattle would touch it, thirsty as they must have been. here we rested 2 or 3 hours till the moon rose, gave them some hay and pushed into the desert, 45 miles to the next water. we took the left hand road or Childs cut off, as it is called and traveled till eleven the next day [September 10], when we stopped and fed the oxen and ourselves. Wide plains of sand salt lying thick on the ground in some places, with here and there a few bushed of grease wood. The mirage exists here. lakes of water, apparently but a few miles from us. About one O'clock, the D--- and I rode off to go thro' leaving the wagons to follow. here commenced the greatest distruction of property. abandoned wagons dead cattle and articles of every description lay strewed along the road. between that time and dark, that is for the next 16 miles I counted 163 head of dead stock oxen mules and horses, 65 wagons, some of them entire, others more of less demolished, about 70 ox chains, yokes, harness, trunks, axes, and all minor things I did not count, and these only while riding along the road. doubtless there were a great many I did not see. holes had been dug in different places for water, but it was strongly impregnated with salt, as to be scarcely drinkable. about dusk we came up with the pioneer wagons [those of the Pioneer Line] left on the road, their mules being unable to drag them further. they had taken them out and drove them on to the river to recruit. the passengers those that were able to walk on. but there were a great many sick, and unable to walk. these had to stay with nothing but salt water to drink. amongst them a Mr. James was expected to die with the scurvey. they like us had nothing left but bread and bacon, and for these they were indebted to the ox teams on the road. three dollars a pint was the offered for vinegar. A soft heavy deep sand commenced here, and continued to the river, (about 10 miles,) thro which our horses labored severely. we sighed for our cattle, and judging from the smell which saluted our nostrils every few hours every few minutes, for it was dark they must have lain pretty thick on the ground. here we met Turner [of the Pioneer Line] going back with a few mules to fetch one of his wagons containing those most severely sick. About 10 O'clock we arrived at the river and found the pioneer passengers asleep around an immense log fire, for here are actually some large cotton wood trees, the first we had seen since leaving the settlements. We toasted a slice of bacon and eat a cracker that we had brought with us, and lay down beside the fire to sleep. I did not rest much it being too cold, but got up and sat by the fire to sleep. I di not rest much it being too cold, but got up an sat by the fire till morng. At day break [September 11] the Dr. returned to meet the wagons, which he met about 6 miles back found several of the oxen had given out, so he concluded to leave them for the day and drive on the oxen to water and grass to recruit.--

Thursday 13th
All day yesterday I was alone huntg our boys, without success till evening. I met E P— — he informed me of the condition of things. several of the oxen still back in the desert. I lent him my mule to ride back and fetch them in, and to bring some bed clothes and provisions, and to meet me at the Pioneer herdsmens camp two miles down the river, where they had driven the rest of the cattle for grass, there being none the nearer. Thither I went

and waited all night but he came not. this morn^g early I set off, determined to find some one that would give me a breakfast. I met E. P—— coming on my mule. it seems they were unable to get the cattle last night but gave the some hay they had, and stayed at the upper camp, or where the road first strikes the river, where he told me to go, and I should find some provisions. I accordingly came on, and got some hot water slightly colored with coffee, and hard bread. to night we shall get up the oxen and fetch in the wagons if we can.--

Sunday 16th

We only left our camp^g ground near the Pioneer's last evening, having been detained by fetching in from the desert 6 or 7 miles back an abandoned wagon, which it was said was much lighter than one of ours, and a good wagon. but after it was brought in and examined by the parties interested, it was risolved to take the old one so by shortening her up and cutting two feet off the bed, and otherwise lightening her, it was thought the teem would pull her thro'. All our cattle are much exhausted and reduced in flesh, as well as other peoples'. I pity those families very much and tremble for their safety that are a week or two behind. Mr James of the pioneers died and was buried yesterday, "with a blanket wrapt around him." what a tale of suffering and neglect he could tell, if the dead could speak. Turner offers 500 $ to any one that will fetch in his provision wagons 3 in number and about 16 miles out, but no emigrants have teams enough to do it. We came 5 or 6 mile last night to better grass. to day we are going to cut hay to take with us. at the commencement of the journey that would be thought nothing of, but here it is "*some.*" Emmigrants make a great mistake in calculating upon the load getting lighter. the team get weaker just in proportion.

Wednesday 19th Sep^r

The nearer we approach the end of our journey the more tedious and irksome does the journey become. But a fortnight I expect will carry us thro'. "*Patience thou rosy lip^d cherrub.*" We are most of us taking the scurvey, myself amongst the rest. the gums bleed and the skin is becoming discoloured in patches, particularly about the legs. I have eaten noting but bread lately, rejecting *fired bacon.* — Carson's river is a small stream of good water about 1 rod wide and 18 inches deep. its margin is marked by a line of cotton woods of large size, lovely to behold to our *desert-weary* eyes, differing from Marys river which had nothing but willows. for 300 miles down its banks I did not see a tree thicker than my wrist. The weather continues hazy, making the hills or mountains on each side difficult to be seen. On monday night we saw a large notice stuck up by the side of the road, informing us the 20 or some said 25 mile desert might be avoided by going about 10 miles around. About 8 miles of the road heavy sand, and then fine grass valeys, besides other information. this was put up by a philanthropic Kentuckian, who had been in advance and returned. A leading man in our party observed he was a fool for his pains, tho' he profited by the information. We went the road and found the best grass we had seen for several hundred miles. it had been observed on this road that a man may have travelled to Santa fee and Chiwawa, and yet derive no information necessary for a trip to California. Of this I suppose Mr Turner can bear witness. speaking of Turner Mr. Garritt of the Planters house Peoria told me that he offered 3000 $ to any one that would take his receipts and pay his expenses for his trip, that he had done all that a man could do for the comfort of his passengers, but what can a man do in the desert. he purchase provisions from the emigrants at an enormous price, that the order passed for reducing every mans baggage to 75 lbs was from a committee of 12 and not from him, that his own private stores that he had laid in to emeliorate the ruggedness of the route, went in the general wreck. That was the time an Irishman observed when the old Cogniac "*watered the plain.*" Besides the wear and tare both of body and mind that Turner went thro' must have been great. Garet observed he had seen him drop asleep as he stood. With watching thro' the night, as he was in continual fear some of the men would steal his mules, and been harassed during the day, he must have had a hard time of it. Most of those able bodied passengers are leaving some taking it o foot, and some on horseback, so that his loads will be light from this onward. And I think he will get through.— –

Friday 21 Sept[r]

Came about 17 miles yesterday 10 over a miniature desert. nothing but sand and sage brush.-- We see notices stuck up warning emigrants, that the Indians are apt to shoot arrows into the oxen, so that they may be left, and then get them for beef. We accordingly sat up with our oxen all night last night. this morn[g] 3 Indians came into camp or rather vicinity for they were a little afraid of coming too close. they were in a *primitive* sate, and appeared to have had very little communications with the pale faces, having no ornaments or articles of dress denoting civilization as the Indians on Marys river had. they carried bows and arrows, the arrows neatly headed with flint ingeniously cut. they could not speak a single English word.-- Our road now lies thro' a valley 40 miles long and from 8 to 10 broad. It is surrounded by pretty high mountains and nearly all covered with pine trees, which altho' looking small from the road, are two and three feet in diameter. beautiful streamlets of clear cold water gush from these hills into the valley, thro' the center of which the river meanders. The soil is rich the grass luxuriant, and take it alltogether it is one of the best tracks of land we have seen since leaving the states. Those who have seen Salt Lake Valley say it is preferable in many respects to that ---

Sunday Sep[r] 23

Again it happens for the third time consecutively that we are making hay on Sunday. Well the Lord will forgive us, I hope. this time we are making it (and I hope it is the last) to carry us thro the dreaded Kanyon. we have now arrived within eight miles of its mouth, and shall go that distance in the cool of this evening, where we shall feed away the hay and start early in the morn[g]. there is no grass fit to cut nearer than this, and no feed for 4 or 5 miles beyond. There are quantities of sand hill cranes and wild geese flying about here, but they are so wild we have not been able to shot one. Yesterday we passed a boiling springs. the hot water gushed up from holes in the ground in several places, tho' not actually boiling was so hot I could not hold my hand in. they ran into a little brook or slough forming a fine hot bath --

Tuesday sep[r] 25

Yesterday morn^r we breakfasted by starlight, and at the earliest dawn of the day, started into the Kanyon. our object in this very early start was to get before many wagons that lay camped near us. for a great part of the road, only one wagon can pass at a time, and if an accident happens to one all those behind are delayed, till it is either repaired or removed. I had seen something I thought of bad roads before, but this capped the climax. He must have had a bold heart and a daring spirit, that first conceived the idea of the possibility of wagons travelling thro' this mountain pass. Imagine a mountain 6 miles thro' at its base cleft in twain, like an immense crack and all the loose rocks and debris thrown together at the bottom, thro' which flows or rather leaks a mountain steam, with here and there patches of scanty soil, bearing lofty pines 4 and 5 ft in diameter amongst these rocks. and sometimes up steep hills loaded wagons had to pass in places where loose cattle could hardly keep their feet. the great difficulty was in steep places and short turns, where only one or two yoke could pull at a time. every man had to put his shoulder to the wheel. here was the place where light loads and strong wheels [were] appreciated. the way all along was strewn with broken wagons. the wheels had in some places to drop as much as 3 or 4 ft onto solid rock. A pretty severe test to try the strength of a wheel. But we got through safely, and congratulated ourselves so much that we took a "horn" on the strength of it. The six miles occupied about 8 hours. We took a short rest, and travelled about four miles further on a good road to grass, where we are now lying. this evening we shall go 4 or 5 more to the last grass, before we ascend the mountain. The scenery in the pass was very sublime. I made 3 sketches, but oweing to my manual exertions being required they were more hasty than I could have wished.--

Friday morn^g 28th

Wednesday morn^g having to ascend the mountain we started at the earliest dawn. there being no good grass within a mile or two of the wagons, we tied our cattle to the wheels the night before, and started without giving them their breakfast, a circumstances which we regretted afterwards. the road thro' not so long as through the Kanyon was if possible steeper and more difficult,

so much so that we had to double teems and take one wagon at a
time. And with all our strength, 6 yoke of oxen and not more than
15 hundred in a wagon, we stalled for the first time since leaving
the Missouri. we had partly to unload the wagon, and carry up
a many articles on our backs. then with the assistance or 3 or 4
fresh drivers with good whips we gained the summit. the other
wagon having less loading, was with some difficulty brought
up. We now had 5 miles to go into a valley to grass, where we
camped. This was a most fatiguing day to men and oxen.--
Yesterday [September 27] we did not get of[f] till 9 O'clock, it
being thought advisable to feed our oxen well before we started,
as we had the second summit to ascend. It is I believe higher than
the first, tho' the road is not so rocky, and fewer short turns on
it. we doubled teams only for a mile or two, and reached the top
about 2 Oclock, where we took a hasty meal amid the snow. The
scenery is sublime, *vastnes*s being the great feature to express in
a picture of it. here on the very summit of the back bone of the
American continent, (and the backbone of the Elephant as the
emigrants call it we were favoured with a storm of hail rain and
sleet. the wind blew icy cold. overcoats were in demand, altho in
the middle of the day, while in the valley below but a few hours
before, the sun was so hot, both coats and vests had to come
off. to add to our difficulties the lady in our company was taken
with the pangs of labour, and we had to descend as quickly as
possible over a most rocky road, to the first grass, which we did
not reach till an hour after dark. The wagon was near upsetting
several times. How she stood the jolting I cannot imagine. I now
hastily pitched my tent, which I gave up for her accomadation,
and before morning she was delivered of a little girl, without any
of those luxuries, nay without the common necessities usually
had on such occasions by the very poorest class, and she an
English woman just from London, and moving in a pretty good
sphere of life, but through the improvidence of her husband now
reduced and penniless. The grass here was exceedingly scanty not
picking enough for a mountain goat, and it was our intention to
tie them to the wheels till morn^g and then dive them a mile or two
to a little valley where we heard it was better. but while we were
eating supper, tho' only left for 10 minutes 12 of them strayed

off, and the hills around being covered with lofty pines and huge rocks, and but a scanty moonlight for the sky was clouded, they could no where be found.

I am now left to watch the remaining 5 in the valley above spoken of, having driven them down there early this morning. While all hands are gone to hunt the others. what makes us more anxious is the Indians in these mountains have a bad name for stealing cattle, notices being stuck up on the trees to that effect. An accident occurred yesterday which nearly proved fatal to one of our party. while ascending a rough rocky hill, the jolting of the wagon caused a loaded rifle to get loose and fell out of the back of the wagon. its muzzles struck the shoulder of the owner, who was pushing behind and immediately exploded, the ball passing over his shoulder and between the Doctor and I, (who were but a few steps behind) into the ground. Some deaths and several severe wounds have occurred on the trip amongst the companics by keeping rifles loaded and capped in the wagons.

ELEAZAR STILLMAN INGALLS, 1850

Ingalls headed west from St. Joseph, Missouri, on May 3, 1850. He and his party traveled with horses. He traveled via the Sublette Cutoff, later, the Soda Springs Cutoff (Hudspeth), and then the main road from Fort Hall over to the Humboldt, and down it, finally arriving at the Sink on August 4. He reached the Carson River on late August 6. After resting, he continued along the river before starting the climb up the mountains on August 15. The summit was reached, and then on August 21 he arrived in "Hangtown" or Placerville.

August 1st.

Remained camped to-day, preparing hay for crossing the Desert, which commences 20 miles from the slough or meadow. There is an abundance of grass at this point for all the stock that can ever reach here. We have to wade to get it, then cart it to the channel, and boat it across that in a wagon box. A man with his wife came into the camp last night on foot, packing what little property they had left on a single ox, the sole remaining animal of their team; but I was informed of a worse case than this by some packers, who say they passed a man and his wife about 11 miles back who were on foot, toiling through the hot sand, the man carrying the blankets and other necessities, and his wife carrying their only child in her arms, having lost all their team.

August 2nd.

We still remain at the meadows. A team came in yesterday evening from Sacramento, loaded with provisions. They ask for rice $2.50 per lb.; for flour $2.00; bacon $2.00; whiskey $2.00 per pint, and brandy $3.00 per pint. We killed a cow this evening which we had picked up a few days ago at a camping ground, where she had been left on account of lameness. She was not exactly beef, but she was better eating than dead mules and horses by the road side; we divided her up in the train and among the starving people who are about us, only saving a small amount for ourselves, which we jerked and dried.

August 3rd.

We are still lying by. About two miles below our camp are some falls in the river, at which point the meadows terminate. There is no more grass from here until we reach Carson River 66 miles.— Some of the teams that left us above Fort Kearney came in to-day, entirely destitute of provisions, and had been so for some days, although they had contrived to starve along somehow. We heard of them before they got here, and saved a little beef for them.

August 4th.

Sunday. Broke up camp and started again. We had stopped three days to recruit our horses before taking the desert, and although we had taken the utmost pains with them, they are weaker now than when se stopped. My advice to all is not to make any stop at this point, but to push on to Carson River, for there is so much alkali in the water and grass here that your stock will not recruit. There is no water for the next 20 miles fit for stock to drink. We lost one horse to-day from watering beside the road, four miles before we got to the sink. He died in thirty minutes after drinking, in the greatest agony. Two others were much injured, so much so, that we could only get them to the

sink with the greatest difficulty. Trimble and Sublet also lost one.
Beware of shallow water along here. 20 miles

August 5th.

Reached the Sink last night about sunset. This is a basin
about 80 rods wide and half a mile long. It is usually the last
water found on the Humboldt, or where it loses itself in the
sand, hence its name, but this year the water is so high that it
runs down several miles further before it entirely sinks. There
is no grass here whatever, nothing but desert. We broke up our
wagon to-day and made pack saddles, being convinced of the
impossibility of getting our wagon across the desert, since the
loss of the horse yesterday and the injury to the others. Last night
while we were making our supper on coffee and boiled corn,
soon after dark, a man came to us and asked for a drink of water.
I gave it to him; after drinking he stood looking wistfully at our
corn, then he asked me if I would take a dollar for a pint cup full
of it. I told him I would not take half a dollar for it, for money
was no consideration for food here. He said no more, but turned
sorrowfully away, when I stopped him and asked if he was in
distress. He said that he had eaten nothing for two days but a
small piece of dried meat which a man gave him. I then told him
that I would not take a half dollar for the corn, but that he was
welcome to sit down and eat his fill; for although we were nearly
out of provisions, we would divided with a man in distress to the
last morsel. He stopped the night with us, and took breakfast,
and although urged to stop and cross the desert with us to-day
or to take some corn with him, he would not do it, but said that
he had taxed our hospitality too much already, and left us this
morning. His name was Bayell, he belonged in one of the central
counties of Illinois, and was a man of standing and influence at
home, and a brother of the I.O.O.F. He said he hailed when he
came up to our camp, but it was so dark that I could not see his
hail, or I should not have put him to the test, to see whether he
was really needy or not. Sublet and company, and Williams & Co.
left us this morning to cross the desert; we got our pack saddles
completed, and took the desert at 2 o'clock P.M., and traveled all
night. Two of our horses gave out, the same that were alkalized,

and we left them. About midnight we reached the first wagon road where we found about four acres of wagons left to decay on the desert; this is the first sand ridge; we passed two other wagon yards before morning at similar ridges, besides great numbers along the road, many of them burning. Who will accurately describe this desert at this time? Imagine to yourself a vast plain of sand and clay; the moon riding over you in silent grandeur, just renders visible by her light the distant mountains; the stinted sage, the salt lakes, cheating the thirsty traveler into the belief that water is near; yes, water it is, but poison to the living that stops to drink. Train after train drag their tiresome course along, man and beast suffering all the pangs of thirst toil on, feeling knowing that if the burning sun finds them on the desert in the coming day, their suffering will be enhanced tenfold, if worn out with fatigue and thirst they do not faint by the wayside and give up altogether. Burning wagons render still more hideous the solemn march; dead horse line the road, and living ones may be constantly seen, lapping and rolling the empty water casks (which have been cast away) for a drop of water to quench their burning thirst, or standing with drooping heads, waiting for death to relieve them of their tortures, or lying on the sand half buried, unable to rise, yet still trying. The sand hills are reached; then comes a scene of confusion and dismay. Animal after animal drops down. Wagon after wagon is stopped, the strongest animals are taken out of harness, the most important effects are taken out of the wagons and placed on their backs and all hurry away, leaving behind wagons, property and animals that, too weak to travel, lie and broil in the sun in an agony of thirst until death relieves them of their tortures. The owners hurry on with but one object in view, that of reaching the Carson River before the broiling sun shall reduce them to the same condition. Morning comes, and the light of day presents a scene more horrid than the route of a defeated army; dead stock line the roads, wagons, rifles, tents, clothes, everything but food may be found scattered along the road; here an ox, who standing famished against a wagon bed until nature could do no more, settled back into it and dies; and there a horse kicking out his last gasp in the burning sand, men scattered along the plain and stretched out among the dead stock like corpses, fill out the picture. The desert! You must see it and feel it in an August day, when legions have crossed it before you, to realize it in all its horrors. But heaven save you from the experience.

An incident occurred this evening which show well of the selfishness of some people on this route. It was soon after dark; we had taken off the packs to rest our horses, and were sitting and lying in the sage bushes beside the road; one of our companions had a few miles back been compelled to leave a horse, which from mistaken feelings of sympathy for the poor animal, he had neglected to kill. While sitting there a company of packers came along the road, when, although it was so dark that I could not distinguish one animal from another, our friend caught up his rifle, cocked and presented it towards one of them, exclaiming in an angry tone, "Get off that horse, you g-d d-n-d scoundrel, or I'll shoot him down under you." The fellow slid off the horse instantly, when our friend gave him one of the "dog-onit-est" blowing up, as the Missourians say, that one fellow ever got for riding the poor animal after he had given out. It was our friend's horse, who, dark as it was, recognized his faithful animal. The fellow sloped without saying a word in his defence.

August 6th.

Morning still finds us dragging our weary steps along the desert, with nothing near but endless sandhills and beds of clay. Passed Sublett's and Trimbles and Williams's wagons, which they were compelled from loss of stock to leave. Reached the last sand 13 miles from Carson's River, about 10 o'clock, A.M., where we found a water station, and brought some water for our horses at 75 cts a gallon. We left the pack of one horse here for the station keeper to bring in at night, and the boys went on with the horses, leaving Fuller, who was pretty much done over, and myself, behind. They reached the river about four o'clock, P.M. We were fortunate enough to find some old friends, P. Welch, and T. Ranahan, who had got up a shelter for themselves and oxen, of tents, cloths, and wagon covers, to protect them from the sun. We stayed with them through the heat of the day, and about night started again, but turned off about a mile from the road to visit a small salt lake, where we found a very good spring of fresh water and a sulphur spring. This lake is about three miles from Carson River; its waters are more salt than the most salt brine, and its shores are encrusted with pure salt. Its bed was evidently once the crater of a volcano. We reached the river about 10 o'clock P.M., but could not find our camp it was so dark, although we found the next day that that we had passes directly through it, but the loss of tents, wagons, & c., rendered it impossible to distinguish our comrades who were snoring away, wrapped in their blankets. However, after straggling around until towards midnight, we found the tent of some old esteemed friends, Esq. Hoffman & son, who gave us a hearty welcome and a spare blanket, which, (having already filled ourselves with God's beverage from the Carson river,) was to us a perfect elysian. 46 miles.

August 7th.
    There are several stations here, at which they sell flour at $1.50 per lb.; meals at $2.00 a head, and liquor at $1.00 a drink, and measure it themselves. There are great complaints of stock stealing here, some of the station keepers having a hand in it.... [Traveling up the Carson for another week, Ingalls continues to the base of the Sierras.]

August 15th.
    Passed the Mormon Station, saw a party of Californians and Mexicans prospecting. There is gold this side of the mountains. Entered the seven mile Kanyon, which begins the real pass of the Sierra Nevada. A branch of the Carson River runs through it, which stream we follow to its head. The Kanyon is wild, picturesque place, with perpendicular wall of gray granite hundreds of feet high, with lofty pines in the bottoms, and a perfect chaos of granite blocks rent from the walls above. We were compelled to camp in it with nothing for our horses to eat, which somewhat destroyed the romance of the thing; as for eating ourselves, it is so long since we had anything to eat that we don't trouble ourselves about it. 23 miles.

August 16th.
    Got out of the Kanyon into the valley, and stopped to bait. Drove about six miles and camped for the night; grass abundant

in this valley. J. Ingalls killed a California partridge to-day. It is larger than a partridge in the States, and finely flavored. 8 miles.

August 17th.

This morning we had the Nevadas to climb; this is the point which will stop the Pacific Railroad on this route, if anything will do it. This rise is said to be 9000 feet in 13 miles. After climbing the first mountain we descended to a lake, which is the head of one of the branches of the Sacramento. It is the crater of an extinguished volcano. The next mountain, the Snowy Peak, is still worse than the last, although both for most of the way are as steep as the roof of a house; in climbing it our road lay over snow, which was 20 feet deep for 80 rods up its side. Having reached the top of the snowy peaks, we took a cut-off, descended about two miles and camped at a small brook where we found good grass. We had the good fortune to shoot three woodchucks (ground-hogs) this evening which, in addition to three lbs. of flour we coaxed out of a Californian, made us feel as rich as the Rothschilds. We have not eaten or the last two weeks (all of us) as much as one man would have eaten if he could have had all that he required, consequently we are living in the greatest luxury and abundance to-night, having all we can eat. It does not take much to make man happy after all; here we have been starving along for the last month, crossing deserts, drinking rotten, alkali or salt water, or deprived entirely, and now we've go to the top of the Nevadas, around our camp fire amid snow drifts, with plenty of good water and three woodchucks for three of us, and we are the happiest mortals alive. We seem to have forgotten that we ever suffered privation. 16 miles.

His diary continues four more days, and then his last entry -

August 21

Leaving packs and horses in camp we entered the town [Hangtown] this morning, where we found great numbers of our friends and country people, as also my brother, who had reached the mines 25 days ahead of us, having started on the Council Bluffs route at the same date that I did, 3 miles.

Chapter Five

Artists

T he old expression that "a picture is worth a thousand words" is one that readily applies to understanding the experiences of the California emigrants. The scenery encountered, the conditions faced, and the dangers endured were vastly different from those that most emigrants left behind. They were both shocking and awesome. Time was critical and few emigrants had time away from their daily chores while traveling down the trail to write extensively; even fewer had the extra time required to stop and draw. Yet, fortunately, some emigrants and travelers did find the time to do so.

Most of the old sketches, drawings, paintings and photos that are in this volume are the works four men: James F. Wilkins, William Henry Jackson, J. Goldsborough Bruff, and William M. Quesenbury. A few of the works are by an unknown artist(s) whose drawings are based on some of the J. Wesley Jones daguerreotypes and other emigrant artists and photographers.

With few exceptions the recent photographs that accompany the early illustrations were taken by the author on his 2015-6 trips along the California Trail. In attempting to duplicate the earlier illustrations a number of problems and conditions had to be contended with and influenced the final selection of the today photos. For some illustrations it was impossible to duplicate the exact view. One of the biggest changes in many areas has been the extensive growth of trees. Sometimes trees have grown so much that they now block the view or exist in areas that were earlier treeless or thinly forested. In a few cases particular trees could be used as references in determining individual sites because they are still alive or recently died or fallen. Vast areas that were once prairie grasses are now farmed, the appearance has changed, and at times, the planted fields are inaccessible except for the perimeters. Rivers have been harnessed, and irrigation has been expanded and the river's flow has decreased. Streams have been diverted, rivers dammed and new lakes formed, smaller lakes enlarged while others have been drained. The physical geography has been altered. The construction of highways and railroads with their wide right of ways has necessitated grading and leveling and the removal of parts of mountains or complete hills and the filling in of depressions and ravines. Energy development from wind farms, mining, oil and gas exploration to the construction of electric transmission lines and pipelines have changed the landscape and viewscape.

Travel and access to certain sites have been restricted as ownerships have changed and developments built. Towns have expanded or grown where none existed before. Another issue that the author had to be aware of was the artists' specific styles, the mediums used, and their ability to depict a subject. Most to varying degrees tended to exaggerate the height of the prominent feature or subject. Even the most accurate of them often seemed to almost double the height. Some were more concerned with specific details while others seemed more concerned with the overall impression. This will become apparent as the reader compares the artists' works and the present photographs. All these conditions had to be considered, and sometimes they made it difficult to duplicate the specific illustration and sometimes necessitated the use of one from a close proximity.

James F. Wilkins joined an ox wagon company and headed for California with the rest of the Argonauts during the gold rush of 1849. He had arrived in the United States about 1836 from England and first set up shop as a painter in New Orleans. Later, he moved to St. Louis where he established a reputation as a respected portrait painter. On April 25, 1849 he set out from St. Louis on his adventure to the gold diggings. He planned his trip with the sole idea of painting scenes along the trail, and then to return east as soon as possible to paint his large rolling murals or panoramas which were a popular form of entertainment for the people at the time.

The large rolling canvases provided a means by which eastern viewers could experience the trail to California without suffering the real discomforts. Wilkins reached the diggings in October and by

December he was on his return voyage. It is believed that he made about two hundred watercolor sketches of scenes along the trail. Upon his return, he prepared his panorama and toured parts of the United States with it for a few years. Little is known about him in the years following his tour or what exactly happened to his panoramas. He died on his farm in Illinois in 1888.

Most of Wilkins' paintings and sketches were not signed, and over the years many of his unsigned trail scenes had often been attributed to other artists. Even the locations of the scenes have sometimes been incorrectly identified in some publications. Of the approximate two hundred sketches he had when he returned, only about fifty of them are presently known to exist. All of these are from the first half of the journey ending with his renderings of Soda Springs, Idaho. None are from the Fort Hall-Nevada-California section of the trail. It is hoped that they are in a private holding or tucked away in a library just waiting to come to light. If found, they would be a terrific resource for trail historians.

As a result of the research work of the eminent historian John McDermott in the 1960s, approximately fifty drawings were identified to have been created by Wilkins. However, some books published during the following quarter century still had them improperly identified.

One aspect to note about Wilkins' work concerned how scale was reflected in his illustrations. Sometimes he made his paintings more compact. Although he did not do this on all his works, this tendency to squeeze the landscape together had the result of exaggerating the height of the formations. At other times the width reflected the reality of the landscape or formation, but the height of a formation or particular aspect was magnified. Thus, he tended to depict mountains more prominently and pointed than they actually were. This may have been done to make the individual scene more appealing or dramatic to the public.

Certain details were included even though his works focused on the overall scene. These will be obvious when one looks at his work paired with modern photos. Once these techniques were recognized, it became much easier to find the specific locations along the trail from which his drawings were made. Today his works are held by the State Historical Society of Wisconsin. Included in the corresponding illustration section are some scenes that have been specifically located and identified for the first time.

William Henry Jackson was born in 1843 when the California Trail was just opening. He did not travel on it until 1866. It was almost past its heyday, yet much of the scenery along the trail had not changed much during the twenty some years that had ensued. Jackson signed on as a bullwacker on an ox freight wagon team and headed west from Nebraska City. Near Ham's Fork in present-day western Wyoming, he quit his job and joined another wagon company and continued with it to Salt Lake City. Then he joined yet another company and headed to California by way of the Salt Lake to Los Angeles Road, which for much of the route coincided with the Old Spanish Trail. He returned from California in 1867, driving a herd of horses. During Jackson's trip he created paintings and drew many sketches which were more detailed. Some became the basis for his later paintings, which were mostly done in the 1930s and less detailed.

Jackson is perhaps best known for his photographic work of the early west, which started in 1869 when he photographed the construction of the Union Pacific Railroad. Then, in the 1870s, he served as the official photographer for the Hayden Survey of the Territories, and was instrumental in making Yellowstone the first National Park. He also used some of his early photos and those of others as bases for some of his later paintings. Some paintings seem to have been based on his other paintings. A major portion of Jackson's original trail sketches and many of his paintings are held by the National Park Service. Copies are on exhibit in the Jackson Memorial Room in the Oregon Trail Museum at Scotts Bluff National Monument. Still other Jackson items are displayed at the Harold Warp's Pioneer Village Museum in Minden, Nebraska.

J. Goldsborough Bruff was the captain of a wagon company from Ohio called the "Washington City and California Mining Association" that headed for the California diggings in 1849. He had earlier trained at West Point as a civilian cartographer. His company consisted of seventeen mule-drawn wagons and sixty-six men. This was typical of the gold rush years when the men went off to make their fortunes while the women remained back home. He kept a diary of his journey, and it is one of the best and certainly longest of all the ones written by the

91

forty-niners. Not only did he make comments about the topography and the conditions encountered on the trail, he also included numerous pencil and pen sketches of scenes and events and even information about the graves and tombstones along the trail. His on-site sketches were very accurate. Sometimes it seems he made a duplicate within a short time and both were later the bases for many of his later paintings. Yet, he too seems to have fallen into the pattern of other illustrators, and when going from his pencil and pen and pad to his brush and canvas he often tended to exaggerate some features making them look even more dramatic than

The Henry Huntington Library, San Morino, CA.
MSSHM8044(144)

J. Goldsborough Bruff

the first sketches indicated. Hundreds of illustrations were finally made, including the many duplicates and triplicates. The two largest holders of his workers are located in The Huntington Library, and the Beinecke Rare Book and Manuscript Library, Yale University Library. Many copies of his original pen sketches can also be found in the book, *Gold Rush*.

Bruff returned east and went to work for the government and topographical engineers. He produced one of the early maps showing the way over the Sierra Nevada by the Lassen-Applegate route and also two maps showing the complete route to California.

As with Wilkins, John Wesley Jones planned to compile a pantoscope and then capitalize on his venture. To this end, he employed many daguerreotypists and other artists to capture the California gold fields and the California Trail with all their challenges and glory for a paying public. *Jones' Great Pantascope of California* was the result.

William Quesenbury was one of the many artists hired to provide materials for Jones. Jones acknowledged that Quesenbury was "the principal sketching artist" for his company. (Jones:48-9) His charge to Quesenbury was to note and illustrate the "scenery, curiosities, and stupendous rocks" along the trail. (Murphy:7) This he did. While the majority of his illustrations are complete and very realistic, at times he seemed to have a tendency to make scenery a little more compact or to increase the scale of his subject as will be noticed when comparing some sketches with the photographs. The Jones' Pantascope held its debut in Boston in late 1852.

It has only been in recent years that the many illustrations by William H. Quesenbury have become more widely known and available and used in publications. Quesenbury had originally traveled to California in 1850. He joined the Cain Hill California Emigrating Company which started on April 9, 1850. During the journey, the company was joined by other emigrants. At other times, some members, including Quesenbury, broke off or joined other companies. They followed local trails from Cain Hill, Arkansas, though Oklahoma and then the Cherokee Trail into Kansas where it joined the Santa Fe Trail. Using the Santa Fe and Cherokee trails until the Cherokee Trail turned off in Colorado, they then turned north to meet the main trail in present-day western Wyoming and then continued down to Salt Lake City.

Quesenbury took the Salt Lake Cutoff and joined the trail coming down from Fort Hall and followed it down the Humboldt. Using the Carson route he neared Placerville on August 20, 1850. During the course of his travel he had made a number of pencil sketches of scenes along the trail. Quesenbury remained in California for almost a year and then returned over the trail to St. Joseph, Missouri in 1851. It was during the time prior to his return and on this return trip that he was employed by Jones. The expedition of artists and daguerreotypists started their eastward journey from Sacramento on July 7, 1851 and arrived in St. Joseph, Missouri in late October.

Quesenbury returned to Arkansas and within a couple of years published his own newspaper for a few years. He then worked for the government and dealt with the Indians. He served with the Confederacy during the Civil War and after his service tried a variety of ventures. During the 1870s he taught art and did some writing. He had had health problems for some time. He died in 1888 with little acknowledgement given to his earlier artistic contributions.

As with Wilkins' work, there is a large portion of the trail where the existence and whereabouts of Quesenbury's illustrations are presently not known. With the exception of a one illustration and a few of those from his 1850 journey west, his 1851 illustrations of the area in Nevada between Elko and the Sweetwater just east of the South Pass in central Wyoming are missing. It is unlikely that he would not have made sketches of that section. Hopefully, someday, if they still do exist, they too will be found. The major holdings of Quesenbury's illustrations are held by McKendree University with more than one hundred, and the Nebraska State Historical Society with over seventy. For those interested in the Jones Pantoscope, they also provide further insight into the scope of his work.

Now, travel west along the trail, and experience it as depicted by these early emigrants and artists. Read what they had to say, and then compare their illustrations with the trail sites today. **Wagons Ho! California or Bust!**

Chapter Six

Maps

Here are the sections of the T.H. Jefferson's *Map of the Emigrant Road* that was first published in 1849. There are four sections to this map. The first two sections cover the eastern half of the route starting at Independence, Missouri, through the South Pass. Section III starts at the South Pass and continues past Fort Bridger and Salt Lake to the Humboldt River. This section reflects the Hastings Cutoff. Section IV shows the rest of the trail from the Humboldt into California via the Truckee route.

There has been some question among historians as to the availability of this particular map for the emigration of 1849. However, it does

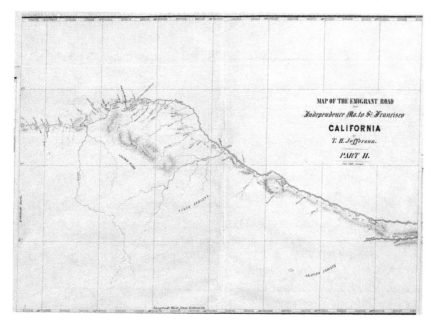

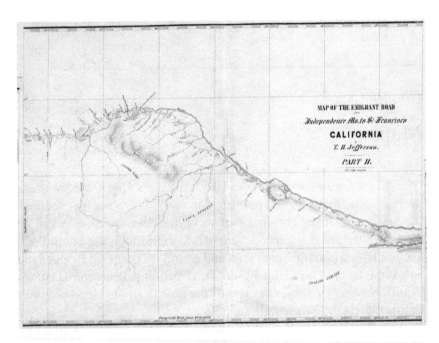

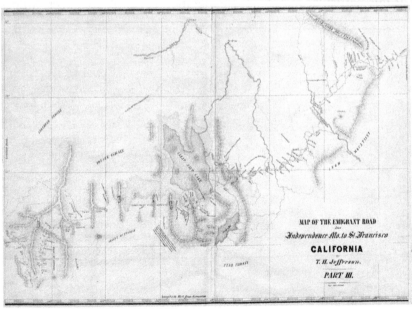

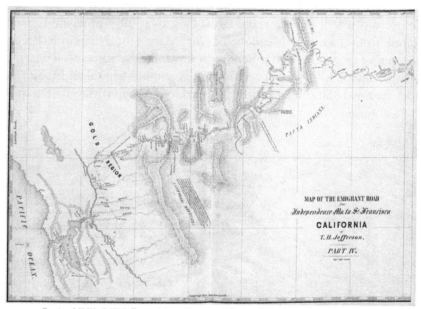

Section I,II III, & IV Jefferson Map – Courtesy, Library of Congress, Geography and Map Division

seem that J. Goldsborough Bruff had a copy of it on his journey, but it is also true that his company was one of the last to leave that year. (Bruff:595) Jefferson had traveled to California in 1846 and was originally part of the Russell Company, which also included Edwin Bryant, the Reeds and the Donners.

However, when the company broke up near Fort Laramie, Jefferson moved ahead. At Fort Bridger he met Hastings and became part of the party that was organized under Hastings' leadership that made it safely to California over the Truckee Route. The slower moving Donner party was never able to catch up to Hastings, due to their own problems and inadequate instructions from Hastings. The fact that Jefferson returned to New York and had his map published in 1849 would seem to indicate that the route was not that unreasonable in spite of the earlier bad publicity because of the Donner disaster. The maps were based on his own work and records together with the Fremont–Pruess maps, *Topographical Map of the Road from Missouri to Oregon* (Sections I-VII). The Fremont maps were also available and used by many emigrants.

Bruff succeeded in traveling to California in 1849. This is one of his maps showing Lassen's Ranch and his route there. If you look closely you will see the route Bruff took over the Applegate-Lassen Trail from Lassen's Meadow on the Mary's or Humboldt River. Sutter's Fort would be farther south down the Sacramento River off Bruff's map. Also shown on his map is another trip taken by him in the area in 1850. Later Bruff also produced a map of the whole trail to California.

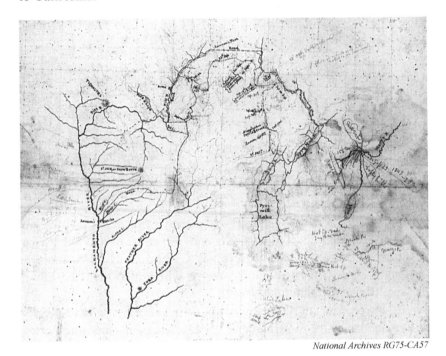

National Archives RG75-CA57

This last map is where it all started. It is a map of the location of Sutter's Mill where gold was discovered by James Marshall on January 24, 1848. It was drawn in July, 1848, by William Tecumseh Sherman who was only a lieutenant at the time. Note that North is at the top, but much of the writing is "upside down."

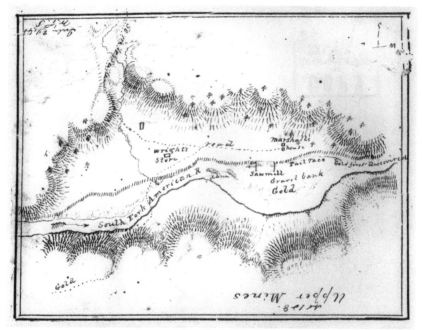

National Archives R677-W8-1

Chapter Seven
A Pictoral Journey

Courtesy, Palace of Governors Archives (NNMHM/DCA)003083 Ben Wittick
Emigrants nooning.

Above are some emigrants "nooning" on their way west. It provided a needed rest for the animals and time for the emigrants to eat a meal that had usually been prepared in the early morning.

Below are some Oregon-California Trail Association members "nooning" during a recent exploring expedition.

Travelers of both yesterday and today welcome a rest and any shade during a long drive in the heat of the day.

Hill – 732-415

Nooning today.

Jackson, National Park Service SCBL-48
Yoking a wild oxen.

One of the daily early morning tasks for the members of every wagon train was the rounding up and harnessing their draft animals. Oxen were the most often used draft animal. They could be especially difficult to yoke.

Hill
Dust on the trail.

One of the constant complaints of the emigrants concerned the dust on the trail. It got into everything. Their eyes burned, and they coughed trying to breathe. In July, 1850 Charles W. Smith wrote, "Our road is very dusty. The dust is so light that the least wind raises it....Sometimes the dust is so heavy that we cannot see the wagon immediately ahead of us in the train." (Smith:71)Even today modern expeditions experience trouble with dust and become strung out to avoid "eating each other's dust."

103

Jackson, National Park Service SCBL-122
Storm on the Prairie

Water and grass were the fuel on which the emigrants' draft animals depended. The trails were usually close to water. Rarely were the trails more than a day's march away. But sometimes there was too much, waer and at other times not enough or it was unfit to drink. Prairie storms were known for their violence. Their downpours were often accompanied by thunder, lightning and hail. Travel could be halted as trails were made "heavy," ie., soft and muddy. Rivers and streams could flood and companies could be forced to wait until they receded before they could ford or be ferried. Jackson depicts a prairie storm experienced in eastern Nebraska.

Digging for water today.

In dry areas they might be forced to dig for water in ravines or in a dry water bed. Howard Stansbury noted, "Encamped for the night on the banks of the Dry Sandy, where we had to dig in the bed of the stream for water, but a very scanty supply was obtained." (Stansbury:70) One can dig for water as shown here at the Dry Sandy. Wagons may have carried small barrels of water, but not those huge barrels often shown in Hollywood movies which would have been too *Hill* heavy when full of water.

104

Hill

Death & grave excavation.

Death was a constant companion for the emigrants. Some historians estimate that there was a grave every five hundred feet. Accidents and disease were the two biggest killers. Indian hostilities accounted for a distant third. Above is the grave of a young woman who was buried in a coffin made from the boards of a wagon box and placed in a stone vault. She was originally buried next to the trail at Emigrant Springs on the Slate Creek Cutoff in Wyoming. The grave was relocated for fear it would be washed out.

Jackson, Smithsonian Institution Photo #1667
Old Shoshoni camp.

Emigrants encountered various Indians tribes along the way. This Shoshone encampment of Chief Washakie was photographed by Jackson near the South Pass. During the early years most encounters were friendly. However, as emigration increased, it negatively impacted the area along the trails.

Kansas State Historical Society
Old Independence Square.

Independence, Missouri, was one of the jumping-off sites for trappers, traders and emigrants heading west. It was here that some of the earliest trading caravans and wagon companies were organized. The high ground, with abundant wood, grass, and its many springs made the area a perfect site for a town. Although about four miles from the Missouri River, it was served by two riverboat landing areas, the Lower or Blue Mills Landing to the northeast and the Upper or Wayne City Landing to its north. Today the courthouse is much larger and occupies most of the old green, but it is said to contain portions of the earlier structures. The square is still a hub of activity. Wagons still roll in the square today taking visitors on a tour of historic Independence.

Hill
Independence Square today.

106

Hill

Brady Cabin & Spring Park today.

Spring Park is located downhill from Independence Square. One of the old springs was relocated from its original site across the street to this small park. In the 1970s the Brady cabin, one of the oldest structures in Independence, was also relocated to Spring Park. There is some talk of moving it to the National Frontier Trails Museum complex.

Hill

National Frontier Trails Museum today.

The National Frontier Trails Museum is located in part of the old Waggoner-Gates Mill a few blocks from Independence Square. It is also on the site of one of the springs that made Independence famous. The first mill was built on this site in 1847. The focus of this very interesting museum is Independence as the jumping-off town for the Santa Fe, Oregon, and California trails, and its important role in westward expansion including the Lewis and Clark Trail and the Mormon Trail. Since its opening in 1990 the National Frontier Trails Museum has slowly expanded to include additional historic structures and displays.

Jackson, National Park Service SCBL-19
Westport Landing .

Another landing area that developed was Westport Landing to the west of Independence. Jackson came west more than twenty years after it had developed as a trailhead or "jumping-off" place. By then it was built up. Here is his vision of it in its early years.

This is the area today at the junction of the Kaw or Kansas and Missouri rivers. The actual landing location was a little farther downstream and can be visited. It was the beginning of modern Kansas City, Missouri.

Hill

Kansas City area today.

Wilkins' sketch of Fort Leavenworth.

Around May 1, 1849, Wilkins passed Fort Leavenworth aboard the steamer on his way to Weston a few miles farther up river on the east side of the Missouri. He may have made this drawing while the steamer stopped to unload some of its cargo. The fort was already twenty-two years old when Wilkins passed it. It had two blockhouses. Note one of the blockhouses on the top left where the trail comes up from the river. Part of that blockhouse can still be seen on the top of the hill if you were to visit the fort today. A number of roads from the fort connected to the Santa Fe, Oregon, and California trails. After the Kansas-Nebraska Act in 1854 the city of Leavenworth was formally platted, and its role as a jumping-off and freighting center rapidly developed.

The large depression or swale going up the hill in front of the car corresponds to the trail which goes up to the blockhouse as depicted in Wilkins' painting.

Hill

Trail swale today.

Hill

Fort Leavenworth Landing area today.

Here is the old landing area today. Trees now block almost the whole view of the bluff. The river's course has moved away from the fort's bluffs, but during heavy rains the area still floods a little. Today this area is part of a nature preserve. Look closely at the face of the bluff on the left side of the photo. A small area of grass shows through the trees. Barely visible on its right is part of the depression identified on the previous page. The low hills by the river bank were leveled years ago for buildings and the construction of the railroad. Note the remnants of a large dead tree in the photo in front of the brick building to the left of center and behind the levee. This could be the same tree that is behind the unloaded cargo in the Wilkins painting.

Mills, Library of Congress, Lee-Palfrey Papers, LCMSS-65612-9
The Rookery .

The Rookery (old barracks) was built in 1832. Today it is almost hidden by trees. Although altered, it is the oldest building still in use in the fort. It faces the old Main Parade. The Main Parade was over the hill past the old Main Gate in the Wilkins landing area painting. Mills took a photo of the Rookery in 1858 when he was selected to accompany and photograph the army's movement west to Salt Lake and then west to California with the Simpson Expedition.

Hill

The Rookery today.

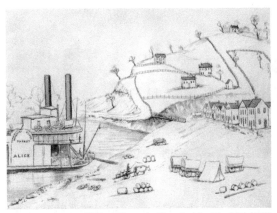

Wilkins, Wisconsin Historical Society, WHi-31437
Landing at Weston.

Weston was another of the jumping-off towns for emigrants. It was a hub of activity in 1849 and in the 1850s. Wilkins disembarked from the steamer at Weston in 1849 and continued north where he ferried the Missouri to the west bank near Old Fort Kearny. By 1850 a ferry was available at Weston. Within a few years more buildings were built on the banks which led down to the river.

Hill
Landing area today.

This photo shows the same corner in the painting barely visible through the trees on the right above the car. Today Weston is a small town proud of its historical past and worth a visit. The river channel no longer runs next to the town. It has shifted about two miles west, and trees have grown on the hills where cleared fields once existed. Old warehouses and abandoned railroad tracks now occupy the site where the riverboats once landed and unloaded cargo and emigrants.

St. Joseph Museum

St. Joseph.

St. Joseph, Missouri, became another jumping-off town for those bound for the west. The city was named after its founder Joseph Robidoux. Wakeman Bryarly, whose diary is quoted in the diary section, left from here. This 1850 view looks west over the city and across the Missouri River. Note the domed building in the far right of the painting. Because St. Joseph was the westernmost terminus for the railroad in 1860, it was selected to be the starting point for the short-lived Pony Express.

Below is a similar view of the city. The city has expanded up the hills with large buildings blocking the view of the river. Note the domed building to the right in both illustrations..

Hill

St. Joseph view today.

Wilkins, Wisconsin Historical Society, WHi-3717

Old Fort Kearny.

Wilkins took the ferry across the Missouri River into Indian Territory near Old Fort Kearny. The fort established in 1846 had been recently abandoned. Wilkins noted that once leaving, "our journey may now be considered fairly commenced as we are out of the united states and in indian territory. we now must travel in the military state with regular guards every night. crossed a fine open rolling prairie near 20 miles. timber very scarce. only a little post oak bordering the creek." (Wilkins:35) After the 1854 Kansas-Nebraska Act, Nebraska City was formally organized in 1855. It continued to grow to be another of the jumping-off and freighting towns. Today trees have replaced the open rolling prairie. Nebraska City is a Tree City and the home of the Arbor Day Foundation.

The replica of the old blockhouse below was situated near its original site. Unfortunately, it burned down and was never rebuilt. Perhaps someday it will be. Today only a historical marker notes the fort's nearby location.

Hill

Blockhouse reconstruction prior to fire.

Mathews, Nebraska State Historical Society, RG 2294-13
Old Nebraska City Landing.

This painting shows the Nebraska City landing areas as some of the later California emigrants would have seen it when it was a busy river port. The view is from the Iowa side of the river. The old fort was situated on the distant hill to the right of center above the main landing.

Here is a view of the area. Trees have grown extensively on the hills and along the river hiding the bluffs. A bridge now connects to the shores where some steamboats once docked. On the hill to the right is the main part of Nebraska City. Today the Missouri River Basin Lewis and Clark Center is located behind the hill to the left up from the bridge. Those also interested in Lewis and Clark should visit this fine center. The small but informative Old Freighters Museum of Russell, Majors, and Waddell is also located in the town.

Hill
Nebraska City landing area today.

115

Nebraska City – Main Street.

The old photo captures the view from near the top of the hill looking east down the main street to the old river landing. It shows Nebraska City during its heyday as a freighting hub. Note the freight caravan formed in the main street. At one time Alexander Majors had his freighting offices in Nebraska City. The site of the old fort painted by Wilkins would have been behind the buildings and off to the right.

Below is the site today. Note the building on the right. It has been altered a little, but it seems to be the middle building in the group of three and the only one still remaining. The center of activity has now moved a few blocks to the west and north. Jackson left from Nebraska City on his first journey west in 1866.

Hill

Street view today.

Jackson, National Park Service SCBL-275
Kanesville Crossing.

Kanesville or Council Bluffs was farther up river from Nebraska City. It was across from present-day Omaha, Nebraska, and it was also an early jumping-off town for the California, Oregon and Salt Lake emigrants. Jackson painted this scene showing the backlog of wagons waiting for the oft unreliable ferries to cross the Missouri River.

This old mill is all that is left of the old Mormon Winter Quarters of 1846-7. The tall elevator section was a later addition. The area became known as the upper or Mormon Ferry, another popular crossing area for emigrants and a riverboat stop. The town of Florence, now part of Omaha, grew where many Mormons had lived before their journey to Salt Lake under the leadership of Brigham Young in 1847. A beautiful Mormon cemetery is on the bluff above and a visitor center is nearby.

Hill
Old Mormon Mill today.

Jackson, National Park Service SCBL-20

Alcove Spring.

For the emigrants that departed from Independence, Alcove Spring became a popular camping area while they were waiting to ford the Big Blue. This is Jackson's view of it. Grandma Sarah Keyes, a member of the Donner Party died here on May 29, 1846. Although her grave was originally marked, over the years its exact location was lost.

This is a similar view of the alcove today. The stream is seasonal, but the spring still flows with reduced volume off to the right under the walking bridge, and more trees cover the rolling hills. The area is being developed with the assistance of the National Park Service.

Hill

Alcove Spring today.

Hill

Alcove Spring carving today.

Here is the rock on which "Alcove Spring" was originally carved on May 30, 1846 by George McKinstry after Edwin Bryant named the spring. Both men were also part of the company that for a while included the Donners. Over the years it seems that some people have tried to restore the original letters as natural weathering occurred.

James F. Reed carved his initials and name and the date, May 26, 1846, at the spring when his family camped nearby. Time and weathering have made them harder to read. Please do not try to improve on the carvings! Reed was to play a major role in the story of the infamous Donner tragedy in the Sierra Nevada that fateful winter of 1846-7.

Hill

J. F. Reed carving today.

119

Hill

Hollenberg Ranch today.

The original portion of the Hollenberg Ranch was constructed in 1857. Within a few years it was expanded to its present form. It sits right along the trail, and was also located after the junction of the Independence Road and the St. Joseph Road. This allowed it to capitalize on a larger volume of the traffic. It also has the distinction of having served as a Pony Express Station from 1860-61. It is one of few standing on its original foundation in an almost unaltered state.

Twenty miles to the northwest the trail crossed Rock Creek, southeast of present-day Fairbury, Nebraska. This is Jackson's painting depicting Rock Creek Station. It appears to have been based on an 1859 daguerreotype, which created a reverse image of the East Ranch.

Jackson, National Park Service SCBL-21

Rock Creek Station.

California State Library, Sacramento
Rock Creek Station, Nebraska, 1859.

This is the earliest photo of Rock Creek Station. It was taken in 1859. The daguerreotype, a mirror like image has been reversed so that it appears with correct orientation. The McCanleses built a bridge over the creek near the early emigrant ford. The ranch also served as a stage station and later as a Pony Express station.

The Rock Creek Station reconstruction was based on the 1859 photo. It was completed in the mid-1990s. Today visitors can step back in time and experience life as it was in the 1850s and see some of the best trail swales on the trail. There is also a fine camping area for those interested in experiencing a night on the prairie.

Hill
Rock Creek Station reconstruction today.

121

Deserted Pawnee village.

This deserted Pawnee village along the Platte was painted by Wilkins. The village was seen by many emigrants in 1849 and in the following years. It was on the Oxbow and old Fort Kearny or Nebraska City Road about seventy-five miles east of the new Fort Kearny. On May 26, 1849, Elijah Howell noted, "We passed the Pawnee Village which is now deserted — The Sioux having a few days previous paid them a war visit." (Howell: 13) Wilkins passed it on May 31. On June 12 Bruff also passed through it and made a drawing of it. He commented about it and described the construction of the lodges.

Jackson's photo could be the Pawnee village on the Loup River on

Jackson, Smithsonian Institution, Photo #124941
Pawnee Lodge.

Wilkins, Wisconsin Historical Society, WHi.-1842

the road from Council Bluffs and Omaha.

This reconstructed lodge below is one of the fine displays at the Archway center on I-80 by Kearney, Nebraska. There are also displays inside the lodge. Another center, the Pawnee Museum, is located near Republic in north central Kansas on the site of an old village and has more information about the Pawnee.

Hill

Lodge reconstruction today.

123

Fort Childs or New Fort Kearny.

Construction on Fort Childs or the New Fort Kearny started in 1848 under the direction of Lt. Daniel Woodbury and C. Mills took the earliest photograph of it in 1858. Wilkins made this painting of the fort Childs. It is the earliest known illustration, dated June 4, 1849. The week before Bryarly noted on May 28, "The fort is at the head of Grand Island. All the buildings at the fort are being made of Sod taken from the prairie, and look comfortable." (Bryarly:88) East of the fort all the different trails on the south side of the Platte had finally converged. After leaving the fort Wilkins noted, "Wagons are now continually in sight. the number supposed to have already passed is

Jackson, National Park Service SCBL-276

Fort Kearny.

124

Wilkins, Wisconsin Historical Society, WHi.-1841

estimated at about 5,000.(Wilksins:41) The emigrants were now in Buffalo country. Bryarly noted, "This is the first time we have used buffalo chips. They burn well." (Bryarly:90)

The fort was much larger when Jackson passed it in 1866. It was situated about one-half mile south of the Platte. As with other military posts, emigrants were not supposed to camp on fort grounds. It was also near the fort that some of those traveling on the north side crossed to the south. Others continued on the north side until Fort Laramie. Some diarists refer to an emigrant register kept at Fort Kearny. Today it is a great resource on emigration. The remains of a dead tree can be

Hill

Main Parade Ground, Fort Kearny today.

125

Hill

O'Fallon's Bluff today.

seen at the left on the ground. It is all that exists of the trees originally planted by Lt. Woodbury and depicted in Jackson's painting.

After about another week of travel up the Platte the emigrants on the south side came to the forks of the Platte. It was the old Indian fording area and became the first of the South Platte crossing sites along the seventy-five-mile section of the trail. Charles Smith noted, "About noon we reached the south fork of the Platte and crossed it immediately. This river...is about one mile wide, with an average depth of about one foot....The bed of the river is a kind of quicksand..." (Smith:31)

Most emigrants did not cross there but continued on. They next encountered O'Fallon's Bluff where the river cut close its face. Some

Simons, Marguerite V. Brown Collection

O'Fallon's Trading Post.

emigrants crossed the South Platte a little before the bluffs and then traveled with those who had crossed at the forks. Most emigrants however continued and chose to ford it at the Lower Crossing or later at the Upper California Crossing. The road along the river's edge at the bluffs was narrow and dangerous and could flood. The main trail followed a safer route which climbed the bluff. Here is part of the display showing the trail swales as it climbed O'Fallon's Bluff. The parallel and sometimes crisscrossing depressions going up the hill are clearly evident. Modern travelers can see the trail display at the eastbound I-80 rest stop east of Sutherland.

George Simons sketched O'Fallon's trading post that was established in the 1850s. It appears to be situated by the bluffs near where the trail dropped back down along the river. The emigrants were now traveling in the territory of the Sioux. The post existed for a few years.

This area just west of Sutherland is in the vicinity of the trading post. Note that the growth of trees has been extensive all along the Platte and blocks the view of the bluffs on the south side of the South Platte.

Some of those emigrants who had already forded the South Platte to its north bank also crossed the plateau to the North Platte near here.

Hill

O'Fallon's Bluff trading post area today.

Crossing the South Platte.

On May 20, the day after fording the South Platte Smith recorded, " We continued our march up the south fork of the Platte, some ten miles, where we crossed over the bluffs which lie between the two streams, and after going two miles we reached the north fork…"(Smith:32)

This shows the area near one of those crossings today. As depicted in the emigrant illustrations the river was from about one-half to one mile wide with treeless banks. Quicksand was a major problem for the emigrants. Lucena Parson travelled as part of a fifty wagon company. She noted, "We had good luck & all got over in half a day & all camped together at night The feed very poor, not much to be seen but white sand, The river is shallow & 1 mile wide. "(Parson: 250) Today flood control and irrigation have nearly eliminated the seasonal flooding.

Hill - 1305

South Platte crossing today.

128

This has reduced the river's width and allowed for trees to grow in the once almost treeless valley.

On July 21, 1850, Lucena Parson noted, "We again are pursuing our teadious journey. For the first 3 miles it was up hill and then we came to a ridge. This extended to Ash hollow..." (Parson:251.) As time passed the two major fording areas dominated the travel. By the 1860s the Upper Crossing had replaced the Lower Crossing as the major one.

After fording at the Lower California Crossing near Brule, Nebraska, the trail climbed up California Hill to the plateau. There are two historical markers in the area of those 3 miles and impressive swales as shown in the California Hill photo near where the trail approached the top and the plateau between the forks. Wilkins forded on June 13, 1849 and described the traffic on the plateau noting, "Find a great many companies continually in sight. in fact, it is one continued stream, as far as we could see both in front and near the horizon is dotted with white wagon covers of emigrants, like a string of beads." (Wilkins:43)

Jackson, National Park ServiceSCBL-23
Upper South Platte Crossing.

The Upper Crossing or last crossing area was near old Julesburg and the site of the later Fort Sedgewick. The Pony Express used this crossing. Jackson crossed there in 1866 and depicted the fording in his painting. It followed Lodgepole Creek west and then cut north until it rejoined the old trail coming from California Hill and Ash Hollow at Courthouse Rock.

Hill

Ruts on California Hill.

Quesenbury, Nebraska State Historical Society, L/A #19135
Quesenbury's view of Ash Creek Canyon.

Those emigrants who crossed the South Platte and climbed California Hill entered the North Platte Valley at Ash Hollow. Quesenbury made this sketch in 1851 from the top of what was later called Windlass Hill. It did not show the drop, but the broad view beyond the drop. That view appears to have changed very little except for the abundance of trees. On June 15, 1849 Wilkins wrote, "Passed to day thro' Ash Hollow, a dry ravine leading to the North Fork, the decent so steep into it that the wagons had to be held back by ropes." Once down they followed the ravine to a spring a mile or two farther but no grass. Wilkins did note, "Here is the last wood of any consequence till we reach fort Laramie." (Wilkins:43-44) Lucena Parson's diary gives a good description of the area from Ash Hollow

Hill

Ash Creek Canyon - View from the top of Windlass Hill.

131

Hill

Ash Hallow today - looking back up Windlass Hill.

to Scotts Bluff to Fort Laramie.This view from the ridge shows the area where the wagons were let down.

This view is looking back up the hill. In the last thirty-five years cedar trees have grown on the once treeless hills and in the old trail swales and scars that were made by the thousands of wagons that traversed the hill. The trees now obscure the hill and portions of the scars. Today if you walk up the hill and back down you will have a similar view and get a feel of the descent. You will also see the wide swale cut by the wagons as they came off the plateau and followed a

C. Hall – Wyoming State Museum, Department of State Parks and Cultural Resources

Outlet of Ash Hallow.

132

Hill

Outlet of Ash Hallow today.

ridge line to its edge and then the many swales left by the wagons as they peeled off for their final descent to the valley floor.

A short distance before the emigrants left Ash Hollow, those emigrants who had earlier forded the South Platte to follow the south bank of the North Platte were forced over the hills into the hollow and joined the emigrants who had come down from Windlass Hill. This sketch by Cyrenius Hall shows the trail as it approached the mouth of Ash Hollow and the North Platte. One of the often mentioned springs was off to the right perhaps in the vicinity of the horse and rider. Emigrants camped along the valley floor. Years ago camping was allowed but not in the past thirty years or more.

Over the years evidence of the trail has been obliterated on the canyon or hollow floor as the creek bed has been altered and straightened and the highway put in. The spring is off the photo and hidden by the trees on the far right. Ash Hollow was a significant site on the trail. It was also often mentioned by the emigrants who

had followed the Platte on the north side.

Past the spring, at the mouth of Ash Hollow Bruff noted on July 1, "Noon'd opp. a train on the N. side riv....Grave on end of bluff terminating Ash Hollow. above,— left of trail leavg hollow — "

"Rachel E. Pattison,

Aged 18, June 19, 1849"

Hill (Bruff:27)

Pattison grave at Ash Hallow.

133

Bruff's journals' entries contained a record of the graves encountered. However, it is interesting to note that he did not mention the grave of Josiah Keeran who had died June 15, 1849 and was buried next to Rachel according to other emigrant accounts. In 1850 Lucena Parson noted twenty graves near the area. (Parson:251) Today the Pattison grave can still be seen in the graveyard at the mouth of the hollow. The modern highway crosses the North Platte, but the old trail turned left or northwest and continued to follow along the south bank.

Wilkins, Wisconsin Historical Society, WHi-31447
Court House Rock.

Farther down the trail on June 19, the same day Rachel died, Wilkins wrote, "Camped tonight in the vicinity of court house rock. This is an immense rock in the shape of buildings standing alone on the prairie, about 4 miles to the left of the road. Although the distance is so deceptive it does not seem to be more than 1 mile away, and many were the mistakes made by the men in going on foot to see it. most of them turning back after walking a mile or two, apparently getting no nearer. From the point I left the road it must have been six miles. took a sketch of it." (Wilkins:45-6) Not all were fooled. Lucena Parson noted, "To day came in view of a splendid looking sight, like a stone castle. Did not go near it as we learned it was five miles off the road." Parsons: 252)

Wilkins would have been just off present highway north of the present entrance to the historical site. The smaller formation came to be referred to as Jail Rock. Cyrenius Hall painted them from nearly the same location in 1853. This view would have also been the same as seen by those emigrants coming up from the Upper California Crossing.

The Courthouse and Jail rocks were the first of the many enchanting eroded shapes that lined the Platte Valley. Travelers often

Quesenbury – Nebraska State Historical Society, L/A #19134
Courthouse and Jail Rock.

commented about them, and many made sketches of the various formations between Courthouse Rock and Scotts Bluff. Although today the valley is heavily farmed and many of the formations have eroded some, the general appearance has changed very little. It is still a wondrous section to drive.

Quesenbury sketched the formation in 1851 from almost a mile farther to the east. His illustration is more realistic. Note also the small dome-like formation at the left in both the drawing and just visible in the photo. Bruff also made sketches of the famous formations, first as they appeared as small formations on the horizon and later as they appeared larger as the trail approached.

Hill
Courthouse and Jail Rock today.

135

Wilkins , Wisconsin Historical Society, Whi -31692

Chimney Rock and Platte River Valley

West of Bridgeport, Nebraska the trail roughly parallels highway 92. As the highway climbs a long low hill and then descends, the Platte valley appears to open up to the west all the way to Scotts Bluff. It seems the area was a natural place for many to record the view.

On June 19, Wilkins came within sight of Chimney Rock. On the twentieth he made a sketch of it. Writing on the twenty-first he recorded, "Passed Chimney Rock Yesterday. it is 12 miles from court house. took our noon rest within a mile of it. it a singular formation about 200 feet high, but as I took a sketch of it, I shall not trouble you with a description." (Wilkins:46) Only his earlier distant view which seems to have been made on the twentieth, west of Courthouse Rock, is known to exist. However, many other close-up illustrations of Chimney Rock created by other emigrants exist. On June 10, 1849 Bryarly described the rock, "It resembles at a distance a large hay stack with a pole running thru it, but upon a nearer approach looks more like a huge chimney of some old furnace." (Bryarly:103)

Hill

Platte Valley today.

136

The present-day photo is the same area as Wilkins' panorama view. As mentioned earlier, Wilkins style that tended to exaggerate the height of his primary object is obvious. Still, Chimney Rock seemed to impress everyone.

Bruff traveled through this region in 1849 in early July. His company and others celebrated Independence Day. He noted, "I delivered an address, and at 3 sat down (on the ground) to a sumptuous repast,— of pork & beans, buffalo meat, sort of rolls, hard bread, bean

Quesenbury, Neb. State Historical Society , L/A #19131

Chimney Rock. View from east.

soup, & stewed apples. Desert— apple pies....the medical stores of brandy and port-wine were used... The ladies honored us with their presence on the occasion; and to them we were indebted for several pounds of dried apples, and decent pastry." (Bruff: 29) This is the view from near where they had their celebration the next morning.

Chimney Rock is the most recorded landmark on the trails. This view by Quesenbury is what emigrants who left the trail and went to see the rock would have seen as they approached it from the east. It was easily identified by its conical base and funnel shape, but its size was harder to determine. Wilkins thought it was 200 ft. tall but others placed it at 500 ft. Wind and water erosion during the past 150 years have reduced its height. There are stories that the military once used

Chimney Rock today.

it for target practice. Lightning has even been known to strike it and knock small sections off. As with other formations emigrants carved and painted their names all over the landmark. Bryarly noted, "A great many names are cut and at least 1000 more are painted upon the Chimney..." (Bryarly:103)

This is a similar view taken *Hill* from north of the visitor center

137

Piercy

Scotts Bluff.

near Bayard, Nebraska. The center is well worth a visit and the displays include many illustrations of the formation. The ravages of time and weather have erased all evidence of the names except for a few saved in museums.

The next major geological feature encountered is the area of Scotts Bluff. As the trail approaches the area, a number of smaller formations are to the south. However, Scotts Bluff is soon hidden by a low rise. Once over the rise to the other side, the view opens with Scotts Bluff looming a few miles to the west. This view is from Piercy's *Route from Liverpool to Great Salt Lake Valley*.

At one time buffalo roamed along the entire Platte River Valley from the central plains to the Rocky Mountains. Today there are still

Mills, Library of Congress, Lee-Palfray Papers, LCMSS-65612-13
Rocky Mountains - Scotts Bluff.

Hill

Scotts Bluff today.

buffalo in the area, but only at the zoo near Scotts Bluff. Even the farms are being pushed back as housing developments are now slowly devouring the lands where the buffalo once roamed. The early trail was headed off to Robidoux Pass to the left or south of the bluffs.

This Mills photo is inaccurately identified as the Rocky Mountains. It is the earliest photo of Scotts Bluff taken in 1858. Frederick Piercy's 1853 illustration was rendered from nearly the same spot. He described it as "…resembling ruined palaces, castellated towers, temples and monuments." (Piercy:119)

Note how similar Mills' photo is to Piercy's earlier view.

This modern view above is after the trail crested the rise mention previously.

139

Quesenbury, Nebraska State Historical Society, L/A #19129
Dome Rock, north of road.

The trail for the emigrants of the 1840s took a turn southwest away from the river. The area near the river was very rugged and cut with ravines. This route was longer, but it was easier to bypass the ravines by the bluffs. On June 21, Wilkins noted, "The road leaves the river for a time and enters an ampitheatre of bluffs, where these castle like rocks are on all sides." (Wilkins:46) He continued to describe the area and a trading post near the pass.

Quesenbury drew some of those "castle like rocks" on both sides when he passed through in 1851. This particular formation was on the north side of the road near where the trail entered the valley and began its gentle climb to Robidoux's Pass. The large portion of the formation, left of center, is known today as Dome Rock. A similar view below is from along Robidoux Road.

Hill

Dome Rock today.

140

Bruff, Yale Collection of Western American, Beinecke Rare Book and Manuscript Library
Robidoux Pass Area.

Farther past Dome Rock, on July 7, Bruff made this sketch of the hills or castle-like structures about halfway up the valley towards the pass. His description of the area was similar to that of Wilkins'. "The basin, among the singular and romantic bluffs, is a beautiful spot. It appears to extend E. & W. about 5 ms. And about 3 ms. Wide. In a

*Hil*l

Castle formation today.

141

Quesenbury, Nebraska State Historical Society, L/A #19127
Scotts Bluff from the west.

deep gulch lies a cool clear spring and brook.— Close by is a group of Indian lodges & tents, surrounding a log cabin....At the W. end of the Bluffs you have the 1st sight of Laramie Peak, about 60 miles off." (Bruff:31)

The hills that appear to be the horizon in his depiction are actually another sketch. Bruff made use of every space he could in his journals. Here is the view of the same formation.

Lucena Parson wrote, "Started early this morn & travelled over beautiful country. No grass or water till we came to Trading point. (Parson:253-4) The climb was gentle. Here is Quesenbury's view of that "beautiful country" looking back through the basin as the trail approached the top of Robidoux Pass. The spring and post were located in the wooded area off to the right of the drawing. Many emigrant diarists noted the valley for its beauty and magical appearance. Bryarly commented about the prices at the trading post,

Today the lower or distant area is heavily farmed. As one approaches the pass the area is used as pasturelands. The trading post area is identified by a sign next the road, also off to the right of both illustrations.

Hill -218 -15   167-15-SPI

Basin view today.

Hill

Trail swales at Robidoux Pass today.

The physical evidence left by the thousands of wagon wheels as they cut into the crest and passed through Robidoux Pass is still clear in the pastureland. From there Bruff mentioned he could see Laramie Peak from the pass and Bryarly also noted this. A little farther up the pass one can still have that experience on clear days in the morning or late afternoon or early evenings.

By the early 1850s the migration route had changed, and those thousands of later wagons would instead leave their mark in Mitchell Pass.

Here is part of the wagon display which includes a variety of types of vehicles used with Eagle Rock as the background at Scotts Bluff National Historic Site. While some Conestoga wagons were used, most emigrants used smaller flat rectangular farm or spring wagons.

Hill

Wagon and oxen display.

143

Jackson, National Park Service SCBL-27

Mitchell Pass

Mitchell Pass through Scotts Bluff was first used in 1851, and emigrants soon made it the main route replacing the original route to the south through Robidoux Pass. The distance was about the same.

Jackson used Mitchell Pass in 1866 and camped on the west side of it. above is one of his paintings looking back east through the pass also showing Dome Rock. The emigrants were now heading for Fort (Laramie) John and the very distant Laramie Peak. The painting looking back eat depicts the rugged nature of the pass that kept the early traders and emigrants out until a route was developed through it.

Today there is a fine visitor center at Mitchell Pass. You can walk on or along the trail for more than a mile and see where Jackson

Hill

Mitchell Pass today.

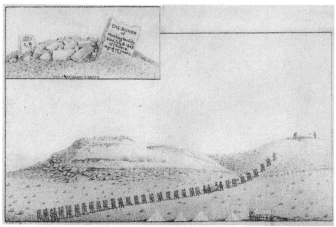

Bruff, mssHM8044(37), The Huntington Library , San Marino, California
Emigrant Burial - Bishop Funeral & Grave-.

camped in 1866. It is also possible to drive to the top of the bluff. The view is terrific.

About a half day's travel west of the passes the sandy road brought the emigrants to Horse Creek. Bruff made this later drawing of the funeral procession and grave of Charles Bishop, a member of his wagon company, based on his earlier sketch of the bluff and grave site near where they had camped on July 8, 1849.

This site was discovered by this author and his wife Jan in 1989. It is located south of Torrington, Wyoming near Jamison Bluff at Hunton's Meadow. Bruff camped off the main trail and remnants of

Hill
Jamison Bluff & grave area today.

145

Wilkins, Wisconsin Historical Society, WHi-3935
Fort Laramie (old Fort John).

the connecting camp roads are still visible in the fields. The grave, on private property, is on the top of the hill to the right. Today trees and ranch buildings block part of the bluff.

Another day of travel and the emigrants would be at Fort Laramie. Wilkins visited Fort John (Laramie) on June 24, 1849, and it appeared to be well maintained. Arrival at the fort indicated the end of the first major leg of the journey. The first wooden fort established in 1834 as a trading post with the American Indians was painted by Alfred J. Miller. It was abandoned and replaced in 1841 by the adobe Fort John painted by Wilkins. It soon became a recruiting area for the westward bound emigrants and their livestock. It was also where the emigrants

Mills, Library of Congress, Lee-Palfray Papers, LCMSS - 65612-14
Mills photo of Fort Laramie, 1858.

Jackson, National Archives, #57-HS-269
Jackson photo of Fort Laramie about 1870.

re-evaluated the contents of their wagons and determined what they needed.

The army had purchased this second "Fort Laramie" in 1849 and immediately began a major expansion of it. The Mills photo shows part of the expansion and the deteriorated adobe Fort John which had served the early emigrants so well. The photo was taken in 1858, and Fort John was demolished in 1862, but the expansion continued.

This Jackson photo of Fort Laramie was taken from near the same spot as the earlier Mills photo, only about twelve years later. The expansion and changes were extensive, and old Fort John was gone save for some piles of rubble.

The photo below was taken from the same spot that Jackson used. Notice the extensive growth of trees along the river and in the hills and the rivers slightly altered course. Today the fort is barely visible.

Hill -1824

Fort Laramie today

147

Hill

Register Cliff today.

Before 1852, those on the trail on the north side of the Platte had to cross to the south side at Fort Laramie where everyone traveled. With the opening of the Childs Cutoff some of those emigrants on the north side did not cross and continued up the North Platte. However, most crossed and followed the south side routes or just to visit the fort. West of Fort Laramie a number of trail variants developed that were used by the emigrants with additional crossovers between the variants.

After about a half day's march those emigrants using one of the variants following the river dropped off the bench, perhaps at Mexican Hill. They were soon forced to cut close to the river bluffs upon which the emigrants wrote and carved their names. Today it is known as "Register Cliff." The wagons passed to the left along the present path and also in the depression or swale to the right of the rock in the center. This area was a favorite camping site.

Bruff noted , "At our noon halt, the [road?] runs close to the foot , (on our left) of brown sand stone, blocks of which lay...scattered about. All accessible faces of the blocks & cliffs, were marked and inscribed with name, initials, & dates. This particular vanity has been displayed all along the route..." (Bruff: 34-35) Some inscriptions are still visible.

Hall, Wyoming State Museum, Department of State Parks and Cultural Resources
Eight Miles West of Fort Laramie.

Another of the trail variants from Fort Laramie seems to have dropped off the hills into the river bottom just west of Register Cliff. The trail arched to the right to meet the variant that passed next to Register Cliff by the North Platte. The river is marked by the horizontal tree line. This wide area on the left was the favorite camping ground. The area was also the site of the later Sand Point Stage and Pony Express Station. The famous Guernsey Ruts are a little more than a mile to the left or west.

Hill

View today.

149

Hill -0240

Guernsey Trail ruts today.

This is the view taken along the present road as it drops off the hills and heads towards Guernsey, Wyoming. Register Cliff is to the right behind the rocky formation near the river.

Charles Gray passed the fort about two weeks before Wilkins passed it. He camped two or three miles east of the cliff. Gray noted, "the character of the road changing from a good hard level road to hills, stones, & rocks which I presume we shall have to encounter for the next 3 or 400 miles. Today we have seen large quantities of every description of article which have been abandoned by the gold seekers. The road and plain strew'd with them." (Gray:35) About a mile farther west from the cliff the river cut next to the hills, and the wagons were forced to climb the bluffs. Here the wagon wheels cut deeply into the rock, and the route was made clear. Gray noted, "...the morning beautiful, cool & pleasant, road very dusty, passed some bad hills, steep & rocky." (Gray:35) This photo of the "bad hills, steep & rocky" is of a lesser visited portion of the well-known "Oregon" or "Guernsey Ruts" park near Guernsey, Wyoming.

As trail traffic increased new splits and crossovers occurred. One such split happened after more than a half day's travel from Register Cliff when the one variant came to Cottonwood or Bitter Cottonwood

150

Wilkins, Wisconsin Historical Society, WHi-31285

In the Black Hills.

Creek. Some turned west to follow it away from the Platte to join the ridge or hill route while others crossed it and stayed closer to the river. Charles Smith described the general area, "we came to a little stream called Little Cottonweed. Our trail led over hilly country, presenting every variety of scenery, from the level plain to the bold bluffs, with here a few shrubs of pine and cedar." (Smith:44)

This is the view as the trail curves to the right shortly after it began its descent down to the creek. Wilkins' style of exaggerating the height of portions of the landscape is most evident in this painting. The hills are not as high and the mountain peaks are barely visible, but

Hill

Approach to Cottonwood today.

151

look closely to the right of center for a white carsonite trail marker. The trails's depression goes from the lower right side to the center, turning a little to the right as it descends a little, then turns again and heads for the distant creek crossing. Then the trail heads up the distant hills. A faint scaring can still be seen near the pipeline route up the hill. The main trail continued through the rolling Black Hills towards Horseshoe Creek.

Although Wilkins' paintings were usually dated correctly, he sometimes made mistakes with his labelling. Sometimes they were even off by up to ten days when paired with his journal entries. The photo below shows Sibley Peak located a few miles south of Glendo along I-25 at Horseshoe Creek crossing. It matches the formation labelled "Black Hills," and the trail passed next to it . However, based on Wilkins' dated diary, he would have been much farther north, almost sixty miles, near Deer Creek. However, the geography of that area does not match his drawing.

After traveling through the Black Hills the trail approached Horseshoe Creek, Ingalls wrote, "five miles from the spring we came to Horse[shoe] Creek. Here were great numbers camped…" (Ingalls: 37) Later a military post and Pony Express and stage station were also built near Sidley Peak where the emigrants camped. Today ranches occupy the area.

Wilkins, Wisconsin Historical Society, WHi-31286
Black Hills (Sibley Peak).

Hill
Sidley Peak today

Wilkins, Wisconsin Historical Society, WHi-31450
Laramie Peak.

Laramie Peak was first seen just west of Scotts Bluff as a small faint object on the distant horizon. As the emigrants followed the North Platte west, it appeared to grow larger. As they approached Horseshoe Creek, the peak loomed large to the west. The trail divided again. One continued north parallel to the river, while the other turned west towards the hill road. Most emigrants turned west.

Wilkins' drawing of Laramie Peak was from near where he made his painting of Sidley Peak. It was also from near where Ingalls camped on June 9, 1850. It was the view he had the morning of June 10 "We

Hill

Laramie Peak today.

102 -Red Hills.

camped last night opposite Laramie Peak." (Ingalls 37) Quesenbury also made a drawing of the peak from across the creek, but he focused on a smaller unique formation off to the left of Wilkins' view called "Anvil Peak" with Laramie Peak in the background.

After two or three days travel over the trail, variations that had developed after Fort Laramie all converged before the crossing of LaBonte Creek. Just to the north the trail entered the Red Earth Country. Wilkins called this painting "Red Hills." The painting shows the trail as it approaches Wagon Hound Creek crossing, located about nine miles south of Douglas off highway 94. William Baker called the area "Uncle Sam's brick yard" and said that "there is between 3 and 4 miles of road that is as red as a brick and the hills the same color." The actual area was much larger.

Hill

Red Hills - Wagon Hound Creek today.

Today power lines mar the beauty of the area. If one were to drive south on the highway as it approached the hill from which Wilkins made his painting, the many trail scars could easily be seen coming over and down the slope where they began to join and turn northwest towards the creek crossing. In the photo they are visible as light parallel lines going downhill from the left. Most emigrants had their last view of Laramie Peak a little before cresting the hill and dropping down to Wagon Hound Creek.

After traveling a few hours more this piled formation of light or white rocks was noted by a number of emigrants. Perhaps that was because it seemed out of place in the Red Earth Country. It was located seemingly only a stone's throw off the trail shown above passing to its right. In 1847 Elizabeth Smith noted it, and Bryarly wrote on June

Quesenbury, Nebraska State Historical Society,
L/A #19119
White River in the Redlands.

Hill
Knob Hill today.

19, "Passed a large conical hill , 200 feet high and nearly solid rock. We nooned on A La Prele River, a narrow & swift stream. Grass very short." (Bryarly 111) Traveling the same area in 1860 Richard Burton noted, "we saw on the left of the path a huge natural pile or burrow of primitive boulders, about 200 feet high and called 'Brigham's Peak'...." (Burton: 167)

Today the formation is more commonly known as Knob Hill or Grindstone Butte. Jackson photographed it in 1870. The trail goes through the gap to the right in the distant hills while the photo is from the old trail where it cuts to the right across the bottom of the photo.

Another five miles brought the travelers to another feature. On July 15, 1849, near the end of the Red Earth Country, Bruff noted, "The road soon sweep(s) around the base of a very conical hill, crowned with a pile of dingy yellow rock and earth, and resembles much such scenes on the Rhine – a great eminence, with a ruined tower on top." (Bruff: 43-4)

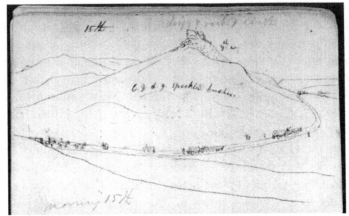

Bruff, Yale University, Beinecke Rare Book and Manuscript Library

Castle Peak .

This was also the area of the later Bozeman Trail junction which is indicated by the monument in the lower right of the photo. Bruff would be surprised to see the new homes now being built in the area. The North Platte and the trail had completed their turns to the west.

Another of Wilkins' drawings labeled the "Black Hills" is shown above. Bruff and Quensenbury also sketched the formation. The name should not be confused with the more famous Black Hills of South Dakota. Here the term "Black Hills" refer to the mountains and the foothills surrounding Laramie Peak from west of Fort Laramie and north to Deer Creek and west again to the Casper, Wyoming area. The

Hill

Castle Peak today.

Wilkins, Wisconsin Historical Society, WHi-31282
The Black Hills.

name comes from the many cedar and other trees on the hills that give them the appearance of a dark or black color when compared to the surrounding lighter grass and sagebrush areas. This painting shows the hills south of the trail near LaPrele Creek.

Near this spot is the earliest identified grave on the trail. It is of Joel Hembree, a young boy who died on July 19, 1843. He was riding on the wagon tongue, fell off, and was crushed by the wheels. Also near this area is Ayers Natural Bridge. About five or six miles to the west is the site of the 1864 Indian attack on a small group of emigrants including Mary Kelly. She and others killed are buried nearby.

Wilkins crossed the North Platte just west of the Deer Creek Crossing. The area north of present-day Glenrock was the first crossing of the North Platte. It was also one of the most dangerous with many drownings. On July 25, 1852, Stansbury recorded, "The ferryman informed me that an emigrant had been drowned here, the day before....this man made the twenty-eighth...this year." (Stansbury:61) The emigrants usually waited for the ferry or continued on. The last

Hill
View today – "curved hills."

157

Wilkins, Wisconsin Historical Society, WHi-31287
Ferrying Wagons at North Platte.

crossing of the North Platte was west of Casper at the Red Buttes or Bessemer Bend. The area around Deer Creek was a major camping area. On July 16, Bruff noted, "…brought us to Deer Creek, which we crossed, passing through hundreds of tents, wagons, camp fires, and people of every age & sex, congregated on its banks and turned down to the right, camped on the banks of the Platte, at the Ferry, 1/3 of a mile above the mouth of the Creek." (Bruff:44) So crowded was the area that Bruff did not cross the Platte until July 20, four days after his arrival.

Bruff and Wilkins would also have crossed the Platte near what appears to be a narrow section. The point is actually part of an island. Today the river is narrower and trees cover the riverbanks, but the north side hills along the river are still the same.

Hill

North Platte crossing area at Deer Creek today.

Quesenbury, Nebraska State Historical Society, L/A #19116
White Rock south of river.

Quesenbury's drawing depicts three identifying features found in the area west of the Deer Creek crossing. On the left is shown the white outcropping seemingly flowing from the hillside, the large rock formation or rock in the glen in the center, and the flat Eagle Butte off to the west. Bruff's camp was north of this, nearer the river and ferry, and he would have seen this view to his south. There was plenty of fresh water, wood, and fishing was noted to be good. The grass was usually decent, except in the years of heavy emigration which 1849 was. Bruff had his mules taken almost seven miles up Deer Creek in order to find sufficient grass.(Bruff:45) His company crossed the next day. This was also the view those emigrants who stayed on the south

Hill

Glen Rock area today.

159

side of the river had as they moved out of Deer Creek west along the trail.

In recent years the immediate buildings around the rock in the glen formation have been cleared, but other structures still stand. This present view from the area of the trail matches Quesenbury's drawing. Unfortunately, from this particular vantage point from the route of the traila house blocks the view of most of the flowing White Rock and trees cover most of rock formation in the center. For those modern travelers who like to camp, there is a new campground in the vicinity of the ferry near where Bruff camped.

Prairie storms were like nothing most people had ever experienced elsewhere. Most emigrants commented about them. On July 21 Bruff wrote, "moved on again, over a high and steep sand-hill, very heavy drag, ascended higher, and gained the level mountain top... on the summit...when, at 3 P.M...two dark clouds discharged their contents on our devoted heads. Rain fell in a perfect sheet, blinding and appalling lightning, crashing thunder. In a few seconds from the commencement of this tempest, the hail suddenly descended, like large gravel in immense quantities...then hail stones of extraordinary size, not only cut and bruised the men, whose hands and faces were bleeding, but it also cut the mules...(Bruff:47-8)

Bruff, mssHM8044(18),. Huntington Library, San Marino, California
Prairie storm.

160

Below is the site from the west. It is east of Casper off the north side trail or Chiles route and a little west of Wyoming 256. The river cut close to the hills and forced the trail up from the valley floor to make a loop before returning to the river. The photo was taken from the edge of the trail as it nears the crest.

Hill

Level mountain top today.

Quesenbury, Nebraska State Historical Society, L/A #19115
Black Hills [Caspar Mountains].

The trails on the north and south paralleled the North Platte. The emigrants were becoming even more conscious about the weight of their wagon loads. The area between Deer Creek and the last crossing area was also another dumping ground for non-essential and heavy equipment and food. Bruff noted, "More beans discarded than any other article of provisions....are heavy freight. Sheet-iron stoves, which every mess of emigrants had, were gradually droped, as useless& troublesome." (Bruff:47) To the south and parallel to the trail was the end of the Black Hills. Quesenbury made his drawing of the range known today as the Casper Mountains. It shows the more distant higher mountains and the lower foothills, but he does not depict the nearly flat land between the river and the foothills which would have been in the foreground.

It seems that he may have made the drawing less than a mile east of the site of the Mormon Ferry and Louis Guinard's trading post and the present Fort Caspar. This view is from inside the fairgrounds next to the river road a little before the entrance to Fort Caspar.

Here is Jackson's Fort Caspar and the Platte River Bridge as well as a photo of the reconstructed fort. The original Guinard Trading Post and bridge were constructed in 1858-9. It was also used by the

Hill

Caspar Mountains today.

Jackson, / Wyoming State Museum , Department of State Parks and Cultural Resources
Fort. Caspar.

Pony Express in 1860-1. The site was soon taken over by the army and expanded. It was known as Platte Bridge Station. It was later renamed Fort Caspar after the death of Lt. Caspar Collins during the Battle of Platte Bridge on July 26, 1865. The site was also the location of the earlier Mormon Ferry. Reshaw's Bridge had been located a few miles to the east. The post was abandoned in 1867 with the construction of Fort Fetterman. The last fording of the North Platte before the

Hill

Fort Caspar today

163

river turned south was about ten miles west at Red Buttes Crossing at Bessemer Bend.

From near Grand Island in eastern Nebraska where all the jumping-off trails had merged, the emigrants had traveled up the Platte on both sides of the river. West of Casper all the emigrants had crossed to the north side of the Platte, and they were headed west to reach and follow the Sweetwater River to the South Pass. The maze of parallel and crossing trail variations that had developed from as far back as Deer Creek all rejoined a few miles east of Rock Avenue.

For most of the route travelers today can drive along the trail

Quesenbury, Nebraska State Historical Society, L/A #19113
Rock Avenue from the north.

to the Sweetwater Valley. West of Casper the trail passed a defile often mentioned by the travelers as "Rock Avenue" or the "Devil's Backbone." It was about a day's travel from Fort Caspar. Few drew the feature. Bruff made a few sketches representing one view while Quensenbury made several drawings from different locations. This is one of Quesenbury's. One of Bruff's drawings was similar. Jonas

Hill

Rock Avenue today.

Hittle made another drawing of it, but it was a very childlike bird's eye-view. He wrote, "we passed through Rock Lane which is two Lines of Rocks Rising perpendicular out of the ground from 20 to 40 feet high. They are about 40 yards apart. At the End of This I Cut my name dated June the 24th 1849." (Hittle:30) Today you can drive through the 'avenue,' but getting out and walking along the trail is more rewarding. Hittle's name is no longer there.

The trail continued west to Willow Springs, a famous camping area

Quesenbury, Nebraska State Historical Society, L/A #19112
View from Summit of Prospect Hill.

and another day of travel. Conditions could vary every year. In June of 1849 it was hot and all the grass had been consumed. (Hittle:30) In June of 1850, Margaret Frink recorded, "while cooking supper a heavy storm of wind and snow came up." The next morning she wrote, "We snowballed each other till ten o'clock....We traveled twenty-two miles, and came to the Sweetwater River..." (Frink: 101) After Willow Springs came the long but gentle pull up Prospect Hill. More discarded items lined the trail. Both Wilkins and Quesenbury made drawings of the view looking to the distant Sweetwater Valley below, the same area Frink traveled and saw. Quesenbury labelled his view,

Hill
View from near Prospect Hill Summit today.

Quesenbury, Nebraska State Historical Society, L/A #19112
Alkaline Lake.

"From the Summit of Prospect Hill." Unfortunately, it appears he may have embellished the view by adding two of his other sketches of alkali flats into the foreground. Those alkali flats are not visible from his vantage point and are actually miles away very close to Independence Rock. (Murphy: 120) However, his drawing was not made from the summit as titled, but from about four miles down from the summit. As a result, it appears he unnecessarily replaced the part of the ravine or depression and the dry flats with his two other drawings.

Emigrants approaching Independence Rock often commented about the nearby alkaline flats. They sometimes collected the saleratus for baking. Quesenbury drew two. (See comment in previous drawing.) One was to the south of the trail and one was on the north. This is the

Hill

Alkaline Lake today.

one on the south side. Thomas Royal's July 21, 1853 entry reads, "It only looked like a frozen lake. It shimmered in the light, but it could not be ice, for this was mid-July. The train halted, all hands rushed to see the strange sight. Great was our amazement, to discover here a lake of alkali that had condensed on its surface until a crystallized sheet covered its surface like a thick sheet of ice. This was a great opportunity to replenish our stores of salaeratus." (Mumford: 85)

Little has changed in the area today. A number of parallel deep windblown trail swales are clearly visible in the foreground as the trail heads towards Independence Rock. The grass, however, would have all been eaten off by the thousands of emigrant draft animals passing through the area.

Quesenbury, Nebraska State Historical Society, L/A #19111
Independence Rock from the north.

This is the view emigrants had as they approached the rock where the trail met the Sweetwater. It was also drawn from right along the trail. Similar views were recorded by Bruff, Jackson, Tappan, and other artists. On July 26, 1849 Bruff noted, "Independence Rock at a distance looks like a huge whale." (Bruff:52)

The trail actually split to round both ends of the rock. Note the trail approaching the left or south side of the rock in the drawing. The other segment curved around the opposite end more like the ranch road today. A Pony Express Station was built in 1860 and later also the military's Sweetwater Station from near where the photo was taken. For a few years the military also had a bridge across the Sweetwater here.

Wilkins noted, "It is a solid dome of granite rising out of the prairie, with thousands of names, painted principally with tar." (Wilkins:53) Today some of the names painted and cut into the rock that Father DeSmet called "The Great Register of the Desert" are still visible.

On July 26, 1849 Bruff, like other emigrants, climbed the rock, noted the many names, enjoyed the view and continued to make some sketches. He wrote," It is painted and marked every way, all over, with

Hill

Looking west at Independence Rock today.

168

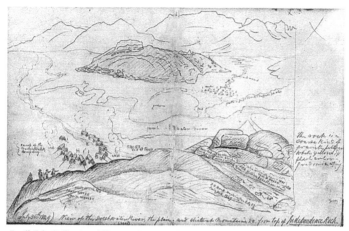

Bruff, Yale Collection of Western American, Beinecke Rare Book and Manuscript Library
View from Independence Rock.

names, dates, initials, &c – so that it was with difficulty I could find a place to inscribe on it: - The Washington Company, July 26, 1849." (Bruff:52)

One June 8, 1850, Charles W. Smith, a former newspaperman on his way to California wrote, "I climbed up its abruptly rocky sides, and spent a few minutes walking about its summit, though I had not time to examine it as I wished." (Smith :49) You also can climb the rock to examine it, but please be careful and don't deface it or the remaining emigrant names.

Hill

Bruff's view today.

Jackson, National Archives # 57-HS-384
Jackson's photo from Independence Rock.

Take your time when examining the rock and be careful. The view is beautiful, but the wind really blows, so watch your hat! You can still find some of the old names on the rock. This Jackson photo was the basis for some of his paintings. Hoffman wrote that "nearly all of our company, large and small climmed to its top to view the surrounding country and inscribe our names on the rocks. Thousands of names are found written there." (Mumford:84)

In the recent photo, it seems the river has meandered a little, some minor rock erosion and one rock slid down a little. Can you find the rock that slid?

Hill

Jackson's view today.

Jackson, National Archives # 57-HS-385
Old Trail at Independence Rock.

This Jackson photo shows the trail that passed on the north side of Independence Rock. It was heading towards the crossings nearer Devil's Gate. The view is looking back "east." The trail can be seen clearly although its use had dropped greatly by 1870 when the photo was taken.

This is the same view. A rest area and new interpretive display has been built on the west side next to the old trail. The present walking bridge crosses the old trail shown in Jackson's photo. The path then leads to the rock, and visitors can walk all the way around it. Those emigrants who continued west along this portion of the trail were heading towards Devil's Gate. Some forded the Sweetwater about one mile west of the rock, while others forded later nearer Devil's Gate. All joined those who had earlier crossed near the rock.

Hill
Old Trail today.

171

Wilkins, Wisconsin Historical Society, WHi-31291
Devils Gate – From east.

Those emigrants who had not crossed the river near Independence Rock continued directly towards Devil's Gate and crossed just east of there. Devil's Gate was a curiosity for most emigrants. Some emigrants walked into the gate for a closer look. Wilkins was one of them. On July 10, he wrote, "the sides of the gap are so perpendicular as to leave no room even for a foot passenger to pass. they are very high (300 feet) and rugid. I regret I could not pass two or three hours to finish the sketch of it more highly." (Wilkins:53) His painting is based on that sketch.

After arriving at Devil's Gate on July 20, 1853, William Hoffman noted, "I went some distance into the gorge from the eastern end, a more wild picturesque and sublime scene I never witnessed." (Mumford:85) In 1858 Mills made the first known photographs of

Quesenbury, – Nebraska State Historical Society
Devil's Gate from north.

Mills, Library of Congress, Lee-Palfrey Papers,
LCMSS-65612-18
Devils Gate, Mills view.

Hill

View from Mills perspective today.

Devil's Gate. Compare this photo with the renditions by Wilkins and Quesenbury.

Here is the view today. It remains nearly impossible to walk through, and it is still picturesque. Note the "little" tree in the top right by the knob in the Mills photo and Wilkin's painting. It is still there today.

Bruff, mssHM8044(56)The Huntington Library, San Marino, California
Rattlesnake Pass.

For the afternoon of July 26 Bruff's diary reads, "... the trail enters a narrow level plain, bounded by piles of rocks & hills, with dwarf cedars scattered over them, and in the crevices. First half mile very sandy. Rocks on the left of the trail, inscrib'd all over; near the outlet a grave attracted my attention, and I pictured it." (Bruff :52-3) This is a later one of his drawings of that area.

The old highway and ranch road follows the old trail in the pass to what was once the headquarters for the Sun Ranch. It seems little has changed. The grave is still there, but with a small new marker by the big old head stone. The headstone has "T.P. Baker, 1864" carved on it, but investigations proved it was the Fulkerson grave. Baker apparently added his name after the original inscription had worn off. The present highway bypasses it but does have another historical site

Hill

Rattlesnake pass and grave site today.

174

Bruff's drawing of Devil's Gate.

pull-off nearby. A little farther is the entrance to the old Sun Ranch and present Mormon Handcart Visitor Center.

The view from the west into the gate was probably more familiar to the emigrants. Smith recorded, "Some of our party climbed to the top of the Gate and boasted of having done some daring climbing." (Smith:80) Sometimes a few unfortunates fell. Many diarists commented about its size. Hoffman described it, "The rocks of granite tower perpendicularly some 400 or 500 feet above the rushing water." (Mumford:84)

Jackson's view of Devil's Gate.

Hill

Jackson site today.

175

Bruff 's sketch was made inside the entrance but up a little near Jackson's later photo. Jackson made a number of photographs in this area looking both directions. This is one of them. It is also from the west, looking east. Bruff's drawing was probably made from near where the two men are in Jackson's photo.

Jackson, National Archives, # 57-HS-289

Jackson's view of Split Rock.

The next landmark on the trail was Split Rock. In earlier years it had other names. It was first visible west of Rattlesnake Pass and then for days from both the east and the west. Alfred J. Miller's painting is the earliest known illustration. Bruff, Wilkins, Quesenbury and Jackson all painted or sketched it. Jackson also photographed it as seen above.

Here is the same view from on the Split Rock Ranch. The trail is off to the left of the photo. It appears that the Sweetwater has meandered very little here and the vegetation patterns are similar.

Hill

Split Rock today.

176

Wilkins, Wisconsin Historical Society, WHi-31694
Wilkins' view of Sweet Water Buttes.

Wilkins made this panoramic view of the Sweetwater Valley a few miles farther up the river. This is the "Old Man" or "Stone Face" as known today. However, it was Sweetwater Buttes to Wilkins. Split Rock is at the extreme right in this painting.

When Wilkins traveled through here he wrote, "Grass very scarce the camping places, as laid down in the guide books as having plenty of grass. we have invariably found none there. it being all eaten off by previous trains." (Wilkins:54) As a result, he noted many dead animals and ejected property along the trail in this area. Today the relics are gone, there is more grass, but ranchers still lose a few animals. A few miles west of Split Rock on the south side was a small square looking sandstone tower known by names such as "Old Castle" or "Devil's Post-office," but the major feature they had to contend with was a short but narrow canyon on the Sweetwater twelve miles from Split Rock. The area came to be known as "Three Crossings," but sometimes emigrants referred to as the "Narrows."

Hill - 391-15　　　　　　　　　　　　　　　　*Hill - 392-15*
Sweetwater Buttes today.

Jackson, National Archives # 57-HS-299

Jackson's view of Three Crossing Station.

This Jackson photo was taken of the abandoned military Three Crossings Station. It also served as the basis for his later painting of "Three Crossings." The site was earlier used as a Pony Express and stage station. The trail actually divided here. One route crossed the river near here and then continued along the river through the small canyon in the photo's center where it crossed two more times close together. The other, the deep sand route, avoided the rocky crossings but had to contend with sand and the climb around and over the hill to the left. Later, a third went south and west around the hills. All later rejoined about ten miles to the west.

Today the tall sagebrush has overgrown the piles of stone which once served as the station's foundation, walls, and chimneys.

Hill

Three Crossing Station site today.

Jackson, National Archives, # 57-HS-246
Tribbetts grave.

Another Jackson photo taken in the Three Crossings area shows the grave of a soldier, Bennett Tribbetts who died in 1862. The grave is on a little hill just west of the station site. A marble stone has replaced the original. The original wooden headstone shown in the old photo is now in the Fort Caspar Museum.

Above the grave is a light smooth looking area between the rocky hills. That area was where the deep sand route climbed over the hill through a narrow pass. William Johnston took that route and noted on June 7, 1849, "…we came to a canon through which the Sweetwater cuts its way, and there our trail diverged through a narrow gap in the granite range, thus avoiding crossing the steam twice. At the mouth of this gap we had our first glimpse of the Wind River Mountains, the great divide between the waters of the East and West." (Johnston: 90-1) Those going all the way through the canyon would have to travel farther before they saw the mountains.

Hill

Tribbetts grave today.

Wilkins, Wisconsin Historical Society, WHi-31292
Wilkins' drawing, Sweet Water [Three Crossings].

Bryarly and Wilkins both took the Three Crossings route. Wilkins made this drawing of the Sweetwater and canyon near where the trail was forced to make its second and third crossing.

Today the willows have overgrown the riverbanks and obscure the view and the flow is considerably reduced. This photo was taken from a point almost near the center of Wilkins' painting, the actual "narrows" where the river took up the full width and the road was in the streambed. When Bryarly entered it was full and deep. He met some ox teams that could not make it and were returning to take the other route. Bryarly and company were able to make it through.

Hill

Three Crossings today.

Wilkins, Wisconsin Historical Society, WHi-31293
First view of Wind River Range.

(Bryarly:121-2) Some travelers noted the mosquitos and rattlesnakes in the area. Both species are still there today.

The emigrants who took the trail through the three crossing canyon got their first view of the mountains about nine miles west before the trail descended to the fifth crossing. On June 22, 1850 Margaret Frink recorded, "During the forenoon, we ascended a long, sloping hill, at the top of which, looking across a wide stretch of rough country covered with sage-brush, we got our first sight of the Wind River range of the Rocky Mountains. They are covered with snow, and appeared to be about fifty miles distant." (Frink:103) Wilkins captured this view in his painting.

Note again the "liberties" Wilkins took by exaggerating the height of the distant Wind River Mountains which are barely visible on the horizon in the photo. Perhaps it was the result of the excitement

Hill
View today.

181

Wilkins, Wisconsin Historical Society, WHi-31294
Wilkins' view of Rocky Ridge, July 13.

Wilkins felt when he first saw them. I know I certainly was excited when they appeared as the trail crested the hill. On the other side of the crossing the trails were reunited.

The trail continued working its way up the Sweetwater River past the famous Ice springs and slough where emigrants sometimes reported that they found ice by digging into the marshy areas. The next features to overcome were the long Sweetwater Canyon and Rocky Ridge. About twenty miles west of the Ice Slough, the Sweetwater passed through a narrow canyon. The early trail bypassed this canyon by ascending some high hills. This section of the trail was often written about, but rarely sketched. Bruff noted, "At 6 A.M. we left camp and I ascended the high hill, moved over it, and ascended

Hill

Rocky Ridge today.

Jackson, National Park Service SCBL-289
Table Mountains.

another, very stony and rough, requiring care of the teamster...."
(Bruff:59) In his diary Wilkins wrote, "the high ridges were rough and
rocky, which had we not forded the river several times the previous
day and so tightened our wheels, we should very probably had some
breakdowns." (Wilkins:55) Wilkins painted this view from near the
top. This vantage point could have been the same that Pritchard had
from near his camp.

The early emigrants walked. Even a modern four-by-four would
have trouble negotiating the rocks. It is much smoother and safer to
walk. This section of the trail is now off limits to vehicle traffic, but
can be hiked.

About twenty miles farther the trail makes its last crossing of the
Sweetwater and then heads towards the great South Pass. The Lander
Road, opened in 1859, branches off just before the last Sweetwater
crossing and heads northwest towards Fort Hall. These buttes had
been visible for a few days. They were also known as Oregon Buttes.
Shortly after the crossing and the climb out of the valley the two flat

Hill
Table Mountains area today.

183

Wilkin's drawing of South Pass,

topped buttes are again seen to the left or south of the trail. Little appears to have changed in the area. Even antelope like those depicted and noted can be found.

Wilkins' diary notation for Wednesday, July 18, 1849, was "Came thro' south Pass yesterday, without scarcely being sensible of any change. the road for eight miles preceeding the summit is very good and nearly on a dead level." (Wilkins:55) A little more than four years later Thomas Royal wrote, "For two months we had been looking forward to this noted pass in the far-famed Rockies. We had pictured it in our imagination. It would of course be a narrow passage between high and overhanging cliffs. It would of course be a dark gorge through the lofty mountains. Happy disappointment! So gradually and imperceptibly had we been ascending for hundreds of miles, that it seemed no summit at all. It was rather a beautiful rolling prairie, and

South Pass, today. To the left is the Atlantic. To the right the Pacific.

184

Wilkins Wisconsin Historical Society, WHi-31695

we were over the divide before we all knew it, and came to Pacific Springs, whose waters flow westward after a long journey through Green River, and the Colorado, emptying at last into the Pacific Ocean." (Mumford:92-3) This reaction to the pass was similar no matter what the year or who passed through. In June 1850 Margaret Frink recorded similar comments, but she also noted that a General James Estelle had established a private post office at the South Pass. For one dollar, letters would be delivered to the post office in St. Joseph, Missouri.(Frink: 105-6)

Hill

Wilkins' painting of Pacific Springs.

The famous Pacific Springs, the first water west of South Pass, were only about three miles west of the summit. Few emigrants stopped at the pass. Many were not really aware when they were in it, and most wanted grass and to get to the fresh water that ran to the Pacific. On August 1, Bruff's company did noon briefly at the pass, and then continued down to the springs. David Leeper, another 49'er, remembered "The spring nourished a beautiful, meadow-like park spread out in gentle slopes." (Leeper:40) Wilkins had camped there on July 17 and noted that most of the grass had been eaten off. His painting is from "the higher and dry ground" showing the "beautiful, meadow-like park."

Pacific Springs area today.

Wisconsin Historical Society, WHi - 316-96

Below is the area today. Pacific Creek shows up clearly in the bottoms. The springs and ruins of the old Halter and Flick Ranch and the site of the Pony Express station are to the east or off the photo to the right.

A few miles to the west after leaving his camp Bruff made his panorama sketch looking back east towards South Pass and Pacific

Hill

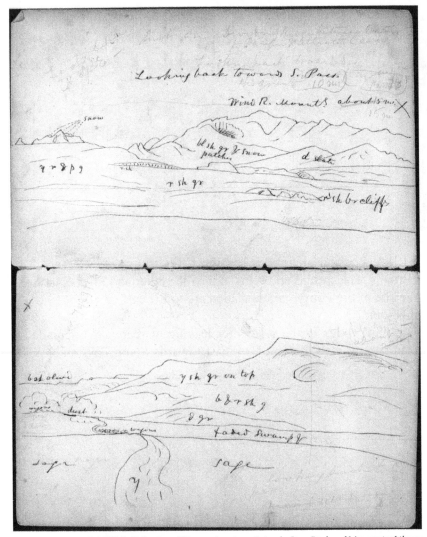

Bruff, Yale Collection of Western American, Beinecke Rare Book and Manuscript Library
South Pass today.

Springs as the trail descends from the pass. The trail crossed Pacific creek and was gradually moving away from it. The view is down and west from the South Pass display and viewing pull-off but along the old trail.

Here is the modern version of Bruff's drawings. The country has changed litlle since he passed through.

Hill

South Pass today.

Named because of its shape and colors, Plume Rock was one of the minor landmarks. It was located about ten miles west from Pacific

Hill

South Pass today.

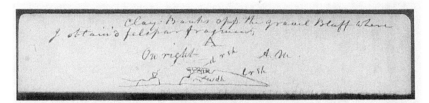

Bruff, Yale Collection of Western American, Beinecke Rare Book and Manuscript Library
Bruff sketch of Clay Banks [Plume Rocks].

Springs where the trail jogged northwest towards the Dry Sandy Crossing. It is two miles from the "Parting of the Ways" highway historical marker. Bruff made this sketch. Howard Stansbury wrote on Monday Aug 6, 1852, "About a mile from the Dry Sandy, some masses of rock were observed on the right of the road, standing up like pillars; they were found to be composed of coarse sandstone, of an orchery colour, under them were white and red shales, the result of the decomposition of the thin ochery rock." (Stansbury:71)

Today the "balanced rock," evident in the drawing, has since fallen off or eroded. Hawks have been nesting on the plume for more than thirty years. The two track is not the trail which is parallel to the bottom of the photo.

This Jackson painting is similar to two areas. This area is about a mile past Plume Rock near the trail's crossing of the Dry Sandy. The

Hill

Plume Rock today.

190

Jackson, Harold Warp Pioneer Village Foundation
Wind River Mountains.

Wind River Mountains are impressive. On July 31, 1853, William Hoffman recorded, "...the Wind River chain fully in view. The perpetual snow bank glistening in the sunbeams and seeming to be but 10 or 15 miles distant, whilst in reality the mountains are said to be 40 miles distant from us. It is reported that a couple of young men set off from this point to go to the mountains and get some snow, and return in a few hours, on they traveled mile after mile, they encamped out in the night and returned the next day without snow. The mountains in the meanwhile appearing as far off as ever." (Mumford:93)

Hill

Wind River Mountains today.

191

Wilkins, Wisconsin Historical Society, WHi-31550
Wilkins' painting of the Green River Valley.

A few miles west was the first real parting of the ways. After 1844 the emigrants could decide whether to take the Greenwood or Sublette Cutoff which branches directly west or to continue southwest on the old trail down to the Sandy towards the Green River and on to Fort Bridger. On June 30, 1849, along this area Bryarly noted, "The road was most awfully dusty & the stench from the dead oxen rendered it rather obnoxious....The oxen strewed along the road as miles stones. We have rolled today 20 miles and passed 20 dead ox. We much pity those coming a few days behind us as the horrid smell...[will] even cause sickness among them." (Bryarly:130)

The old trail crossed the Sandy River in present-day Farson, Wyoming. The highway west out of Farson crisscrosses the trail and follows it to the Green. The drive gives the modern traveler a pretty good feel of the journey. The landscape remains nearly unchanged. Wilkins labeled this "Green River Valley," but its date would put him by Fort Bridger. Here is a similar view at the Green River where the present highway and near where the old trail drop down into the flat river bottom.

Hill

Green River Valley today.

Wilkins' depiction of the Ferry at Green River.

Wilkins appears to have crossed the Green River at the Lombard Ferry. Each year, depending on the river conditions, the specific location of the ferry might vary. During low water the emigrants could ford the river. Wilkins wrote, "Some Mormons have established a ferry here, a very unsafe flat boat, a heavy wagon comes near sinking it, for which they charge 4$ per wagon, but there is no help for it." On July 23 he wrote, "We passed the ferry for a miracle without accident, as a more crazy thing to call a boat I never saw. it required one man to bail all the time, while another at every trip kept stuffing in bits of rag. we had a great dispute about paying the full amount of ferage, which is still unsettled...," (Wilkins:57)

Today the site looks much the same. It is part of the bird sanctuary and has a display about the ferry. It is located just south of the highway bridge crossing.

Wilkins' next painting shows the bluffs along the Green River. They are located a few miles south of the Lombard Ferry near where

Hill

Lombard Ferry area today.

193

Wilkins, Wisconsin Historical Society, WHi-31697
Wilkins' view of bluffs Near Green River.

one variant of the trail leaves the Green River Valley. Coincidently, it was the site of the old Bridger-Fraeb trading post. The different variants continued southwest towards the Ham's Fork crossings near Granger, Wyoming. This section between the two rivers was hot, dry and desolate. The photo is from off the trail, but Wilkins appears to have been closer to the Green River.

This Wilkins painting labeled "Clay Bluffs" also includes the first view of Church Butte or Cathedral Rock which appear as the

Hill

Bluffs near Green River today.

Wilkins' view of Clay Bluffs.

three small peaks at the right. The seemingly large single formation is actually a long flat butte with the mountains rising directly behind them. Due to atmospheric conditions it is often difficult to see the mountains. There are only three good vantage points from the trail where the Uinta Mountains appear directly behind the clay bluffs.

Today the old Lincoln Highway generally follows the trail from Granger to its junction with I-80. This area has been experiencing extensive energy development and an improved dirt road closely parallels or follows much of the route and replacing portions of the old Lincoln Highway.

Hill

Bluffs today.

195

Wilkins' drawing of Cathedral Rock.

Cathedral Rock or Church Butte was a noted landmark on the trail to Fort Bridger after crossing the Ham's Fork. Wilkins saw it on July 24.

The formation has continued to erode, but it is easy to see how it got its name. At sundown when the light bounces off it, the colors are vibrant and briefly seem to glow. Part of Mariett Cummings' entry for June 29, 1852 reads "Passed the most magnificent curiosity I have ever seen on the road. It was a stupendous rock of petrified clay and sandstone of blue and light and dark brown color. There are spires and domes, grottoes and caves of every form and size. It was immensely high and colonnaded. One's voice would reverberate several times. We called it "Echo Rock." (Cummings: 146)

It still has its identifiable shape, and the area remains much the same save for all the energy exploration.

Hill

Church Butte today.

196

Jackson, National Park Service SCBL-39
Jackson drawing of Bridger Butte.

Jackson made this sketch looking west towards Bridger Butte on July 4, 1867, on his return trip from California. He was camped about four miles east of Fort Bridger. The fort was down in the valley east of the butte. The early trail was down in the valley, but a later one followed the ridge on the left along the telegraph line.

The photo below was taken from the edge of location where Jackson camped. It is east of Fort Bridger on the edge of the ridge in Urie, Wyoming. A new house and storage unit now occupies the site.

Wilkins' painting shows the fort before the Mormons obtained it and built a larger stone fortification. Wilkins camped nearby and described the original structure as "...merely a few log houses built in a square...a few goods are kept here at most exorbitant prices." (Wilkins:57) Charles Gray visited the fort about three weeks earlier. He described it, "This place is situated on the *Black Fork*...& has a

Hill

Bridger Butte today

197

Wilkins, Wisconsin Historical Society, WHi-31549
Wilkins' drawing of Fort Bridger.

beautiful location, 4 or 5 splendid brooks flowing around the Fort in every direction. Trout are to be had here....The Fort is quite a large one & many traders are here employed." (Gray:55) Captain Howard Stansbury described the fort, "It is built in the usual form of pickets, with lodging apartments and offices opening into a hollow square, protected from attack from outside by a strong gate of timber. On the north, and continuous with the walls, is a strong high picket-fence, enclosing a yard, into which the animals belonging to the establishment are driven for protection from both wild beasts and Indians." (Stansbury:74)

The drawing of Fort Bridger is from Stansbury's *An Expedition to the Valley of the Great Salt Lake of Utah*. Only a small portion of Bridger Butte is visible at the right.

When Jackson first visited the fort it was a military post and its appearance very different from the original trading post. However, this is his version of it. Note its similarity to Stansbury's drawing. It was here in 1846 that some emigrants were persuaded to listen to Hastings

Stansbury – Fort Bridger

Jackson painting of Fort Bridger.

and follow his cut-off southwest. Later California bound emigrants had to decide whether to take the Hasting's Cutoff to the southwest through the Salt Lake Valley or head north along the established route to Fort Hall before turning southwest to California.

This is the reconstruction of Bridger's original trading post. Enter the gates and step back in time to the period of the trappers and emigrants. Be sure to see the visitor center where one can view the archeological work showing part of the original and later Mormon portions of the fort. Bridger Butte is just above the fort.

The route down Echo Canyon was originally part of the Hastings Cutoff that headed southwest from Fort Bridger. The trail crossed the Uinta Mountains and dropped down into the Bear River Valley, crossed the river and climbed the hills and passed Cache Cave a little before entering Echo Canyon above Castle Rock.

Hill
Fort Bridger replica today.

Mills, Library of Congress, Lee-Palfrey Papers, LCMSS-65612-15
Early photo of Castle Rock.

This 1858 photo is possibly the earliest photograph made of Castle Rock. The immediate area looks unchanged. Jackson also photographed the area in 1870 and Moran drew it.

Mariett Cummings crossed the Bear River early in the morning and entered Echo Canyon late that morning. She wrote, "On the north the most stupendous cliffs of red rock, of gravel cemented together and sandstone, some of them indescribable beauty and magnificence. At noon we camped opposite the entrance to a cave high in the rocks, which we explored. The entrance was an arch, the cavern 30 by 25 feet and high enough for a person to stand erect....The rocks at the side towered hundreds of feet above. The sides were full of holes...." (Cummings: 148-9)

Hill

Castle Rock today.

200

Charles W. Carter , CJCLDS-Church Archives
Wagon Train in Echo Canyon.

This well-known photo shows a wagon train winding its way through Echo Canyon on part of the Hastings Cut-off. For years it had often been misidentified and always mislabeled until the site was correctly located by this author. Although representative of westward moving trains, it is an "out & back" eastbound wagon train in Echo Canyon near Sawmill Canyon. It was designated to pick up Mormon emigrants from back east and to bring them to Salt Lake.

The building of I-80 and the earlier transcontinental railroad altered the position of the stream and trail. What was once the stream bed is now a marsh. The trail scars, however, are still evident although they are being eroded and overgrown with trees and willows.

Hill
Echo Canyon today.

Jackson, National Archives, # 57-HS-33
Jackson photo of Amphitheater, Echo Canyon.

Jackson took the route through Echo Canyon to Salt Lake on his trip to California. He returned a couple of years later and took photos of the construction of the railroad. Note the railroad tracks parallel to the old road in Echo Canyon.

The photo shows the "amphitheater" area today. The modern Interstate 80 has been cut on the other side of the valley. However, much of the older narrow paved road is raised and straightened some, but it follows the bed of the old dirt trail very closely for many miles in the canyon.

Describing his journey down Echo to the Weber River and canyon Frederick Piercy noted on August 8, 1853, "We crossed Echo

Hill

Amphitheater today.

Jackson, National Park Service SCBL-125
Jackson's drwing of the junction of Weber & Echo canyons.

Creek from 15 – 20 times, most of the crossings were difficult."
(Piercy:125) Mariett Cummings noted on her second day of travel
down the canyon, "Went fifteen miles through this canyon, the wildest
and most magnificent scenery, surpassing anything I ever dreamed
of, constantly crossing and recrossing the stream, in some places the
rocks hanging over our heads in every form, and the valley constantly
narrowing until finally we came to Weber river It runs directly across
the foot of the canyon." (Cummings:149) Jackson's drawing shows
the trail as it approached this area before the railroad was constructed..

Hill
Canyon junction today.

ackson, National Archives, # 57-HS-29
Jackson photo of Pulpit Rock.

Now the Interstate, railroad, and earlier highway all run parallel or on top of the old trail. The trip down Echo Canyon, especially on the old highway, is still magnificent with the sun bouncing off the walls.

Pulpit Rock marked the mouth of Echo Canyon and junction with Weber Canyon. Legend holds that Brigham Young spoke from this rock to his followers on their 1847 journey to Salt Lake. Most historians discount the story noting his illness at the time.

Jackson made this early photograph showing some of those who later did climb Pulpit Rock. The rock was destroyed to make room for the railroad and highway. Some of the features are still visible in the present photo.

The trail turned north or down the Weber where it passed another landmark. These odd-shaped formations are called "Witches Rocks." They were drawn or photographed by a number of travelers. This drawing was made by Captain Albert Tracy in 1859 during the army's march to Salt Lake. The construction of

Hill
Pulpit Rock area today.

204

Tracy, Idaho State Historical Society, Photo #T-6
Witches Rocks.

the modern highway and railroad cut into the hill and weathering has
occurred, but the view is much the same. The formation is off I-84 a
short distance south of Henefer, Utah.

Hill

Witches Rocks today.

History Colorado

Jackson's view of Devil's Slide.

Devil's Slide is located farther down in Weber Canyon. Hastings had first told emigrants taking his cutoff to go down the Weber all the way through the canyon. Those early 1846 emigrants passed this landmark. However, he told the Donners not to take this route down the Weber because it was too difficult. Instead he told them to turn off before the canyon narrowed and to cut over the mountains which would be easier. After the Donners cut a route over the mountains, it became the main route and replace the one continuing down the Weber.

Here is Devil's Slide today as seen from I-84 past Henefer at the viewing pull-off.

Hill

Devil's Slide today.

Jackson, National Park Service SCBL-41
Jackson painting: Approach to the Valley of Salt Lake.

At present-day Henefer, Utah, where the Donners turned off, the Hastings Cutoff began its climb over the Wasatch. The easy rise soon changed. The Donners had to chop their way up to Big Mountain Pass and over the Wasatch and down to Salt Lake. The route was long and laborious. When they intersected Parley's Creek they were forced to climb up and over to another canyon, now known as an Emigration

Hill
Emigration Canyon today.

207

Jackson, National Park Service SCBL-127
Jackson painting of Parley's Canyon.

Canyon. They had to cut their way down and through the canyon and followed it into Salt Lake Valley.

Jackson's painting depicts emigrants on their descent into Emigration Canyon after climbing over Little Mountain Pass. The passage down the canyon proved to be extremely difficult adding to the Donners' delay. Just before the Donners entered the valley the canyon narrowed, the trees and brush got even thicker, and the creek became even more treacherous with cataracts. They were forced up and over a small hill now known as Donner Hill at the mouth of the canyon. In 1847 the Mormons followed their trail, but they were able to cut through those trees and heavy brush skirting the cascades and the hill. For July 14, 1849, Charles Gray recorded, "…journey'd down the creek *crossing it 19 times* — some of the mud holes being very bad, so steep…others were full of large stumps & rocks & logs; at length as we turned the corner of some rocks the '*Great Salt Lake*' burst upon our sight!" (Gray:62) The photo looking west is taken from above the pass. The trail going down is just over the sagebrush in the foreground.

Jackson's painting shows the trail in Parley's Canyon, the route he traveled down in 1866 and up on his return in 1867. Parley Pratt successfully cut the route to Salt Lake in 1850. This soon became the major route, and the parallel route down Emigration Canyon was bypassed and used mostly for local traffic.

Today Interstate 80 follows the route up the Weber and over to Parleys Canyon to Salt Lake City. Note how the valley floor had to be raised and leveled and some of the mountain sides cut to make room for the interstate highway. For the Mormons, the Valley of the Great Salt Lake was their goal and become the center of their Zion. For those traveling to California, the city was a place to pass through but also could be a source of needed supplies.

For the Donner Party and others on the Hastings Cutoff, the journey west of Salt Lake was almost unbearable. Hastings had reported it to be only forty miles across, but in reality it was over eighty miles. The trail wound around the south side of the Great Salt Lake hugging the hills and mountains away from the marshes along the lake's edge. Then it began a low climb to Redham Spring in the foothills and crossed the low, but difficult Cedar Mountains at Hastings Pass. Sarah Davis noted,"we left the springs and started over the mountain…then on and had the rufest road we have had atall….we had to duble teams twice coming over and then it was vary harde" (Davis: 193). Greyback, a low range of hills, was next.

Hill

Parley's Canyon today.

209

Hill

Salt Lake Desert & Floating Island today, Looking East.

Once over the hills, it headed into the white salt flats towards Pilot Peak which was mostly hidden behind Silver Island on the far horizon. At Pilots Peak they would finally find life-giving water. After their sixty mile long dry road with no grass, no water, and no shade they still had completed only about half of the Hastings Cutoff since leaving Fort Bridger.

The view below looking east shows some of the hummocks the emigrants had to contend with after crossing the salt flats that stretched to the horizon. Floating Island is the large dark formation on the right. Below is the view from near Donner-Reed Pass looking over the area from which they had come. The trail, after passing Floating Island and passing through the hummocks, reached Silver Island at the point in

Hill

Salt Flats looking back east from near Donner-Reed Pass.

210

Hill

West towards Pilot Peak.

the far right. It then more or less followed the present road hugging the mountain to the pass.

After the harrowing experience on the salt flats the emigrants crossed a low saddle, known today as Donner-Reed Pass. On August 29, 1850, Davis wrote, "we traveled all night of the twenty eight and all night of the 29 buy this time I have got use to it a little we have now got all most a crost the desert it…the grounde is white with salt all over… we are now in sight of a mountain" (Davis:193-4) But they also had another eight miles of the white playa before they reached the spring. Here is that view that she would have seen. It is looking west from a trail marker towards the mountain – Pilot Peak.

Hill

Donner Springs today.

The famous life-giving springs are known today as Donner Springs. Davis wrote, "we rived at land and water about eight o'clock this morning   we are a cross ... the men all tired nearly to death as well as the catle   the men are all a sleepe and the catle are resting themselves   we [lost] no catle nor horses   we got through safe and are thankful" (Davis::194) After recuperating, the emigrants continued south, rounded Pilot Peak, crossed Bidwell Pass and headed west toward Silver Zone Pass.

Had the Donner Party then turned west northwest instead of west and then south after the pass, in a few days they would have rejoined the main trail coming down from Granite Pass and Goose Creek at Humboldt Wells. Instead, they had to travel farther, looping farther south around both the Pequop and Ruby mountains. Hence, they were still more than two weeks away from rejoining the main California Trail near Carlin Canyon west of present-day Elko, Nevada.

Hall, Wyoming State Museum, Department of State Parks and Cultural Resources
Green River Ferry as viewed by Hall.

West of South Pass a maze of trails soon developed that crossed the Green River at different places in hopes of saving time. One of these, depicted by Cyrenius Hall in 1852, appears to be the Case Ferry on the Baker-Davis Cutoff. This cutoff was associated with the Kinney and Slate Creek cutoffs that bypassed both the long dip in the old trail to Fort Bridger and the long dry section of the Sublette Cutoff farther to the north. These variants ultimately connected with the Sublette Cutoff.

In periods of low water the wagons forded the river. Today the Green is dammed a few miles upstream and the flow is controlled.

The photo below shows the area today. An unnamed grave is located on the bluff from near where the photo was taken. The big trees have died but still lie near where they fell, and horses still graze in the area.

Hill
Case Ferry area today.

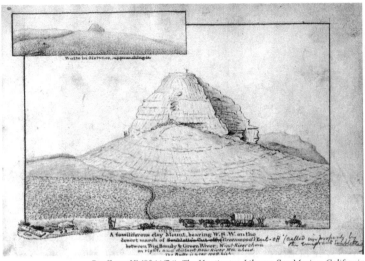

Bruff, mssHM8044(74), The Huntington Library, San Morino, California
A Fossiliferous clay Mount [Haystack Butte].

On August 4, 1849 Bruff passed this "clay mount" and made his first sketches of it. This illustration was done later. This landmark was on the Greenwood or Sublette Cutoff which had split from the old trail to Fort Bridger a few miles west of the Dry Sandy Crossing. It was the first to develop to save time and the loop south.

Haystack Butte today.

It looks pretty much the same today, only eroded a little more. His painting, unfortunately, made it appear larger than his more accurate original pen sketches. The clay mount is located about nine miles north of Farson, east, off U.S. 191, a little south of where the cutoff crosses the highway and two miles west of the cutoff's crossing of the Big Sandy. That crossing provided *Hill* the last reliable water for over forty miles until reaching the Green.

214

Bruff, mssHM8044(75), The Huntington Library, San Marino, California
Descent to the Green River.

This is another of Bruff's later drawings. It is his "Terminus of the Greenwood Cut–off. – descent to Green River valley." His company had crossed Sublettes Flat. On August 5, 1849, Bruff noted, "...look down on a perrilous descent the wagons had to make....From the crest, down to base, right and left were fragments of disasters, in the shape of upset wagons, wheels, axles, running-geer, sides, bottoms, &c. &c. –Nothing daunted, we double-locked, and each teamster held firmly to the bridle of his lead mules, and led down, in succession... without accident." (Bruff :70-1)

Hill

Similar descent area today.

215

Emigrants descended to the bottomland in a variety of locations. The specific site of his drawng of the descent is hard to pinpoint based on his diary entry. However, this area is similar to his drawing and near the location of his first sketch. It could just be a more elaborate version of his other more basic sketch.

As mentioned, the emigrants descended to the Green at a number of places. This seems to be Bruff's early rough sketch of the descent. Here the trail paralleled the river along the top of the ridge and then dropped down on its side away from the river and then turned towards the river.

Bruff, Yale Collection of Western American, Beinecke Rare Book and Manuscript Library

Descending into Green River Valley.

Following the trail on the river bluff, its descent appears to match perfectly with Bruff's early sketch. It is also near where Bruff camped on August 6.

Hill

Descent area today.

216

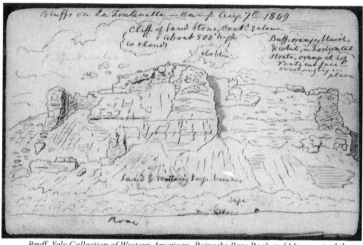

Bruff, Yale Collection of Western American, Beinecke Rare Book and Manuscript Library
Bluffs on La Fontenelle.

Depending on the year and the condition of the river, the Green was either forded or ferried. Bruff forded. Once across, the trail cut southwest up a short steep bank known today as Names Hill, down parallel to the river, and then over the high bluffs to the Fontenelle's Creek. Fontenelle, of French descent, was an early fur trapper and trader. One of his men is reported to have had a camp and perhaps a small cabin on the creek by the bluff. Above is Bruff's sketch of "Fontenelle Bluffs".

It appears that little has changed. Bruff camped there on August 7, 1849. He mentioned the French camp but no cabin. On the 8th he wrote, "There is An immense perpendicular, clay cliff alongside our

Hill

Fontenelle Bluff today.

217

Bear River Peaks.

camp, which with some trouble and danger, I managed to scale; and was well compensated by the magnificent birds-eye view of the stream and valley. . .(Bruff:77-78).

Here we are back on the old main trail heading up the Bear River Valley toward Fort Hall. After leaving the Green, the Sublette Cutoff took a west southwesterly route following the ridges and up or across the valleys and up and down the high hills. Wilkins made this painting he called "Bear River Peaks" north of the junction of the two routes.

The present view is from off highway 30 after it enters Cokeville. Wyoming. Much of the trail is under or parallel to Highway 30 all

Hill

Bear River Peaks today.

218

Wilkins ,Wisconsin Historical Society, WHi-31553
Descent of Bear River Mountains.

the way north to Soda Springs, Idaho and Sheep Rock. Bruff also sketched this area and much of the scenery from here to Fort Hall.

June 29, 1850, Ingalls noted, "...some very bad hills to descend.... emigrants of last year had to let their wagons down some of them with ropes. We got down with out accident, by locking our hind wheels." (Ingalls:44) Wilkins wrote, "I made a sketch of the descent on the other side, but owing to the clouds of dust, it was anything but pleasant to sit sketching." (Wilkins:60) This is the drawing of the descent of the trail after it had climbed the "Big Hill" or "Sublette's Hill" and descended again into the valley of the Bear River. The photo

Hill

Descent today.

Wilkins, Wisconsin Historical Society, WHi-31684
Bear Mountains Sun Rise.

was taken near the interpretive sign and pull-out on highway 30 just east of Dingle Station in the vicinity of Peg Leg Smith's cabin. Note the scars on the mountainside where the wagons came down. Some emigrants turned right or north once down and others, as depicted in the painting, headed towards the Bear River near the present farm road.

Conditions for travel along the Bear were pleasant for most travelers. In July of 1852 Enoch Conyers noted, "On the bottom lands of the Bear River is found the best grazing that we have had on the whole journey." (Conyers:467) However, as the emigrants approached Soda Springs it became much drier. On August 2, Wilkins camped at present-day Bennington and saw the sunrise and recorded it as "Bear

Hill

Bear River Mountains today.

220

Wilkins, Wisconsin Historical Society, WHi-31699
Wilkins' painting of Beer (Soda) Springs.

Mountain Sunrise." Baldy is the present name given to the larger of the mountains to the left of center.

Wilkins painted the larger area known as Valley of Fountains, Beer Springs or Soda Springs. Joel Palmer in 1845, and Chester Ingersoll in 1847 also noted many large white mounds with soda water in them. Some described them as being between fifteen and thirty feet tall and were located off to the right of the trail. In 1849 Wakeman Bryarly wrote extensively about the whole Soda Springs area. Wilkins noted, " nearby were eminences of rock from 4 to 15 f' high, or rather cones like a sugarloaf , and on the top of all but the highest was a spring of water strongly impregnated with oxide of Iron. the cones had evidently been formed from the water depositing the rocky sediment till it got so high that it dried up and commenced another opening...." (Wilkins: 61) The cones and springs seem to have been mentioned by most diarists passing through.

Hill

Pyramid Spring & Geyser today.

221

Today the town of Soda Springs has developed surrounding the area of the white mounds or cones. Many of the old cones have been graded away, and the Bear River dammed, covering parts of the trail and some of the springs. Below left is part of the Pyramid Spring in Geyser Park. It appears to be part of the cones painted by Wilkins which were climbed by many of the emigrants. Today visitors may also climb on the cone. There is no sign of a spring in the tallest cone, but a shorter one next to it has a basin in it, Someone plugged the spring long ago by driving a post into it. In the other direction is a man controlled geyser depositing its "rocky sediment."

This is Hopper Spring, one of the few soda springs left in the area. Another is Octagon Spring. When drinking from some of the springs

Hill

Hopper Springs today.

Wilkins noted, "we took out tin cups and some sugar and drank repeated draughts of excellent soda water." (Wilkins:61) The modern traveler can also drink from this spring as those earlier ones had done. Use some Tang or Crystal Light and you won't notice the taste of the iron so much. People still come from miles around to fill containers with the water.

Emigrants were fascinated by Soda Springs. Wilkins painted the famous Steamboat Spring on August 4, 1949. Bruff sketched the spring on August 17, 1849. One of the earliest was made by Father Nicolas Point in the early 1840s. The name was derived by the sound made which resembled steam escaping from an exhaust pipe. (Conyers:469) Bryarly wrote, "The greatest curiosity of all, however, is what has been named "The Steamboat Spring." This is situated upon the edge of

Wilkins, Wisconsin Historical Society, WHi-31685
Steam Boat Springs.

the river....Out of a solid rock, with a hole 1 foot in diameter, gushes forth the water, foaming, whizzing, sizzling, blowing, splashing & spraying. It throws it up from two to three feet high." (Bryarly:145) He notes two others nearby, just as Wilkins painted. Conyers described an incident where one of his fellow travelers made a wager that he could stop the geyser by sitting on it. After the water subsided he took off his pants and seated himself on it. Soon he began "bobbing up and down at a fearful rate." His friends tried to hold him down and added more weight, but to no avail. He kept "on bobbing up and down like a cork. Finally Doyle cried out, 'Boys, there is no use trying to hold the devil down....I am now pounded into beefsteak.'" (Conyers: 469)

The trail seen here is approaching the site of Steamboat Spring. It was about a mile farther west. The once famous Steamboat Spring and geyser are now under the water of the Soda Springs Alexander Reservoir. On days when the reservoir is fairly calm, the bubbles and ripples made by the famous spring's eruptions can be seen.

Hill

Trail & reservoir area today.

223

Just west of Soda Springs was Sheep Rock, the tip of the range shown at the far right in Wilkins' painting and also in the above photo. There, another trail variant developed, the Hudspeth or Myers Cutoff which Wilkins took. It bypassed the main trail's northern loop to Fort Hall. The cutoff actually saved little time or mileage. Bruff took the old road to Fort Hall.

Bruff's drawing shows the adobe Fort Hall. When a scene was larger than his paper he continued under it or on the next page with "X"s" where the segments join.

Fort Hall was another milestone for the emigrants with its own landmarks nearby. "We have now reached the most northerly point of our wearisome journey….We are now to turn to the left at right angles, and travel the rest of the way in a nearly southwest direction, until we reach Sutter's Fort, which is still seven hundred miles distant; and from all accounts, the worst part of the road is yet to be passed over." (Frink:118) When emigrants saw the Three Buttes, they knew they were near Fort Hall. Margaret Frink noted, "the 'Three Buttes'

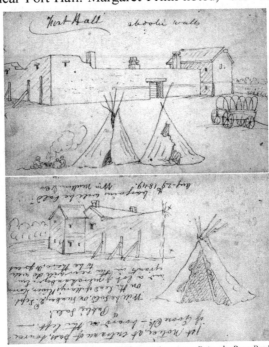

Bruff, Yale Collection of Western American, Beinecke Rare Book and Manuscript Library

Bruff's drawing of Fort Hall.

224

Jackson, Harold Warp Pioneer Village Foundation
Fort Hall.

rise high and bold out of the lava plain, and can be seen for a long distance. Our first view of them was from the high ridge south of Fort Hall." (Frink:119)

Jackson, like many later emigrants, never saw the original Fort Hall. Some emigrants took a different route or cut-off. Then, in 1855 the fort was abandoned. It finally succumbed to flooding, and the trail bypassed the site. Jackson's painting is similar to Bruff's sketch and also to one made by William Henry Tappan in 1849. Note that Jackson does show one of the three buttes at the far right that were mentioned by Frink.

This reproduction of Fort Hall is in Ross Park south of Pocatello, Idaho. The original site is marked with a monument and is on the Fort Hall Indian Reservation. Permission is required to visit the actual site.

Hill
Fort Hall replica today.

225

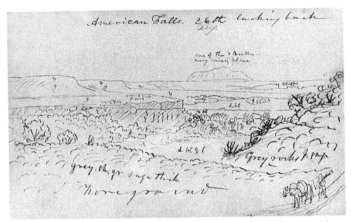

Bruff, Yale Collection of Western American, Beinecke Rare Book and Manuscript Library
Bruff's sketch of American Falls.

After leaving Fort Hall the trail followed the Snake River. The next major wonder was American Falls about two days away. Bryarly noted, "The distant rumbling of these Falls broke the monotony of our march yesterday evening & last night, & we felt anxious to see them. The fall was about 30 ft., & reminded one of a miniature Niagara. (Bryarly:156) Margaret Frink noted, "This stream, which is nine hundred feet wide, is inclosed by high walls of black volcanic rock, and has a perpendicular fall of fifty feet. Beyond is a wide plain of black lava..." (Frink: 149) Bruff wrote, "The 'American Falls' of the Columbia [Snake] are very pretty cascades, but with more rapids and froth than fall of water at this season....I sketched the Falls & scenery." (Bruff:111) Note one of the famous Three Buttes in the background above the falls. Here the trail was right along the edge of

Hill

American Falls today.

226

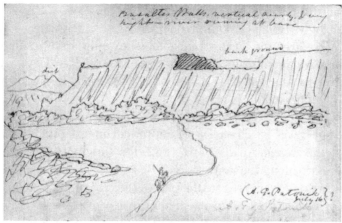

Bruff, Yale Collection of Western American, Beinecke Rare Book and Manuscript Library
Basaltes Walls [Massacre Rocks].

the river. Today the town of American Falls has grown up there. The river has been dammed and the falls harnessed. The view is from near the cemetery. The falls' name is based on a story of early American trappers who were swept over them and died.

About ten miles past the falls Bruff noted, "On our right, outside this walled up area, we could see the perpendicular basaltic banks of the river; the high dark wall very regular, with a rock at an angle – looking like the turret entry box, on the wall of a castle." (Bruff:111) Bryarly, also traveling in 1849, described the area, "The banks of the river here is well marked, being high rocky bluffs, resembling those of

Hill

Massacre Rocks today.

227

the beautiful Hudson River. Six miles from the Falls, the road passes through two 'Buttes' of solid rock with just enough space for the road." (Bryarly:156-7) Bruff's sketch shows the trail heading for a very narrow gap in the rocks, know earlier to some as "Devil's Gate." Over the years the gap has been enlarged, and today I-15 cuts through the "walled up area."

The present name Massacre Rocks first appeared in the early 1900s, but it was based on a series of Indian attacks on four emigrant trains in the area on August 9-10, 1862. Ten emigrants died. Massacre State Park is along the north side of I-15, and there is also a pull-off that allows one to investigate the part of the area of the attacks. About 15 miles farther the trail reaches the Raft River. Here those going to California split off and headed south towards City of Rocks, a little more than a day's travel farther.

Wilkins camped in City of Rocks after taking the Hudspeth Cutoff from Soda Springs. He made many sketches of the area he called "City of the Rocks," but none are known to have survived. Bruff noted that many of the rocks had names written on them such as "Napoleon's Castle" and "Hotel Rock." (Bruff: 116). Margaret A. Frink wrote on July 17, 1850, "During the forenoon we passed through a stone village composed of huge isolated rocks of various and singular shapes, some resembling cottages, others steeples and domes. It is called 'City of

National Archives, # 77-kS-44-105
Sullivan photo of the City of Rocks.

Hill

City of Rocks today.

Bruff's sketch of the City of Rocks.

Rocks' but I think Pyramid City more suitable. It is a sublime, strange, and wonderful scene—one of nature's most interesting works." (Frink:121)

An early photo, by Timothy O'Sullivan, shows the north end of the Valley. Note the extensive growth of trees and sagebrush. It is still a popular camping area.

Bruff also made many sketches of the rocks. Fortunately his have survived. This sketch was described as "singular formations of disintegrated granite" and on August 29, he rested in a cave-like portion of one he describe, sketched and named "Sarcophagus Rock.

229

Hill

Hill

Helmet Rock today.

Rock today.

Jonas Hittle also traveled here in 1849. He noted the rocks, "Some like Large Churches and all most Every Size and Shape Some had overhanging Caverns here are many names mine among them in a Cave on the Left of the Road"(Hittle:55)

Perhaps it was the same cave Bruff referred to. However, the location of Sarcophagus Rock remains elusive.

Bruff sketched the trail heading south to Pinnacle Pass where it left the City of Rocks. The present road exits at the southwest corner of the park farther to the right of his sketch. Bryarly described his passage and exit from City of Rocks as sketched above by Bruff, "Four miles brought us to the coming in of the Mormon Road [Salt Lake Cutoff]. Half [a] mile before striking it we passed through a narrow pass of rocks, just wide enough for the wagons..." (Bryarly:161)

Bruff, Yale Collection of Western American, Beinecke Rare Book and Manuscript Library

Bruff's sketches of Pinnacle Pass.

Photos of the area show how little things have changed. Although

230

Hill

Pinacle Pass formation today.

the formation was photographed from a different spot, a faint scar of the old trail is still visible. If you were to walk through the pass, you would see where the wagons left their marks on the rocks and ground and follow it down the hill.

Probably the most famous landmark at City of Rocks is Twin Sisters at the southwest corner of the" city." During the emigration period it was known by other names: Steeple Rock, Cathedral Rock, or Twin Steeples. William Hoffman noted, "The Circle is a great Natural curiosity, being about five miles long by three wide, in which are many isolated masses of rocks, of a great variety of shapes and forms. Some like a dome, others pyramidal and some overhanging. One especially attracted my attention giving the idea of a place of worship." (Mumford:112)

After nooning in City of Rocks Hittle noted, " we drove on and intercepted the Salt Lake Road" (Hittle:55) Steeple Rock marked the junction of the Salt Lake Road, first blazed by Sam Hensley, with the old California Trail coming down from Fort Hall and the Hudspeth Cutoff. The sketch is based on an early J. Wesley Jones daguerreotype.

Courtney, California Historical Society, CHS2010.20
Steeple Rocks.

The area appears to have changed little.

Francis Sawyer had used the Hudspeth Cutoff and rejoined the route from Fort Hall and passed through City of Rocks. He wrote, "We are in camp to-night at Steeple Rock. There are a great many names on the rocks….The Salt Lake Road meets us again and all the California emigrants are now on this road." (Sawyer: 105)

In 1852 Mariett Cummings had taken the Salt Lake Cutoff north out of Salt Lake around the lake and then west to the Raft River to

Hill

Steeple Rocks (Twin Sisters) today.

232

Quesenbury, Nebraska State Historical Society. L/A #19102
Steeple Rocks.

meet the main California Trail. She wrote, "Went up the stream some distance and up through a canyon opposite Steeple Rocks, magnificent conical rocks as white as marble, glossy and bright, several hundred feet in height. (Cummings : 155)

This view by Quesenbury is that which would have been seen by Sawyer, Cummings and others using the Salt Lake Cutoff as they came to its junction with the trail from Fort Hall. The Hastings Cutoff went west out of Salt Lake City skirting the marshes and Great Salt Lake on the southside and then aimed for Pilot Peak.

Hill - 743

Steeple Rocks today.

233

Hill

Granite Pass today.

The next major geographical feature the emigrants had to contend with was Granite Pass. The trail's climb up the mountains west of Steeple Rocks was rather gentle when compared with its descent to Goose Creek. Below is the view from the trail down from the summit and just before it begins to get rough. Table Mountain at Goose Creek can be seen in the distance.

On July 8, 1849 James Pritchard described the route, "Our corse since noon has been over broken ridges & steep precipices. We had to ease our wagon down some of these hills by hand...reached the vally of Goose Creek." (Pritchard:111) Hittle noted "we Came to the

Hill

Descent to Goose Creek Valley today.

234

Quensenbury, McKendree University -
Goose Creek.

Summit and in descending we find it to be much the worst Mountain we have passed" (Hittle:56) July 14, 1852, Francis Sawyer wrote, "We camp with some company every night now and keep a strong guard out all the time, for the Indians will steal the animals....We traveled over the Goose-Creek mountains today, and had a very steep one to descend. We are in camp on Goose creek." (Sawyer:105) . William Hoffman wrote on August 27, 1853, "...travelled nearly 6 miles rising a mountain the descent of which was exceedingly steep with deep jogs, but not rocky. We continued...to Goose Creek." (Mumford:113) The emigrants seemed in agreement about the descent. It is impossible to drive the route today and walking it is difficult.

Quensenbury made a drawing of Goose Creek. It is the only 1851 drawing of his that is presently known to exist of the trail section between Carlin Canyon in Nevada and the Sweetwater in Wyoming. Here is a view similar. Francis Sawyer noted, "We traveled over the

Hill
Goose Creek area today.

Moran, Picturesque America

Humboldt Plains.

Goose Creek mountains to-day, and had a very steep descend. We are in camp on Goose Creek. Distance traveled, twenty-four miles." (Sawyer:105) This is the view as they neared the creek.

After traveling up Goose Creek, the trail crossed to Thousand Springs Valley and then over the divide into the Humboldt River Valley. Before reaching the Humboldt the trail split. One branch continued in a more southerly direction to meet the river near present-day Wells, Nevada, while the other branch followed Bishop's Creek southwest to join the Humboldt about ten miles to the west. The emigrants often commented about the good grass and water. But that would soon change as they moved down the Humboldt.

Conditions on the Humboldt grew worse the farther they followed it. This is a view of the Humboldt Valley where most emigrants were happy for the water. However, some saw only a monotonous plain with mountains in the distance. By the time the emigrants reached

Hill

Humboldt Plains today.

the distant mountain the complaints were becoming commonplace. The alkali, the deep sand, the heat, the dust, the lack of feed, the increasingly warm and poor quality of the water all took their toll on them as they moved west. The Hastings Cutoff continued west from Donner Spring to Silver Zone Pass and then southwesterly and over and around the Ruby Mountains to join the main trail west of Elko, Nevada before entering Carlin Canyon.

Elko Mountain appears in the plain.

West of present-day Elko the river flowed towards Carlin Canyon. The main trail continued along the river where it had to make four crossings. However, another alternate route, which came to be called the Greenhorn Cutoff, climbed the mountains on the north side before the trail entered the Canyon. It was used by many, but best used during periods of high water. Nearing the first crossing Frink noted,"...we stopped for the night, The water was too high....we had taken what is called the 'Greenhorn Cut-off,' which required fifteen miles' travel to gain six...What is called a 'cut-off is a shorter road across a bend. A 'greenhorn cut-off' is a road which a stranger or new traveler takes believing it would be shorter, but which turns out to be longer than the regular road. There are many such on the plains." (Frink:125) It rejoined the main trail at present-day Carlin. The meadows west of Carlin were a major camping area.

Quesenbury, McKendree University
North end of Carlin Canyon.

   This drawing shows the rock formations north of the trail and a little west of the Greenhorn Cutoff and junction of the Hastings Cutoff. It is near the first crossing before the river makes a horseshoe bend to the north.

   Below is the view north off I-80 west of the California Trail Center and east of where it enters the tunnel that bypasses the river and trail's horseshoe loop.

   John Gibson had camped and successfully fished just west of Elko. On August 8, 1859, he noted, "Ten miles more through the dust, and we reached a rugged canon, through which the travel passes only at certain seaons....we took the canon and crossed the river four times during the passage. The road composed entirely of large cobblestones, was pretty severe on the feet of our cattle....The canon is six miles long, two miles on this side and we are again camped in splendid grass." (Gibson:84) The photo is the view he had before the third crossing. The drawing appears to be from just after the third crossing.

Hill
Carlin Canyon today.

238

*Quesenbury, McKendree University*Carlin Canyon from the south.

The formation can be seen from the west bound I-80 looking north before one enters the tunnel. The horseshoe bend was narrow with steep walls that forced the trail to cross the river twice inside the curve. He camped near present-day Carlin.

West of Carlin the trail bypassed the Palisades Canyon. For August 9, 1859 Gibson's journal reads, "…we had to leave the bottom and take a cut-off over 18 miles, up and down hills of the steepest, stoniest , and roughest description. Ten miles out we found some muddy springs but no feed, so we only rested the cattle, and then put out till we reached the river, and camped…" (Gibson:85) They had traveled up to Emigrant Pass, down a little to a spring, and then down Emigrant Canyon to the river where some emigrants forded. After Gravelly Ford, emigrants traveled on both sides of the river.

Hill

Carlin Canyon from the south, today.

239

Quensenbury, McKendree University

South of the Humboldt River.

This drawing and view off I-80 are to the west from near the spring and before the trail turned south and dropped down into a side ravine or canyon to return to the river. He made other drawings after reaching the river. Wilkins also sketched this area but those illustrations have not been found. (Wilkins:66)

Hill

View from near Emigrant Pass today.

240

Bruff, Yale Collection of Western American, Beinecke Rare Book and Manuscript Library
Bruff's sketches of Battle Mountain.

After about two days of travel west from Gravelly Ford the emigrants saw these formations on the south side of the Humboldt or Mary's River. Bruff drew these formations from the north side trail. They are located south of I-80 between present-day Mosel and Argenta, east of Battle Mountain, Nevada. Quesenbury drew the same formation from a different angle a little farther west.

The photos on the following page show the same formations from near the south side trail. The triangular formation is not quite as perfect as he drew it. Silver is now being mined in the area the emigrants passed on their way to strike it rich in the California goldfields. It has altered part of the formations, but otherwise the area has changed little. The small pointed formations have now been leveled.

Hill

East of Battle Mountain.

The view is looking back east from the south side trail. Emigrants sometimes described the hot springs near Stony Point in their diaries. Travelers on the north side passed right by the springs. Quesenbury even noted it on his drawing. Argenta Point is in the distance to the right of center. Traveling through this area Bruff noted, "our drive was over a trail of deep white powder, on a Westerly course, generally near the river; close to the stream some fertility, green willows, reeds, grass &c, but off from it, all dusty barrens." (Bruff:134)

The harsh conditions on the trail were beginning to take their toll. Wilkins recorded, ".... From what I can hear, and I speak to almost every company I see, I don't think there ever was a body of men … that had so much quarrelling and fighting...." (Wilkins:67)

Quesenbury, McKendree University
Valley of the Humboldt, from the south.

For two days the emigrants traveled in the wide valley. The area was hot and dry and the trail dusty with deep sand. After Iron Point they would be forced to contend with a narrow canyon. First, the north and south side trails had to round Iron Point. On the south side, the trail was forced to climb over the point because the river cut into its edge.

It was near this area that Wilkins commented about the increase in fighting among his company members. It was also there on October 8, 1846, as the Donner Party climbed a short steep hill where James Reed and John Snyder quarreled. In the photo the trail goes from the lower left corner to the top center, and the soil changes from deep sand to hard rocks near the crest. In the ensuing fight Reed killed Snyder. While some members wanted Reed hanged, after much disagreement he was ultimately banished from the wagon train.

Recent research indicates that Snyder was buried near where the trail began its ascent up the hill. The probable site is by the pile of rocks near a Trails West marker at the junction of the old railroad bed and trail from where the photo was taken. (Grebenkemper-1:102)

Hill
Humboldt Valley today (Battle Mountain area).

243

Hill

Hill at Iron Point today.

Reed made it safely to California and led one of the rescue parties to bring back his family and others in the Donner Party who had been stranded for the winter near present-day Donner Lake.

The view on this page is from near the top of the hill looking back down the trail to the car. It shows the trail and dirt road parallel to the river coming to the point and hill as it intersects with the later abandoned railroad bed and present "road."

Hill

View from the hill.

244

Quesenbury, McKendree University

Emigrant Canyon.

After passing Iron Point, the trails headed into a short canyon. Quensenbury's view is from the south side trail looking west with the infamous hill and Iron Point behind it. The south side trail actually cuts to the left and over the distant hill to bypass the very narrow section of the canyon near the center of the photo, but it docs return near where the river leaves. Aside from some ranch fences, the immediate area has not changed much since then. The north side trail had split after passing Iron Point as it approached Emigrant Canyon. The river road went into the canyon along the base of the hills while the other branch climbed up and over and was behind the hills on the right north of the river.

Bruff made this sketch labeled "Pauta Pass" a little more than five miles east of Golconda, Nevada as the trail wound along the Humboldt west of Iron Point inside the canyon. Bruff was traveling along the north side river road in the canyon while the other northern

Hill

Canyon area today.

245

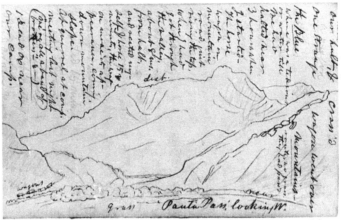

Bruff, Yale Collection of Western American, Beinecke Rare Book and Manuscript Library
Bruff's sketch of Pauta Pass.

branch climbed over the hills on the right north of the river. With the exception of this narrow canyon the Humboldt Valley was wide before and after this point. Traveling in this area on September 20, 1853, Hoffman recorded, "Commenced our journey this morning at 6 ½ oclock and travelled thro a very barren mountain region (Kanyon) until 1 oclock making a distance about 14 or 15 miles and encamped on the river Bottom, having good grass, and remained during the day" (Mumford:126).

One of the major problems the emigrants faced along this region of the Humboldt was the loss of stock due to the Indians. Bruff frequently commented about the problem of theft confronting the emigrants. T.

Hill

Pauta Pass today.

Quesenbury, McKendree University

Humboldt River from east.

H. Jefferson, whose 1846 maps are included earlier, lost a significant portion of his stock and warned emigrants to be constantly on guard, especially at night. (Bruff:137)

Today the river bottom of Emigrant Canyon is farmed, and the railroad and highway often overlaps the trails. A few miles west were some hot springs near present-day Golonda. It was another favorite camping area. A large island in the Humboldt River was known for its good grass. That area is now also farmed, but it is no longer an island.

West of present-day Winnemucca, Nevada; the trails were going through a very dry and sandy area. Margaret Frink camped in the area on August 3 & 4, 1850. She described it, "Feed is becoming scarcer then ever....Away from the river, the soil is hard and dry void of any vegetation except sage-brush, which is worthless for any purpose but fuel....Constant travel over rough road, through suffocating dust makes any rest welcome..." (Frink:127-8) Lucena Parson traveling in

Hill

Humboldt Valley - Blue Mountain today.

247

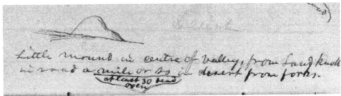

Bruff, Yale Collection of Western American Beinecke Rare Book and Manuscript Library
Bruff's sketch of Little Mound.

the same area on May 16 recorded, "We still find sandy roads winding among the hills...Found better roads this afternoon. The valley is 30 miles wide. Came to the river crossing. Here there is a sage pain.... [the next day] Nothing but sage and sand as far as the eye can reach." (Parsons:285-6) The view drawn by Quesenbury was what Frink, Parson, and others would have seen to the north over the sage plains.

Both the north and south side trails were approaching Lassen Meadows from the east and the bend of the Humboldt where it turned south. Here emigrants were able to find and cut some hay. John Gibson was on the north side and had followed the Dry Cutoff away from the river. On August 18, 1859 he noted, "...left the river for something like 17 miles, road deep, heavy and stony. Another two miles brought us to Lassen's Meadows, making 25 miles in all, feed good." (Gibson:88) After 1848 it was also time for the emigrants to make another decision. Those emigrants who decided to use the Applegate Trail to Oregon and those who chose to use the Applegate-Lassen route to California separated here. Near the split, north of the trail, was this small mound in the center of the plain. Yet, it could be seen and was known by both those emigrants turning south and those heading northwest. The junction or dividing points of the trails were south of the formation and is now under the waters of the Rye Patch Reservoir.

Elijah Howell recorded, "...soon came to the Forks of Road. We took the right hand road, leading nearly due west, towards a Gap in

Hill

Little Mound and Lassen Meadows areas today.

the Mountain—a valley leading up towards the north, in the middle of which arose a hay-stack looking mound. The river and old road bore off to the South West." (Howell: 100)

Bruff also followed the Applegate-Lassen Trail. Bruff's notation reads, "Little Mound in center of valley, from sandy knoll in sand a mile or so in desert from forks." (Bruff:539)

The lower left view is from a knoll on the north side trail. It is about a mile and a half east of the trail junctions. It is also near where the emigrants could have had their first view of the little mound after passing the point of the mountain seen in the photo at the right. The lower right view is a close-up from the south side trail, and it is also near where they could have first seen the mound as they moved towards Lassen Meadows. The north side view was taken from the low dark knoll to the right of the light meadows below the little mound.

Those following the Applegate-Lassen Trail would soon have to contend with the Black Rock Desert. After leaving Lassen's Meadow, the next water was at Antelope Springs over thirteen miles away. The route was hot and dry and nearly devoid of useable vegetation. Next it headed for another spring about seventeen miles or a day's drive. Bruff made this drawing and wrote, "Road-powder blinding & choking one." Coming to Rabbit Hole Springs, he noted one hand-dug well "filled up with a dead ox, his hind-quarters & legs only

Bruff, mssHM8044(109), The Huntington Library, San Morino, California
Rabbit-Hole Springs.

Hill

Rabbit Hole Springs today.   Rabbit Hole Springs Tank.

sticking out, — above the ground. Dead oxen thick about here, and stench suffocating." (Bruff: 147)

Here is Rabbit Hole Springs today. In 1860 the army under Colonel Frederick Lander improved the springs and dug a tank that held 80,000 gallons. (Brooks:17) Over the years and into the mining period, it was improvements and expanded even more. The springs derived their name from the rabbit trails that led to the springs. Rabbits and their trails can still be found there today. Remnants of holes can still be

Hill

Dead cattle.

seen in the sagebrush and also the expanded spring and tank first dug by Lander.

Dead oxen often lay along the road before and after Rabbit Hole Springs. Even today dead cattle are seen along the road as this one was. Ellen Burt's entry for September 27, 1853 was, "Our pet cow got alkalized or poisoned, and we had to leave her at Rabbit Hole Springs

at one o'clock." (Mumford:137) . The next water and grass was at the Boiling Hot Springs at Black Rock. But first they had to cross the Black Rock Desert, named for the large black formation's contrast to the lighter coloring of the surrounding flats and mountains.

Bruff wrote, "Course, after halt, for 6 or 8 miles, N.W. the plain generally level. A plain apparently more elevated, ahead of us, is very level and smooth, and in the sun, looks like a vast field of ice....When we reached the plain I found it was not elevated ...but cover'd with a smooth white encrustation, probably alkaline.(Bruff: 149) Crossing that plain he counted more than 103 dead oxen. On September 21, he

Hill

Trail towards Black Rock today.

wrote, "A little after Sun Set we reached, on our right, a hight volcanic promontory, and went...3/4 of a mile to the "Great Boiling Spring," and a grass valley, a distance of 21 miles from the "Rabbit Hole Springs," and terminating the great desert stretch, so much dreaded." (Bruff:151) He camped in the area moving a little during two days to recruit. This was the view as the trail approached the desert with Black Rock in the distance.

Bruff made a number of sketches of the features in the area. This one is part of three of a panorama series that looks back over the desert they had successfully crossed. Most emigrants spent time at the rock to recover, but they had to contend with the hot water. Hoffman noted, "In this vicinity there are numerous hot and luke warm springs, some of them of great depth. They smell strongly of sulfur. The soil near the springs seemed to be good so as to afford some grass, doubtless owing to the moisture produced by the springs as well as by the warmth of

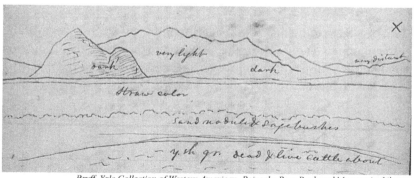

Bruff, Yale Collection of Western American, Beinecke Rare Book and Manuscript Library
Black Rock Desert sketch.

251

the water. Sometimes the mules were hesitant about approaching the smelly hot water. (Bruff:154)

The principal hot spring at Black Rock was 8 or 10 feet in diameter, and of considerable depth, and the water quite hot. I had to go some distance down stream from the spring, before the water was cool enough to wash my feet." (Mumford:138-9) On September 28, 1853, Mr. Lacon wrote, "The spring is boiling hot. It will cook meat. One of the boys put in a sheeps tongue for an hour and it was perfectly done." (Mumford:138)

Near the springs or after a rain the playa could turn to mud. Wagons sometimes got stuck in the mud that could be under the dry cracked plains as they neared the springs. The same could be true for modern vehicles. It is still dangerous and desolate. Don't travel there alone.

Black Rock Desert today.

After the emigrants rested, they continued north past a white formation high on the side of the mountain to their right. Bruff dubbed it "Fremont's Castle," Now they were headed Mud Meadows and Mud Lake Basin, one day's travel away.

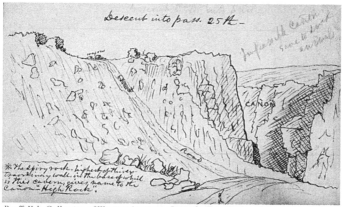

Bruff, Yale Collection of Western American, Beinecke Rare Book and Manuscript Library
Descent into Pass [Fly Canyon].

After the climb from Mud Lake Basin, on Sept 25, Bruff wrote, "While ascending this elevation, I had a fine view around, but the harsh angularly ruptured country close on mi right, attracted my particular attention, and extorted a sketch. All volcanic. The road terminated, as it were, at the edge of the very apex of this hill, and from a big rock on the left of the trail, at crest, I looked down, and for a while thought it must be *'the jumping-off place'*! Here down this very steep descent, must our wagons roll." (Bruff:160) His company made it down successfully, but he did note the broken wagons littering the canyon floor. An alternate route over the hills to the north bypassed the canyon. Today his sketch is known as "Descent to Fly Canyon."

The present road cuts across the side of the hill on its way to High Rock Canyon. A later painting made the descent and canyon appear much steeper and deeper. Again, it seems his first sketches were more accurate than many of his later paintings.

Hill

Canyon descent today.

253

"Singular Rock."

Continuing northwest the trail passes through the rugged High Rock Canyon and back into rolling hills and dry sage plains. On September 29, Bruff sketched a rocky formation which he labelled, "Singular Rock" which later became the site of Massacre Ranch. According to folklore a massacre occurred near there, but there is no historical proof of any happening in the area even after the supposed gravesite was excavated.

Below is the area today. The view remains much as it was for the emigrants. The depressions of the old trail are now overgrown by sagebrush. The BLM has an emergency camping cabin in the area of the old ranch just off the trail. From there the trail begins to follow a westerly direction in the unchanged landscape.

Hill

Singular Rock today.

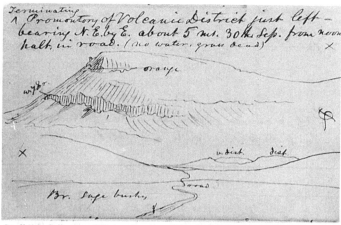

Bruff, Yale Collection of Western American, Beinecke Rare Book and Manuscript Library
Terminating promontory.

On October 8, 1853, Mr.Lacon notation was, "We Traveled 17 miles. We came to another lake which is called Mud Lake. [A different one than that mention earlier northwest of Black Rock at Mud Meadows.] Again the road was good but rocky in part. We are now in sight of the Sierra Nevada Mountains." (Mumford: 146) As the trail descended into Long Valley Painted Point was to the north, Mud Lake [Fortynine Lake] was eight miles west, and two miles farther the mountains [Forty Nine Mountains]. Bruff made this close-up sketch looking back at the area known today as Painted Point.

This view, from by the trail near where it enters the mountains to the west, is looking back east across Mud Lake towards Painted Point from where Bruff made his sketch. The travelers would have had a view of the Sierras spread out before them as they came over the low saddle in Bruff's drawing.

Hill

Across Long Valley to Painted Point today.

255

Bruff, Yale Collection of Western American, Beinecke Rare Book and Manuscript Library

The mountain in plain.

Continuing west, the trail passed through Surprise Valley and then northwest to Fandango Pass, which Bruff climbed on October 3, and then continued down to Goose Lake. Those going to California turned south. The trail entered the valley of the Pitt River. Part of Bruff's October 6 entry was, "A few hundred yards N.W. of our camp, a tall symmetrical butte, or isolated mountain, rises from the level, like a tent....Water, and good grass, but dry fuel scarce. Extensive camps here." (Bruff: 180-1)

Emigrants often complained about the Indians in this area as they had along the Humboldt. Charles Gray noted, Sept. 8, 1849 , "Last night the greatest misfortune...happened to our teams. The Indians eluded the guards & seized 11 head of cattle...they seemed to have selected our best ones..." (Gray:97) From here the emigrants continued to head south towards Lassen's Peak, then to Lassen's Ranch, and finally, to Sutter's Fort.

At Lassen's Meadow the Applegate-Lassen Trail turned northwest, while the main California Trail turned south following the Humboldt. The California Trail on both sides of the river was on the flat plain traveling straighter usually away from the winding river which had cut itself into a deep canyon. Sometimes the trail or camp roads dropped

Hill

Rattlesnake/Centerville Butte today.

briefly down to a lower bench or to the valley floor in an attempt to get water. At this point good and sufficient amounts of grass and water were again becoming harder to find. The trail was sandy and very dusty. It was littered with dead and dying animals and broken and discarded items. It was taking its toll on the emigrants. Wilkins noted, "Since I last wrote, I have taken another peek at the elephant. Dr D-- and I travelled on in advance of the wagons, searching every hole and corner in the river bottom for grass, without success. we finally however agreed upon a camping place…where they might get a few willows and a little dry picking, down a steep declivity to steep to take the wagons down."(Wilkins:69)

Below are some of the best examples of trail swales in the area where Wilkins had "another peek at the elephant." They are located a few miles west of the Rye Patch Dam across the Humboldt River running north and south. The area still looks much the same. However, nearby, development could threaten the area and the view.

Hill

Trail swales along Humboldt today.

John Grantham wrote this poem expressing the emigrant's feelings which many expressed in this area.(Potter:190)

The Humbug
From all the books that we have read
And all the travelers have said
We most implicitly believed,
Not dreamed that we should be deceived.

That when the mountains we should pass
We'd find on Humboldt fine Blue-grass
Nay that's not all[;] we learned moreover
That we'd get in the midst of clover.

Nay, more yet, these scribbing asses
Told of 'other nutricious grasses'
But great indeed was our surprise
To find it all a pack of lies

But when we to the Humboldt came
It soon with us lost all its fame
We viewed it as a great outrage
Instead of grass to find wild sage.

The route was dry, dusty, with little if any grass for the animals, and if they were lucky, a scant few willows for cooking and almost no drinkable water. Ingalls wrote about the area noting, "From this place is a desert, the river running through narrow clay banks, void of vegetation except the Artemesia or wild sage. The road generally follows the plains back from the river, only approaching occasionally for water. (Ingalls:58) But, ahead of them was the "Pyramid" or Lone Mountain, the landmark they were headed where emigrants could find a spring nearby with good water, and then south of present-day Lovelock, Nevada, the meadows. Quesenbury made this drawing looking south off the south side trail or from a camp road about thirteen miles north of Lovelock near Oreana, Nevada. On July 31 Ingalls noted,"...no grass, only an arid sage desert.... The pyramid at a distance resembles an ancient Mexican pyramid, rising by steps. It may be seen for up to forty miles up the river, and serves as a beacon, for the slough or meadows.(Ingalls:59)

Humboldt River Valley from the east.

The view here seems almost unchanged. However, today as one gets closer to Lovelock, agricultural improvements due to irrigation and construction have replaced dry sage plains.

The Big Meadows was critical for most travelers. The Humboldt spread out in the flat plain and grass grew. Most emigrants would stop, rest, recruit their animals, and cut hay at the Big Meadows. It was the last good major source of feed for the animals. Ingalls wrote, "We found two cities of tents at the slough quite populous…The road for the past few days has been strewed with dead stock." (Ingalls:59) On September 13, 1857, Helen Carpenter wrote, "Decided to lie by today in such good grass. This is called the Big Meadows. Some are cutting grass to carry along to feed when crossing the desert which is 25 miles ahead." (Carpenter:174) By the mid-1850s traders often appeared with supplies for sale which made the journey easier than it was for these early emigrants.

Hill
Humboldt Valley today.

259

Quensenbury, McKendree University

Mountains west of the Humboldt River (at the Big Meadows).

This is a closer view of the once distant "Pyramid," but now looking west across the river and part of the meadows. Note how its profile has changed.

The next day Carpenter wrote, "Came 15 miles and camped at what is called the lake. It is where the Humboldt River spreads out in a lake like a body and there is no longer any current. There is little grass and that is covered with alkali and the water is so impregnated

Hill

Mountains today.

Quesenbury, McKendree University
Humboldt lake, viewed from east.

with it that it cannot be used for drinking, and...there is no wood."
And the next morning she noted, "When the cattle were driven up...
two laid down and in a few minutes were dead. A great many are sick
from alkali." (Carpenter: 175)

Margaret Frink recorded," In a few miles we came to where the
river...spreads out on the level plain and forms a broad shallow lake....
called the 'sink of the Humboldt'....the end of the most miserable
river on the face of the earth. The water of the lake, as well as that
of the river for the last hundred miles above, is strong with salt and
alkali, and has the color and taste of dirty soap-suds....unfit for the use
of either animals or human beings; but thousands of both have had to
drink to save life..."(Frink:136) Trees in the area were rare and still
are today. The tree in the drawing by Quesenbury was lucky to still
stand in 1852. Perhaps it was worth more for its shade than as wood
for a fire. What was once the shallow lake is now a dry basin.

Humboldt Lake area today.

261

Quesenbury, McKendree University
Humboldt Lake from north.

Quesenbury was on the south side where the trail ran close to the mountains. The formations on the hills could change shape dramatically as one moved along the trail. Today this area is near the Indian Caves. What appears to have been either the shallow stagnant water or flats in the drawing is now covered with sage and alkali.

The photo is from the location near that of the drawing. Death was common along this area of the trail. The post appears to mark a grave. Sagebrush has overgrown an east-west out-of-place pile of rocks in the sand. Very few graves are still marked or identified. Perhaps this is one of the 953 graves recorded in the 1850 survey of the desert. A second one is nearby in the general area. Another half day's drive would bring the emigrants to the Humboldt Bar or Dike and to where the emigrants had to decide whether to use the old Truckee and newer Carson trail.

Each year the size of the lake changed. During some years there was almost no water in it. But during wet years the lake was large and the Humboldt continued south through the Humboldt Bar or Dike into

Hill

Grave near lake area today.

Quesenbury, McKendree University
Humboldt Lake from south.

the Carson Sink. When Quesenbury traveled through there seemed to have been a fair amount of water in the lake.

Today the lake area is considerably smaller than that encountered by the emigrants. An alkali plain and sage have replaced most of the water. His view of the sink and lake is looking north from on the dike or bar.

The present dirt "road" on the right closely follows the main portion of the south side trail.

The Humboldt River grew sluggish and foul and finally "sank" into the ground. Randolph Marcy's guidebook states, "This desert has always been the most difficult part of the journey to California, and more animals have probably been lost here than any other place. The parts of wagons that are continually met with here shows this most incontestably."(Marcy: 276) That was an understatement [Note the sign and remember the conditions encountered and emigrants' comments that you also read in the diary section.]

The Forty Mile Desert started after the sink of the Humboldt and Dike and the nearby Carson Sink. Here emigrants had to select either the old route over to and up the Truckee River or the one to the Carson River. No matter which route was selected, they crossed sections of

Hill
View north from the Humboldt Dike today.

263

Hill

Forty Mile Desert sign.

the Forty Mile Desert. Conditions proved to be as bad, if not much worse than those on the Black Rock Desert on the Applegate-Lassen route. There was one last source of water south of the Dike. Two small wells had been dug a few miles into the desert on the east side. Perhaps these pictured here could be the same ones mentioned by Wilkins in the diary section. Describing the slough he painted Hall wrote on July 28,1852, "The water is uncommonly bad having the taste of Sulphur and salt. There are some wells near by them. The water is a little better." Note the distant hills in the painting and to the left of the car in the photo.

Describing the desert crossing in 1850 Frink noted, "Both sides of the road for miles were lined with dead animals and abandoned wagons. Around them were strewed yokes, chains, harness, guns, tools, bedding, clothing, cooking-utensils, and many other articles in utter confusion." (Frink:138) Today most of the broken wagon parts and discarded items and animal bones that once littered the desert routes have disintegrated or have been removed. Although rarer and rarer as the years have passed, fragments of discarded items, such as bits of china, thick broken bottle glass, pieces of rusty iron and barrel hoops can still be found. Please leave them for others to find and observe.

Crossing the desert to the Truckee there was one life saver—boiling hot springs, but they could be dangerous too. On September 4, 1852 Eliza McAuley recorded, "After feeding some hay we started for the desert....stopped at noon, fed and water from the store in

Hall, Wyoming State Museum, Department of State Parks and Cultural Resources

Last water east of the desert.

Hill

Double Wells today.

our wagons and drove on again… rested…started and drove the rest of the night, passing boiling springs about midnight….as it was dark we could not examine them closely. We hear a woman & child have got scalded very badly by stepping into one." (McAuley:75) The next day she recorded, "We are now seven miles from the Truckee River, but the road here becomes very sandy and heavy. After traveling three miles the teams begin to give out, so we had to unhitch them…and send them on to grass and water….." (McAuley:76)

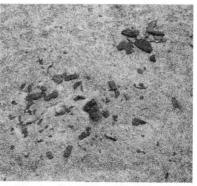

Hill

Forty Mile Desert reminders.

This is the modern view looking ahead from where the trail was "sandy and heavy" and the animals gave out. The Truckee could be seen after the trail rounded the point in the center.

Hill

Trail approaching the Truckee today.

After arriving at the Truckee, the emigrants welcomed its cool, clear water. There they rested for a day or more, waiting for stragglers to catch up and to recruit and reorganize before continuing. The trail up the Truckee to the Sierra passes was difficult. The canyon was rugged, narrow at time, forcing the travelers to cross the river, as many as seven times a day. It usually took more than a week to make the journey and they still had the pass to climb.

Donner memorial.

After following the Truckee River, passing through the Meadows [present-day Reno, Nevada], and continuing into the mountains, the trail came to its last obstacle. At the foot of the final climb, the trail followed the north side of the Truckee [Donner] Lake and then ascended the steep mountainside to the pass. Pictured is the Donner Monument at Donner Pass State Park. It was placed on the site of the Breen family cabin. It is situated near the lake where the Donner Party was forced to spend the winter. Some believe the height of the base represents the depth of the snow that winter.

Hill

A large rock served as a wall for another of the cabins occupied by Murphy family of the Donner Party in the winter of 1846-7. On the rock is a large plaque with some of the names of the party. These two sites are also mentioned in the Bryarly portion of the diary chapter. The Donner families spent the winter about six miles back on the trail.

For years emigrants frequently referenced the Donner incident. On Sept.13, 1852, Liza McAuley wrote, "This afternoon we passed Starvation Camp, which took its name from a party of emigrants....

Hill

Cabin Rock today.

There were the remains of two or three cabins...surrounded by stumps ten to fifteen feet high....Donner Lake, a beautiful sheet of water... was named in remembrance of the party. We camped in a small valley about three miles west of this place." (McAuley:78-9) It seems her party used Roller Pass to cross the mountains.

In recent years there has been a growing controversy about and

Hill   *Hill*

Traditional Donner camp tree.   New Donner camp tree.

research into the exact location of the Donner family campsites at Alder Creek. The traditional site was thought to have been by what is now the remnant of the tree in a meadow. However, recent archaeological work and the use of specially trained human remains dogs, has caused assumptions about this site to be questioned. No artifacts were found there, but some artifacts have been found nearby. A different meadow area with an old large living tree has been identified through the use of dogs as a likely location. This old tree could be the one that George Donner camped under. (Grenbenkemper-2:83)

The Stephens-Townsend-Murphy Party had opened the Truckee route in 1844 and crossed the Sierras in the area that is now known as Donner Pass. In 1846 an additional route was developed using the nearby pass now called Roller Pass. It was a little longer and higher, but the climb was actually easier. By 1847 the Truckee (Donner Pass) area was used less and less. As the result of recent research and related physical evidence the traditional route up Donner Pass has come into question. Based on the newly found physical evidence and

Hill

Looking east from near Donner Pass.

reinterpretation of the old, many historians now believe the route to the top was slightly different. The traditional twisting route went to the right of the center rock formation up through a notch later blocked by the China Wall that was built to support the railroad (far right) and continued up to the low area. The route supported by the recent research was straighter and a little easier. It went up left or north of the formation and continued up going over the mountain less than a mile north of the traditional Donner Pass. (Hollecker :14) The Trails West trail marker identifies it as Stephens Pass.

Quesenbury, McKendree University
Carson Desert, north of road.

Back on the Carson Route the emigrants were no better off, or perhaps worse, than those who had decided to take the Truckee Route. Few emigrants described the scenery and fewer drew the area. Quesenbury, however, made a number of sketches of the crossing. The last possible water had been the two wells referred to earlier a few miles south of the dike or bar. In the early years there was no other source of water until they reached the Carson. Traveling at night was preferred to the heat of the day, but there was no way to avoid daytime travel. In 1850 Frink wrote, "It was long before sunrise when we left camp....At six o'clock we halted and rested....We set forward again at ten o'clock and soon realized what might before us. (Frink: 138) The land was generally pretty flat and the trail was as direct as the geography would allow.

This feature would have been passed shortly after they began the crossing. This view, from near the Salt Creek Crossing west off highway 95, was what they would have seen looking back near their morning stop.

Hill
Hills north of road today.

269

Quesenbury, McKendree University
Carson Desert, south of road.

Their route was hot and dry during the day and cool at night. At times the ground could be rocky, at other times it was sandy or over alkali or salt flats. It sometimes ran closer to the hills or mountains. The only shade might come from that of a wagon, a large hummock or sand dune or the nearby hills when the sun was lower in the sky. A few miles after Salt Creek or the Humboldt Slough the emigrants approached a vast white expanse. The drawing shows the trail cutting straight across one of the alkali or salt flats. The glimmering flats were hard on their eyes during the day and mirages could appear. At night under a full moon the trail was clearly evident. As the emigrants traveled farther into the desert the conditions took their toll on emigrants their stock and equipment.

This area is west of U.S. 95 about 16 miles south of I-80

Hill

Desert flats today.

Quesenbury, McKendree University

Carson Desert.

Describing her march through the desert crossing Margaret Frink wrote, "For many weeks we had been accustomed to seeing property abandoned and animals dead or dying. But those scenes were here doubled or treble....The owners had left everything, except what provisions they could carry on their backs."(Frink :138)

Quesenbury's drawing illustrates that the line of march and some of the debris left along the road. The route here is over fine black gravel and in other places fine sand. It is still very hot, dry, and sunny with no natural shade. On August 16, 1850, Frink wrote, "The living procession marched steadily onward, giving little heed to the destruction going on, in their own anxiety to reach a place of safety. In fact, the situation was so desperate that, in most cases, no one could help another. Each had all he could do to save himself and is animals." (Frink:138)

Here is the same area where the "living procession marched." In front of mountains in the far distance flowed their goal – the Carson River. Here the trail paralleled the formation now called the Upsal Hogback.

Hill

Upsal Hogback and desert today.

271

National Archives # 77-KRP-32

Soda Lake.

Sometimes travelers were lucky. Traveling in 1850, Frink wrote, "we met a wagon...loaded with barrels of pure, sweet water for sale.... hauled from a newly discover spring, four or five miles southeast of the road. Mr. Frink bought a gallon of it for which he paid $1.00" (Frink:139) That was certainly a life saver.

Here is one of the salt lakes in the Forty Mile Desert on the Carson Route. Randolph Marcy's 1859 guidebook notes, "At 9 ½ miles beyond the mail station, on the desert, a small road turns off the main trace towards a very high sandy ridge, and directly upon the top of the ridge is a salt lake. Upon the extreme north end of this lake will be found a large spring of fresh water, sufficient for 1,000 animals. From thence to "Ragtown" on the Carson River, is three miles." (Marcy:276)

The old photo was taken in 1868. Below is a similar recent photo of the area.

Hill

Soda Lake today.

Quesenbury, McKendree University
Western termination of desert road.

The journey across the desert had been very difficult as noted by Wilkins in the diary section. Many emigrants had to abandon their wagons. The worst sand was within the last five to ten miles. In May 1852, Lucy Cooke recorded, "Well, our good wagon was left on the desert. But such was the prevailing custom…to destroy anything that you might not need, and so prevent the next person from benefiting (She did mention that only some did it, not everyone. The owner of the oxen that were pulling her wagon feared the animals would not pull it anymore, and that it had to be left and burned.)….We reached the Carson River in the early afternoon, having traveled the whole night. Teams and men pretty well jaded. We found a shanty or two and several tents here, and the place was given the not inappropriate name of "Rag Town," for such described the appearance of most of the emigrant arrivals." (Cooke-99) On August 7, 1850 Frink reached

Hill
Ragtown area today.

the river in 37 hours and noted, "Its water was clear, cool, and pure, free from salt or alkali, as different from the Humboldt soap suds is from night." (Frink:140)

Quesenbury sketched the end of the desert crossing. The immediate river bottom is now farmed and with many more trees growing along the river, but the hills in the background seen above the trees are the same.

Quesenbury, McKendree University
Quesenbury's drawing of the Dry Sink.

The Carson Trail now followed the river, sometimes parallel to it and at other times taking a more distant path to avoid following its larger twists and turns. This is one of Quesenbury's drawings where the trail was avoiding one of those twists in the river, and it passed through a dry sink or alkali bed. The emigrants sometimes mentioned the sinks. This location became the later site of Hawes Station, a few miles east of Silver Springs, Nevada. The immediate area has changed very little today. The ruins of the station can be seen in the photo. A mile farther west the trail split. The river or wet route, about 37 miles long, turned south to follow and meet the river near where

Hill
Dry sink at Hawes Station ruins today.

Fort Churchill was built in 1860 and then turned west along the river. Wilkins wrote, "we saw a large notice stuck up by the side of the road, informing us the 20 or some said 25 mile desert might be avoided by going about 10 miles [more] miles around. About 8 miles of heavy sand, and then fine grass valeys....We went the road and found the best grass we had seen for several hundred miles."(Wilkins:74) The other, the shorter but dry route, continued about 26 miles southwest to the Dayton area where it rejoined with the river route. As with other dry crossings, night travel was preferred. Mary Karchner took the dry route and wrote, "...are not going to start from here till 5, O, had it very cool and pleasant traveling drove till 11, O, then fed and drove on till 4, O, in the morning...." (Karchner:145)

Old Fort Churchill display.

Fort Churchill was built in response to increased Indian attacks during the Paiute or Pyramid Lake War. It was also located near the western end of the recently opened Central Overland Route that had been explored by Captain James H. Simpson between Salt Lake, Utah and Genoa, Nevada in 1859. After the fort was finished, it was also used by the Pony Express in 1860-1. The road along the river was sandy but usually considered to be good and water was near. While originally known for its good grass, it varied based on weather conditions and the volume of traffic. Travelers even then had

275

Hill

Fort Churchill ruins today.

to contend with government regulations. Phebe Carleton noted, "…entered Fort Churchill. This is a very beautiful place…The houses are alike and the streets neat and clean….We went about 2 miles out of the Fort and camped, we had not been there long when one of the soldiers came and ordered us from the Government Reserve, so we hitched up and went three miles farther…" (Carleton:211)

The drawing in the photo is from a display showing how the fort appeared after its completion. This similar view is from the trail to the right of the wagon shown at the bottom of the drawing. The dry alternate route was on the north side of the mountains in the background. The fort's ruins have been stabilized. The visitor center is nice, but small.

From the junction of the dry and wet routes the trail continued south-southwest towards present-day Carson City.

The trail's route seemed to alternate between a dry sandy or a stony and rocky road. The emigrants were warned by word of mouth or posted signs to take extra precautions to guard their oxen. The local

Quesenbury, McKendree University
Carson Valley from north.

Hill

Formation today.

276

Quesenbury, McKendree University

Carson Valley from the north.

Indians would try to wound the cattle forcing the emigrants to leave them, and thus, enabling the Indians to get the beef.

Quesenbury drew this rocky formation along the side of the trail. The formation can be seen from a park, the Moffat Open Space Property, in Carson City, Nevada. The river makes a bend south and then southwest. The emigrants left the river for about seven miles to across the valley and to cut out the bend. The next drawing shows the view they had near where they encountered the river again.

"Our road now lies thro' a valley 40 miles long and from 8 to 10 broad. It is surrounded by pretty high mountains and nearly all covered with pine trees, which altho' look small from the road, are two and three feet in diameter. beautiful streamlets of clear cold water gush from these hills into the valley, thro' the center of which the river meanders. The soil is rich the grass luxuriant, and take it alltogether it is one of the best tracks of land we have seen since leaving the state. Those who have seen Salt Lake Valley say it is preferable in many respects." (Wilkins:79) Quesenbury drew that area.

Hill

Carson Valley from the north today.

The decade after the gold rush brought many changes to Carson Valley. Both gold and silver mining were having an impact. Increased pressure was placed on the Indians as traffic increased and populations grew. Carson City grew up and ranches were starting to appear in the valley. Trading houses were also found along the trail to take advantage of the passing emigrants. The telegraph line connected Carson City with San Francisco, and there was even talk about building a railroad. (Gibson:95-6)

This particular area is still undergoing significant change. Suburbanization is rapidly expanding in this part of the valley. Today a lush green golf course and housing developments have replaced much of the sagebrush along the river and valley bottom and nearby hills. However, the mountains on the west side of the valley seem to look much the same. Genoa and Mormon Station are located at the foot of the Sierras about half way down the valley.

This is the famous Mormon Station in Genoa that Ingalls mentions in his diary as did others. It was built in 1850 two years after the Carson Route of the California Trail was opened to capitalize on the emigrant

Nevada Parks, Mormon Station

Mormon Station.

traffic. The 1860 photo is displayed in the replica. Francis Sawyer arrived here on August 9, 1852, and noted, "The Mormon Station has been built one or two years. It is a boarding house and store together, in a pretty location at the edge of the mountains with tall pine trees all around it. There are gardens here. I bought some more turnips, at five cents each. We have arrived at civilization, though things are still

278

very high." (Sawyer:113) On September 1, 1859, John Powell noted, "We passed Genoa, contains about twenty homes, one good store and some small trading houses….We passed some hot springs close by Genoa."(Powell:156)

Hill

Mormon Station replica.

The replica, minus the later false front, has been reconstructed on the old site. Enjoy a snack or refreshing drink in the cool of the trees, or step inside, and step back in time. The tall pines are still there, only even more of them, and a resort encompasses the hot springs about two miles down the road.

Courteny, California Historical Society, CHS52009.141
Carson Canyon.

Before Mormon Station was established, the emigrants continued south and stopped at the hot springs. The trail continued hugging the foothills of the Sierras, up from the valley floor where the trail was drier. It would be about fifteen more miles before the wagons turned west to enter the canyon and start their difficult climb.

This sketch based on a Jones daguerreotype depicts the trail as it enters the dreaded Pass Creek Canyon known today as Carson Canyon. Some emigrants called this the Mad River because of all the difficulties faced in the canyon. August 4, 1849 Pritchard recorded, "…at an early hour, we commenced the trying ascent through the Canon. And in about One mile we began to meet and brave the difficulties. We have the River to cross 3 times, the first and second time it was bridged by falling to large tree across and the laying puncheon & poles

Hill

Entrance to Carson Canyon today.

280

Quesenbury, McKendree University
Coming to Canon from west [Hope Valley].

on them, which made a tolerable safe bridge….the 3rd and last place where the road was forced across it, we were compelled to ford it…" (Pritchard:131) Note the bridge in the sketch.

The route followed today has had the rocks removed, the twists and turns cut out, and most of the river crossings removed. There are, however, some places along the highway where the old trail can still be found. Walking along them, one wonders how the emigrants ever made it. This site is located near the canyon entrance where a local road pulls off the highway and bridges the river.

On July 31, 1848, Azariah Smith, part of the Mormons who going east opened the Carson Trail, noted, "…encamped at the head of a canion, that we expect to pass through about fifteen miles long, called pass canion. There is also a river runs through the canion which is called pass River….Some of the Boys have been ahead to fix the road,

Hill

Hope Valley today.

Quesenbury, McKendree University
Mountains at Reed [Red] Lake.

today and they say it is very bad, and seemingly imposible for wagons to get through. (Smith, A:133)

The California bound emigrants were now through the difficult canyon and could rest. Margaret Frink wrote, "...to our great relief, we have gotten out of the granite jaws of the mountain and had come to an open, level, beautiful vally, sprinkled over with trees. This is known as Hope Valley, which we thought an appropriate name. We went a mile further and camped. (Frink:148.) This is part of the view they would have had from near their camps. The top of the canyon mentioned by Smith and Pritichard can be seen near the far left of the photograph and just off Quesenbury's drawing.

Leaving their camp the next morning Pritchard wrote, "The road was rough, hilly & stony. At noone we reached Reed [Red] Lake, One of the fountan heads of Carson River. This lake is about one half mile

Hill

Mountains at Red Lake today.

282

Quesenbury, McKendree University
Red Lake.

long and about one forth wide" (Pritchard:132) And lies immediately at the base of the Mountain that we have to ascend. (Pritchard:132)

The lake has since been enlarged to include the original Red Lake and smaller nearby ponds that are shown later in the illustration "Red Lake & Summit." The recent draught has lowered the lake and the trunks of formerly cut and submerged trees are visible. Part of the old trail has been submerged, but the mountains surrounding the lake remain almost unchanged. The modern highway is cutting diagonally from the base of the mountains and rising to the left. These mountains were not the ones the emigrants ascended. They were off to the left at the other end of the lake. This view is from the far end of the lake in the Red Lake & Summit illustration looking at the mountains behind the large cliff formation on the left side of the drawing and photo.

Hill

Carson Pass mountains today.

283

Courteny, California Historical Society, FN-13639
Red Lake & summit.

The trail passed between these two peaks of the mountains to the pass. It started at the lower left at Red Lake and climbed the very steep grade, sometimes referred to as "Devil's Ladder."

The western end of present Red Lake is visible in the lower left of the photo. Trees block the view from down in the valley. The photo was taken from the modern highway before it made its turn to the left where it can be seen on the right as it cuts across the face of mountain and makes another turn to the right around the mountain.

This old drawing shows the trail as it nears the summit of Carson Pass above Red Lake. The climb had been very steep and hard on the animals. Pritchard noted, "This Mountain by the road is about one mile high and appearatly perpendicular. We have to go nearly … strait up it winding first to the right & then to the left....We have to lift our wagons round frequently....Many of the places have such perpendicular falls, that , if a mule were thrown off or a wagon & team

Hill

Carson Pass today.

Courteny, *California Historical Society, CHS 2009.142*
Sierra Nevada Great Summit – Snow.

they would fall from 50 to 100 feet without touching anything....We commenced the ascent with 14 mules hitched to one wagon and all the men of the train pushing chocking & holding on, & by sunset we had suceeded in takeing 2 of our wagons to the top of the *hill* Mountain where we found good water & in 2 miles good grass for our animals. Distance 5 miles." (Pritchard:132-33)

Note the rock formation and cliff behind the wagon in the drawing which is evident in the modern photo. Today an old pull-off and parking lot near the summit have flattened and filled the part of the area and altered the rock formations.

above is another drawing based on a Jones daguerreotype. It appears to show the approach towards the base before the climb.

Hill

View towards Great [Second] Summit.

Quesenbury, McKendree University

North Summit.

Today the old trail in the valley floor is flooded by a greatly enlarged Caples Lake, and the mountain forest is larger and denser making it difficult to photograph close up. This is a similar view but from much farther away and a different view point. The trail comes in from the left below the shoreline and goes diagonally up the valley behind the bare hills to the pass off to the far right.

The view at the summit or West Pass is something to behold. The altitude was over 9,600 feet. It was the highest wagons were taken on the trail. The Wilkins' painting from the top is lost, but this is Quesenbury's drawing of the formations at the top. The trail crosses in the foreground and then follows along Squaw Ridge for a few miles before descending. After the climb and traveling for a few hours Pritchard wrote," We are now upon the topmost ridges of the Sierra Nevada Mountains. Language is inadequate to describe, the striking contrast between this grand and magnificent Alpine and Elysian Scenery. Nothing in nature I am sure can present Scenery more wild,

Hill

Summit formations today.

286

Quesenbury, McKendree University
Volcanic rocks west of Sierras.

more rugged, more bold, more grand, more romantic, and picturesquely beautiful, than this mountain scenery. . ." (Pritchard:134-5)

The emigrants were on the home stretch. The trail often followed along the crest and up or down the ridges, but headed downhill. They had fresh water and wood from the cool, tall forests. The route could still be rocky and dusty, but their goal was near. Trading posts were being built by enterprising traders selling goods and drinks to the emigrants.

A few miles west of Tragedy Springs the trail crossed a saddle. This volcanic formation was alongside the north side of the trail and is almost across from the site known today as the Maiden's Grave. Part of the outcropping was removed during the grading and construction of Highway 88.

Hill
Volcanic rocks today.

Courtesy of the Bancroft Library, University of California, Berkeley

Sutter's Mill.

By August 10, 1849, Pritchard had descended from the mountains and wrote, "The roads have been down hill pretty much & compairitively good all day. We nooned in the neighbourhood of the diggins, then came on a forks of the road—the left hand leading to Sutters Fort & the right hand to the mills or Coloma. It is 50 miles from this point to the Fort—and 15 miles to the Mills. We here took the right hand road…" At the "Saw Mill" he bought lumber to make a gold washer. (Priticard: 137)

Hill

Sutter's Mill replica today.

Quesenbury, McKendree University

Sutter's Fort.

James Marshall, who discovered gold on January 24, 1848 is shown standing in front of Sutter's Mill four years later. By then California had changed more than either Marshall or Sutter would ever have imagined in 1848.

Today the mill has been reconstructed near its original location in Coloma, the town that grew up at the site. The river has changed its course since the gold rush era, and there appears to be more trees.

This is Sutter's Fort, the center of Sutter's "New Helvetia" as it appeared to many of the early emigrants. It had been built on a small rise near a seasonal stream and at the site of an Indian village. Here emigrants found Sutter's helpful hand after their long hard journey across the plains, deserts, and mountains. Inside a variety of goods such as food, clothing, tools and equipment could be obtained. Also farrier and medical services, and sometimes even employment opportunities were available to emigrants. They could acquire everything they

Hill

Sutter's Fort today.

289

Sutter's Fort

Main Building at Sutter's Fort.

needed to start their new lives. The gold rush, however, would soon change almost everything.

Once in the middle of the countryside, Sutter's Fort now is tucked away, surrounded by the city of Sacramento. Only when you enter inside can you get a sense of what it was like many years ago.

Within a few years Sutter's empire was overrun and his fort soon fell into disrepair until only the main building remained. This is a photo of it in 1867. Fortunately, there were those who wished to preserve it and restore it to reflect its proper place in history.

Hill

Main building today.

Placerville.

This is the building today, part of a fine reconstruction of the fort. Inside the restored main building and reconstructed walls and other buildings are exhibits and displays that explain its history and what business and life was like at the fort when the emigrants came. Here visitors can take a step back in time.

This is another sketch based on an early J. Wesley Jones daguerreotype of a site along the California Trail. This is Placerville, the end of the trail for many gold seekers, and also for "Betsey" and "Ike!" It was also the beginning of a new adventure and life for them. A few emigrants sought employment here, but most would spread out to the different gold fields to seek their fortunes. Few would strike it rich. The tree shown in the drawing near the flagpole in the center of

Hill

Placerville today.

291

town was the one used for the hanging which gave Placerville its other name – Hangtown!

Today the town still bustles with activity! The view is from the edge of the old cemetery on the hill. The trunk of the infamous tree is in the basement of one of the buildings in town.

The journey is over.

Chapter Eight

Parks, Museums and Displays

For those traveling along the California Trail there is an ever growing number of sites that can be visited to learn about the journey west. Large or small, some of these have been in existence for a number of years, while others have been recently developed; hopefully more are coming. At the same time the pressure on what is left of the old trails is increasing with new developments in agriculture, expanding urban populations, the subdivisions of large ranches onto which second or summer retreat homes are constructed, and the growing energy needs met by the development of wind farms and gas and oil exploration. It is harder to find and see the old trails as experienced by the emigrants. The cumulative effect of these factors is the reason that the identification, preservation and interpretation of those existing sites are becoming more important.

Many of the historic trails west overlapped in places. Sometimes a center or museum may place more emphasis on a particular event related to its focus. As a result, some sites or centers are not included in this chapter. For those who do drive along the trail, the National Park Service's *National Historic Trails Auto Tour Route Interpretive Guides* are highly recommended. These booklets are generally organized by state and include a great many more sites than are mentioned here, but even they are not able to include them all. It is hoped that this chapter's selections will allow the traveler to experience the trail and the emigrants' journeys through significant centers and relevant interpretive sites while following the trail along the highways. Many of these sites are open seasonally, and it is advisable to check to find the days and times in which they are open.

Jefferson National Expansion Memorial, St. Louis, Missouri

Here is the location of the gigantic Gateway Arch which commemorates St. Louis as the "Gateway to the West." It is situated on the site of old St. Louis. Under the arch is the Museum of Westward Expansion. In it can be found well designed exhibits that cover the whole period of westward expansion including the California Trail era. It begins with displays related to the Lewis and Clark Expedition's exploration of the West and continues with others about American Indians, trappers, emigrants, cowboys, homesteaders, and railroads until the West was settled and "closed."

The park is located on the west bank of the Mississippi River just off I-55 and I-70. Other Points of historical interest are also within walking distance of the memorial park.

Independence, Missouri & the Greater Kansas City Vicinity

The area is unique in that the three major trails to Santa Fe, Oregon, and California began in this area while the Lewis and Clark Trail passed through it, and it also played an important role in the history of the Mormons. There are many different museums, historic buildings, and points of interest within the area, which, if all were visited would take a few days for travelers to enjoy. Independence Square is often considered to be a starting point for the Santa Fe, Oregon and California trails. Here is the present-day courthouse, which contains parts of the early courthouse. Near the square is the National Frontier Trails Museum. It houses fine displays providing information about the whole westward journey including all five of the above mentioned trails. Its expansion program has just begun. It also houses an excellent and expanding Merrill Mattes research library about westward migrations topics. In addition, it has been increasing its online capabilities. The headquarters of the Oregon-California Trails Association is located on site. This organization is dedicated to the preservation and interpretation of the historic trails related to westward expansion. Around the block from it in a park, the trail is evident. Parallel impressions in the ground, caused by the hundreds of wagons that left Independence, can be seen. Also near the Square, but in different directions are the old log courthouse and Spring

Park, which contains the Brady Cabin, one of the earliest structures built in Independence. A few miles away the two major riverboat landing areas, the Upper Independence and Westport Landings, are identified with interpretive signs. Westport, which is often considered to be the beginning of Kansas City, has its small Pioneer Park with its interpretive sign. A number of historic homes related to the trail period are open. These include those of Moses Grinter, Alexander Majors, and Archibald Rice-Tremonti. Near the Rice-Tremonti house is the Cave Spring site in Klein Park. Jim Bridger lived in the area and is buried in Mount Washington Cemetery. The Shawnee Methodist Mission in Fairway was a site frequently visited by the emigrants before they began their trek over the prairies. There are numerous small parks with trail remnants, while Minor Park has the famous immense trail swales. In recent years the various local governments working together have embarked on an extensive program of marking of more than fifty continuous miles of the route of the trails. They have placed numerous interpretive displays describing related sites. Small booklets or leaflets are becoming available and more are planned to help locate and learn about the numerous sites and routes. All of these allow tourists to learn about the trails as they follow them. Thousands of emigrants arrived at the jumping-off towns by steamboat, and the Arabia Steamboat Museum in Kansas City displays the thousands of artifacts used by people on the frontier. It is a terrific museum.

And for those interested in Lewis and Clark, President Harry Truman, or the history of the Mormons, there are numerous historic sites associated with them, which are well worth the time. Independence was once the center of the early Mormon Church and presently is that of the headquarters for the Church of Christ with its Mormon Visitors Center.

PARTING OF THE TRAILS, GARDNER, KANSAS

About thirty miles southwest of Kansas City and about two southwest of Gardner, the Oregon-California trails split off to the west while the Santa Fe Trail continued southwest. While no physical evidence is evident, interpretive panels explain this important site.

The roadside park is located by the intersection of U.S. Highway 36 and 183rd Street.

FORT LEAVENWORTH, KANSAS

This is the oldest continually operated military post west of the Mississippi. It was first constructed in 1827. This area was also used by emigrants. On his way to California in 1849 James Wilkins, the artist, painted the landing area of the post. Today the post museum, with its emphasis on the fort's military role and the opening of the west, can be visited. One can also walk on the old main parade ground that was the site of early councils with the Indians. A large trail swale leads up from the river from where steamboats landed to the remnants of the old blockhouse. The impressive monument to the Buffalo Soldiers is also on the grounds. The fort is an active post and the location of the Command and General Staff College for advanced military training.

The fort is located off Highway 73 just north of present-day Leavenworth, Kansas, which had first been named Douglas City in 1854. Visitors are welcome but leave extra time to gain access to the grounds.

WESTON, MISSOURI

During the early years of the gold rush Weston was one of the disembarking points for emigrants who came up the Missouri by steamboat. Many people thought it would become the greatest port city, but that never came to pass. In later years, the river channel moved due to flooding, and Weston was left "high and dry." Today it is about two miles from the river. The old town is presently a Registered Historic District and has a nice museum. There are several buildings from its heyday period, and many of the older homes are periodically open to the public. Numerous shops catering to tourists line the main street. You can stand at the main intersection down the hill and imagine the riverboats pulling up to the area where the railroad tracks lie.

The town is located off State Highway 45, a few miles northeast of Leavenworth, Kansas.

ST. JOSEPH, MISSOURI

St. Joe was another of the "jumping-off" towns for the westward traveling emigrants. Within the city are numerous historic sites and museums. The Robidoux Row Museum (Third and Poulin Streets) is located in a building built by Joseph Robidoux in the 1840s to temporarily house emigrants or new settlers. Its focus is on Joseph Robidoux and family and their role in the West. The Pony Express

National Museum (914 Penn St.) deals with the Pony Express period as does the Patee House Museum just up the hill. The St. Joseph Museum (11th & Charles) deals with the town's relationship to the westward movement, along with exhibits about the Indians and Civil War. The town is also associated with Jesse James. His house is open to the public.

NEBRASKA CITY

This was the site of the first Fort Kearny and another of the "jumping-off" towns. James Wilkins passed through here as did William Henry Jackson. The town also became a major freighting center. For a few years Alexander Majors' office for his freighting business was here. The city is the location of the old Freighters Museum which has displays about the town's history and its commercial role. Also located here are the Arbor Day Foundation Visitor Center and the very good Missouri River Basin Lewis and Clark Interpretive Center.

COUNCIL BLUFFS, IOWA & OMAHA, NEBRASKA VICINITY

This was another of the "jumping-off" areas for the emigrants and the principal point of departure for those following the trail on the north side of the Platte River. Before it was known as Council Bluffs, it was Kanesville. The Western Historic Trails Center is focused on the story of the westward migration and trails passing through the area: Lewis & Clark, Oregon, California, and Mormon. It is located at 3434 Richard Downing Ave, off I-80/29. Other sites and museums related to the Lewis and Clark Expedition, the railroad, and the Mormon Trail can be visited in Council Bluffs.

Across the river in old Florence/Omaha is the site of the Mormons "Winter Quarters" in 1846-47. The Mormon Trail Visitor Center and old Mormon Cemetery are located near Thirty-sixth and State Street. Mormon emigrants follow the Council Bluffs road of the California Trail and the Hastings Cutoff to the valley of the Great Salt Lake in 1847. The site of the old Mormon Ferry was by the present I-680 bridge or "Mormon Bridge." The ferry was used by many of those leaving Council Bluffs for California, Oregon or Salt Lake. The old Mormon or Florence Mill, which is open on a limited basis, is also near there.

The Joslyn Art Museum's holdings are vast and include many Karl Bodmer paintings and exhibits on early Indian life and early expeditions in the area. It is located at 2200 Dodge Street, Omaha.

The "Pioneer Courage and Spirit of Nebraska Wilderness" sculptures are an impressive tribute to the westward movement and the early pioneers. They are located downtown off Capital Avenue between 15th and 17th streets in Omaha. They will certainly get you into the spirit and should be seen!

TOPEKA, KANSAS AREA

The crossing of the Kaw (Kansas) River occurred in this area. One of the more recent sites marked with interpretive displays is Papin's Ferry. It was established in 1842 and continued until 1857. The site on the river is near the Topeka Avenue Bridge.

Just west of Topeka is the Kansas Museum of History. Of special interest are the exhibits and displays about the different American Indians, the various trails, and military forts. Also on the site is the Potawatomie Baptist Mission. They are located north off I-70, exit 356.

OREGON TRAIL PARK, WESTMORELAND, KANSAS

The Scotts Springs area was a favorite camping site of the emigrants. There are a number of interpretive panels and displays identifying the site. The park is located about one mile south of Westmoreland on Kansas highway 99. Travelers can picnic where the emigrants camped.

Also nearby is a local museum related to the history of the area. Trail swales are in the area, but they are on private property.

MARYSVILLE, KANSAS AREA

Marysville has a number of sites related to the historic trails. For those California bound emigrants traveling west from St. Joseph and Fort Leavenworth, the Blue River was crossed here in Marysville. In 1852 Francis Marshall established a ferry near the old ford. A reconstructed wagon ferry is located in a roadside park near the crossing area off highway 77. Also in Marysville is the fine Pony Express Barn Museum on 8th Street. The barn was constructed in 1859.

South of Marysville is Alcove Spring Park. Plans are underway to expand this park to include a hiking or walking path along part of the trail. Here was the "Independence Crossing" of the Big Blue where the emigrants who had departed from Independence and Westport crossed. This is the location of the spring associated with John F. Reed, Grandma Keyes' grave, and the Donners. During the summer months the falls are usually dry, but the spring still flows. It is a great place to picnic.

HOLLENBERG RANCH, HANOVER, KANSAS

A Kansas State Historic Site, this ranch was constructed by Gerat Hollenberg, a German emigrant, who had originally gone west to the gold diggings of California, but left there after not having much success. He came to Kansas in 1857. He built his ranch on the main Oregon-California Trail from Independence, just west of its junction with the St. Joseph and Fort Leavenworth roads. The ranch house is basically unaltered since the late trail period and on the same site as it was during the trail days. This structure also served as a store for emigrants, a stage stop, and a Pony Express station. The displays inside are primarily devoted to its role during the Pony Express years. There is also a small visitor center with displays.

It is located about one mile east of Hanover, Kansas, off Kansas 243.

PAWNEE INDIAN VILLAGE, KANSAS

This museum is a Kansas State Historic Site. While it is located off the California Trail, it is included here because many of the emigrants to California remarked about seeing an old abandoned Pawnee village along the Platte River. James Wilkins' drawing of it is included in the pictorial journey chapter as well as a Jackson photograph of a Pawnee village. It is possible that the photo is of the new village established after the older one was abandoned.

The museum was constructed over the site of one of the larger lodges of the village, and the floor of the lodge can be viewed with the artifacts left as they were uncovered by the archaeologists. The museum is devoted to showing how the Pawnees lived in this region of northern Kansas and southern Nebraska during the 1800s when the emigrants were traveling through the area. It is located about three miles southwest of Republic, Kansas.

ROCK CREEK STATION, NEBRASKA

A Nebraska State Historic Site, Rock Creek Station was first developed in 1857 by S. C. Glenn who built a small cabin and established a store for emigrants at the ford of Rock Creek. By 1859 David McCanles had purchased the place and established a ranch there. It later became a stage and Pony Express station. At the same time he built a bridge across the creek near the old ford. The ranch is possibly most famous as the location of the infamous Hickok-McCanles shooting of 1861. The reconstruction of both the east and west ranch house complexes was done to appear as they did at that time. There is a fine museum, campground, and picnic area. The trail swales are on both sides of the creek, but those on the west side are the most vivid and dramatic. It is one of this author's family's favorite places to camp. You can still hear the coyotes!

The park is located about five miles east of Fairbury, Nebraska off highway 8 on County Road 710.

STUHR MUSEUM OF THE PRAIRIE PIONEER, GRAND ISLAND, NEBRASKA

While the focus of this museum is the late 1800s, there are exhibits and structures dealing with the local Indians and the early pioneers that make this a worthwhile stop for our trail followers, and especially if other aspects of the old west are of interest. The museum is located on the north side of the Platte River trail system coming from the Council Bluffs area.

It can be found south of Grand Island, east on U.S. Highway 34 off U.S. Highway 281.

KEARNEY AREA, NEBRASKA

A great place to stop, rest, and learn about the history of the West and Nebraska.

THE ARCHWAY, KEARNEY, NEBRASKA

For those traveling on I-80 you can't miss seeing the Archway. It is east of Kearney and goes from one side of the interstate highway to the other. There is a terrific center inside. You can take a walking tour of the history of the Platte River Valley. You start by taking a modern esculator up and through a wagon, and then your journey back in time begins. You hear and see the buffalo, American Indians, trappers, Oregon & California emigrants, Mormons, Pony Express, the railroad, Lincoln Highway, and the Interstate Highway. This cleverly designed and constructed exhibit is entertaining and educational for every member of the family. Outside is a reconstructed Pawnee lodge and homesteaders' cabin.

Take Kearney exit off I-80 and head for the Archway.

Fort Kearny, Kearney, Nebraska

This fort is a Nebraska State Historic Park. It originally was named Fort Childs and was constructed in 1848 by Lieutenant Woodbury. Today the visitor center has displays about the fort's history and the westward migrations. A blacksmith shop has been reconstructed along with the powder magazine over its original site, and a stockade. One can walk the main parade and see the locations of many of the other buildings. The last of the trees planted by Lt. Woodbury died a few years ago, but the remnants of it lie where it fell. The visitor center also has some displays related to the Pony Express. The area surrounding the fort is quite different from trail times when it was dry and sandy. Today irrigation has transformed it into a rich agricultural area.

The fort is located south and east of Kearney about four miles off Nebraska 10 on V Road.

Also located in the town is the Trails and Rails Museum. The office is the old train station. Many other old buildings have been moved to the site and can be visited where an individual can get a feel for earlier town life.

Although Harold Warp's Pioneer Village in Minden is not in the immediate vicinity, it is about an hour away and worth a visit if time allows. It has a number of William H. Jackson paintings and old historic structures and buildings full of displays of every type of item.

North Platte, Nebraska

Although there is no specific site related solely to the California Trail here, there are a number of places that may be of interest to those following the trail and are interested in related topics. Buffalo Bill's Scout Rest Ranch, a state historic park, has displays about his life and legend from his days as a scout and hunter to his Wild West shows. The Golden Spike Tower and Visitor Center is at the largest railroad yard and switching center in the United States. The Lincoln

County Museum has a reconstructed railroad town with some of their buildings originally from the old Fort McPherson, road ranches along the Oregon-California trail, the Pony Express and many other sites. Just off Interstate 80 is the Fort Cody Trading Post which has not only great items for tourists, but also displays with many interesting historical artifacts associated with the old west.

CALIFORNIA HILL, BRULE, NEBRASKA

Today a historical monument and roadside sign identify this location. California Hill was climbed after the emigrants using the Lower Crossing had forded the South Platte River. A monument by a farmhouse marks the beginning of the climb. A roadside Nebraska Historic Site sign located by a section line farm road tells the story. For those who wish to see more, drive about one-half mile north up the hill on the farm road to a small pull-off on the left. In the field are the windblown ruts made by the wagons as they climbed the rest of the hill to the plateau.

The marker and signs are on the north side of U.S. Highway 30, 4½ & 5 miles west of Brule, Nebraska.

JULESBURG, COLORADO

Later, the main fording of the South Platte, often called the Upper Crossing, was made in present-day Colorado near old Julesburg. This is the ford depicted in Jackson's painting. Within Julesburg are two small museums, the Fort Sedgwick Museum and the Depot Museum. They focus on the later period of the trail, including early settlements, the military, railroads, and the Pony Express. On U.S. Highway 138, east of Ovid, there is a historic sign about Fort Sedgwick. About one mile east of it was the crossing area. A marker notes the site of old Julesburg, the Pony Express station & Upper Crossing.

The Colorado Welcome center off I-80 has information about the various museums and trails in the area and a recommended driving route.

ASH HOLLOW, NEBRASKA

Today this site is a Nebraska State Historic Park. Ash Hollow is where the trail which had come north from the California Crossing and Hill dropped off the plateau into the North Platte River Valley. At Windlass Hill, looking up one can see the vivid scars of the trail as they comes down the hill. From a climb to its top, one can look back and see the scar cut into the top of the ridge coming from the plateau. Also in the park is Ash Hollow Spring that welcomed the emigrants and their animals after crossing the dry plateau between the forks of the Platte and their arduous descent. At the mouth of the valley is a pioneer cemetery. Unfortunately, the visitor center on the bluff is open on a limited basis.

Ash Hollow is located on U.S. Highway 26 just before it crosses the North Platte River as the highway approaches Lewellen, Nebraska, from the south. The old camping ground in the park closed years ago, but a private one has opened on the north side of the river.

COURT HOUSE & CHIMNEY ROCK, NEBRASKA

Both Nebraska State Historic Sites, these prominent landmarks on the trail are still a wonder to be seen by modern travelers. Driving west, Court House and Jail Rock are the first to come into view. There is no visitor center at the site, but the drive to it gives one the sense that the emigrants had as they walked miles off the trail to see it. Today, one can drive to its base.

Chimney Rock holds the dual distinction of also being a National Historic Landmark. Just east of the site is a fine visitor and interpretive center. Chimney Rock was the most recorded landmark of the trails west. The focus of the center is the emigrant experience in the area with related displays. Especially interesting is the display of sketches made of the site by both early travelers and young visitors today. However, it is the view of this landmark that still excites the modern traveler. As you approach the area, strain your eyes to be the first to get a glimpse of "something" just sticking up on the distant horizon—that is the real thrill! For those driving by at night, they will see something the emigrants never did: Chimney Rock is now lit up and can be seen for miles. For those interested in camping there is a private campground just off Highway 92 after turning towards Chimney Rock.

Court House and Jail Rock are located about five miles south of Bridgeport, Nebraska on highway 88. Chimney Rock is located about fifteen miles west of Bridgeport south off Nebraska Highway 92 near Bayard, Nebraska.

SCOTTS BLUFF NATIONAL MONUMENT, GERING, NEBRASKA

The early emigrants and forty-niners did not go through Mitchell Pass here at Scotts Bluff National Monument, but traveled a few miles south through Robidoux Pass. There are some markers there noting the location of certain historical sites. Information about Robidoux Pass is included in the Oregon Trail Museum. The trail museum is in the Scotts Bluff Visitor Center. Today modern travelers can walk along the swale of the trail through the pass that was opened in 1851 to one of the emigrant camping grounds. After its opening the route was heavily used, and the route through Robidoux Pass fell into disuse. This was also the route used by the later Pony Express and then the telegraph. Within the museum is one of the finest displays of paintings of scenes along the trail by William Henry Jackson. Until recently, it held possibly the single largest collection of Jackson illustrations in its research facilities.

Mitchell Pass and the Oregon Trail Museum are located on Highway 92 just west of Gering, Nebraska. Next to it is the North Platte Valley/ Legacy of the Plains and Farmer and Ranch Museum which has a variety of exhibits related to the history of the area and is also worth a visit.

FORT LARAMIE NATIONAL HISTORIC SITE,
FT. LARAMIE, WYOMING

Today Fort Laramie is a National Historic Site and has perhaps some of the best displays along the California Trail. It is the pride and joy of the National Park Service. This was the site of the first Fort William (Laramie) and the second, Fort John (Laramie). On the grounds are buildings from the third Fort Laramie. The sutler's store and old Bedlam, both constructed in 1849 are the oldest buildings. Other structures from the military period have been restored and are also full of interesting displays. Plan on spending a few hours there in order to walk around and take in all the exhibits. Depending on the day, one may be able to speak with the sutler, the wives of officers and enlisted men, trappers, laundresses, cavalrymen, or infantry men. Within a few miles of the fort are fine examples of trail ruts and an emigrant grave.

The fort is located three miles west of the town of Fort Laramie off U.S. Highway 26.

REGISTER CLIFF & OREGON TRAIL RUTS, GUERNSEY, WYOMING

These two areas have no physical visitor centers, but should not be missed. They are Wyoming State Historic Sites, and both offer the impressive physical evidence of the westward trek. The trail swales are next to Register Cliff which is full of names carved by emigrants and travelers. A couple of miles farther west is the Oregon Trail Ruts site. Here are the excellent examples of the effects of the thousands of wagons that cut their way deep into the hills and rocks. In places, the wagon wheel cuts are more than three feet deep, and the tire and wheel marks are vividly evident. Here you can walk along the trail ruts and imagine the sights and sounds of the oxen bellowing, the wagon wheels scraping, and the emigrants shouting as they pulled up and over these rocky hills.

Both areas are located on the south side of the North Platte in Guernsey off U.S. Highway 26. Local signs will point the way.

WYOMING PIONEER MEMORIAL MUSEUM, DOUGLAS, WYOMING

This fine museum covers the Oregon-California Trail period and more! There is something for everyone, including exhibits about pioneer life, ranching, Indians, period clothing, and cartography. It is located on the Douglas County Fairgrounds/Wyoming State Fair Park at 400 W. Center, near the main entrance in Douglas.

About nine miles north of Douglas on Wyoming 93 is Fort Fetterman. It is associated with the Bozeman Trail. Eleven miles west of Douglas and four miles south off I-25, exit 151, is Ayers Natural Bridge, a site visited by some emigrants.

CASPER AREA, WYOMING

Within the area of Casper are some important sites. One is **Fort Caspar**, which has been reconstructed on site and has many displays. The visitor center has even more exhibits about the history of the fort. Also on the fort's grounds is a partial reconstruction of the Guinard Bridge, and one can see some of the remains of the earth and log crib on which the rest of the bridge stood. Within the city are the sites of the Mormon Ferry established in 1847 and the Reshaw Bridge. Fort

Caspar is located on Fort Caspar Road just before it crosses the North Platte in the western part of Casper.

The **National Historic Trails Center** interprets the four National Historic Trails that passed through the Casper area: Oregon, California, Mormon and Pony Express. The learning experience begins as one approach and continues inside. There are a variety of multimedia and interactive displays and exhibits that will please and inform everyone. The center is on a hill on the north side of Casper off exist 189, I-25 at 1501 Poplar Street.

Southwest of Casper off Highway 220 is the site of the last emigrant crossing of the North Platte—Red Buttes/ **Bessemer Bend**. It was the fording area used by the emigrants until 1847. Today there is a small interpretive display and walk. Across the dirt road on the hill is the site of the later Red Buttes Overland Stage and Pony Express station and Goose Egg Ranch. (See also Oregon Trail Road below.)

Between Casper and Fort Bridger there are no major museums focused solely on the California Trail, but there are a number of interpretive sites and landmarks along the trail, that will be noted. Such landmarks helped to keep the emigrants and trappers headed in the right direction. Interestingly, the City of Casper was named in honor of Lieutenant Caspar Collins, who had been killed in Battle of Red Buttes. However, his name was misspelled in the process of the naming of the town.

OREGON TRAIL ROAD (COUNTY ROAD 319)

While Highway 220 is the main paved road west out of Casper, there is another road for those who don't mind a little adventure and "a little dust." It is a dirt road, the Oregon Trail Road. It can be joined by two approaches, one in Casper and the other at Bessemer Bend. A good local map would be useful. The connecting road out of Casper on the north side of the river is the Poison Spider Road. For the Bessemer Bend connection take Bessemer Bend Road (CR 308), now a dirt road, north from the interpretive area. It will make some 90 degree turns but will connect with County Road 319. Driving the Oregon Trail Road will give you a feel for the trail and the conditions the emigrants faced. It is not a well-traveled road and has no services and much of it passes through private property. Stay on the road, but look for the swales and white and/or concrete trail markers along . On it you will pass through Rock Avenue, aka Devil's Backbone, which is on state land. Here the road is on or near the visible trail swales. Farther down the road past Willow Springs, at the top of Prospect Hill is a BLM pullout with panels. The view towards Independence Rock and Devil's Gate is impressive and trail ruts run through it. Other trail sites are also marked. The road joins Wyoming Highway 220 a few miles east of Independence Rock.

INDEPENDENCE ROCK, WYOMING

This Wyoming State Historic Site rivals Chimney Rock, Nebraska, as claimant to being the most famous of all trail landmarks. Many century-old carvings and paintings of the names of emigrants and trappers can still be found on the rock. One can climb the rock as thousands of emigrants did. There is an interpretive site and display. Trail swales are next to the parking area in this beautiful rest stop where emigrants camped.

The site is about fifty miles west of Casper on Wyoming Highway 220 and is a must see stop.

DEVIL'S GATE, WYOMING

This was a famous landmark and a curiosity to the westward emigrant. Many emigrants took time to try to climb it or walk through it. There is an interpretive site off Highway 220 about five miles west of Independence Rock.

The site is also associated with the Mormon Trail and is the location of the Mormon Handcart Historic Site and Visitor Center. It is concerned with the Mormon handcart migration, disaster, and Martin's Cove. The site is the former headquarters for the famous Tom Sun Ranch. Rattlesnake Pass is just to the east of the former Sun Ranch. This center's entrance is less than a mile from the Devil's Gate interpretive site off Highway 220. Trail ruts are visible in the area as well as walking paths to Devil's Gate. All the trails — Oregon, California, Mormon, and Pony Express followed the same route here.

SPLIT ROCK, WYOMING

From Devil's Gate on the western horizon the next landmark that becomes visible is Split Rock. As was the case with many of the other landmarks, a Pony Express station was also located nearby. The Interpretative site is located on U.S. Highway 287.

From this point west to the highway crossing of the Sweetwater, the trail is wiggling, more or less parallel to the highway, usually between it and the river.

ICE SLOUGH, WYOMING

This site is easy to drive by. There is only a small interpretative panel. The trail crosses the highway here. The trail marker is there but difficult to see. The site is located a little more than nine miles west of Jeffrey City. From here the paved highway begins to turn northwest towards Lander, while the trail continues west. The next easily accessible site associated with the California Trail is South Pass.

SOUTH PASS, WYOMING

Today South Pass can be viewed in two ways. The interpretative site and displays are located four miles west of the actual South Pass on Highway 28, about forty-five miles southwest of Lander. Here you look back east. The visible green area is the indicator of Pacific Springs and behind it up on the saddle is the South Pass.

The actual South Pass can be visited by driving back east about four and a half miles from the interpretive site. Turn to the right on Oregon Buttes Road, a dirt road. At the sign to South Pass, go three miles, turn right again on a dirt road on the trail and drive about one mile to the pass itself. A little more than two miles west from there is the famous Pacific Springs. Be sure to check the trail roads, they can be a little rough!

Also in the area are the old mining towns of South Pass City and Atlantic City. Much has been done to restore these old towns in recent years to make them interesting stops.

"PARTING OF THE WAYS," WYOMING

About five miles west of the South Pass interpretive site is a highway historic marker. For many years this had been identified as the "parting of the ways" where the Sublette Cutoff started its westward route to the Green and then Bear River valleys. The actual split is farther west, but the trail ruts are clearly visible in this area. The more recent trail markers are in the trail. The trail crossed Highway 28 just east of the pull-out and can be seen continuing to the west and then northwest from the pull-off.

BIG SANDY & FARSON, WYOMING, TO THE GREEN RIVER

Present-day Farson, Wyoming, was the site of the trail's crossing of the Big Sandy. The main crossing was just west of the intersection with Highway 187 near the Pony Express station marker. Farson is also the home of the "Big Cone," If you like ice cream, you'll love the Farson Mercantile. It is the perfect place to rest and cool off after a long hot drive along the trail.

West of Farson one can now drive very near the trail on a paved road (Highway 28) all the way to the Green River. For those who did not drive on the Oregon Trail Road west of Casper to near Independence Rock, this will allow a safer, but similar experience (Still no services.) Once out of Farson, the area has changed very little all the way to the Green River. Be sure to stop at the historical markers on the road. After crossing the bridge over the Green there is another interpretative site. This describes the Lombard Ferry Crossing. A replica of the type of ferry used is there. There are other nearby sites such Seedskadee National Wildlife Refuge & Visitor Center and, for those interested in camping on the Green, the Slate Creek campground.

FORT BRIDGER, BRIDGER, WYOMING

This is the location of Bridger and Vasquez's early trading post. Today it is a State Historic Park. Extensive archaeological work has identified the location of Bridger's trading post and also more of the Mormon stone fort. There is an open display area of the site. There is a fine replica of Bridger's post a short distance from its original site. The visitor center has very good displays relating to the fort's history — mountain men, Indian, emigrant, stage, Pony Express, and military. A number of buildings from the military period have been restored and are open. It was here that the emigrants had to decide if they were going to California by way of Salt Lake or Fort Hall.

Fort Bridger is located off I-80, Exit 34 on the business loop in the western part of the town of Fort Bridger.

PIONEER TRAIL STATE PARK

This park is on the branch of the old trail into Salt Lake City through Little Emigration Canyon. There is a visitor center and picnic grounds available for the modern traveler. Most of the displays are related to the Mormon migration into the area and their development of the region. "Old Deseret," a recreated pioneer village, depicts life

309

from 1847-69, and it also includes Brigham Young's farmhouse. Here is the Mormon monument "This is the Place," commemorating the Mormon entrance into the Salt Lake Valley and Promised Land.

The Park is located off Highway 186 at the mouth of Emigration Canyon in the eastern part of Salt Lake City. Within the city are more sites of historical interest for those interested in the Mormon migration.

NATIONAL OREGON/CALIFORNIA TRAILS CENTER, MONTPELLIER, IDAHO

The center is located on a former camping area on the trail. Within this fine center one can really get a feel of the trail in a simulation ride, crossing, and campfire. You'll also get a chance to visit the mercantile and blacksmith. It is a terrific interactive experience for young and old alike. Don't miss it! Additional displays are also in the center.

The center is located on U.S. Highway 30 and its junction with U.S. Highway 89, 320 North 4th Street.

SODA SPRINGS, IDAHO

This was the location of the famous Steamboat Springs and Geyser that many emigrants wrote about. Unfortunately, today it is covered by the Alexander Reservoir and not visible, except for ripples that show on the surface on very calm days. However, just north of the city, a little more than one mile and half miles off 3rd Street East, are the famous Hooper Springs. They are located in a city park. One can drink the water there just as the emigrants did. Within the heart of the city are the remnants of the old cones of Pyramid Springs like that painted by Wilkins and a man-controlled geyser which is of special interest to young children. The present geyser is more like "Old Faithful" than the Steamboat Spring and Geyser seen by the early emigrants. The park with its exhibits is on Geyser Park Street off Main Street. Nearby is Octagon Spring, another soda spring. The swale of the trail can be found as it traverses the present golf course and also in the Oregon Trail Park by the reservoir at the west end of town.

A few miles west of town is Sheep Rock the western most point of the range. This is where the Oregon–California Trail turned right or north to Ft. Hall and where the Hudspeth or Myers Cutoff continued west to bypass Fort Hall. It is also where the California bound emigrants of the 1841 Bartleson-Bidwell party turned South and then traveled down the western side of the Great Salt Lake. Near the split are two old low volcanic cones mentioned by many of the early emigrants.

FORT HALL REPLICA, POCATELLO, IDAHO

The site of the actual fort is on the Fort Hall Indian Reservation and is identified only by a marker. Permission to visit the site and old trail sites on the reservation must be sought and granted by the Shoshone Bannock Tribes. However, a full-size replica of the 1834 fort has been built and can be visited. In it are displays from the trapping era and the emigration period. The 49er J. Goldsborough Bruff would feel right at home.

The fort is located in the upper level of Ross Park. It is off I-15, Exit 67, north on business loop for a little more than a half mile, and then left on Avenue of Chiefs. Also next door are the Pocatello Zoo and the Bannock County Historical Museum which has informative displays on the history of the area.

The small but informative Shoshone-Bannock Tribal Museum tells the story of the Shoshone and Bannock peoples, their culture and history and is worth a visit. Plans are being developed to expand it. It is located just off I-15 at exit 80 on the reservation north of Pocatello.

MASSACRE ROCK STATE PARK, IDAHO

Within the park grounds is a visitor center with displays and interpretive panels about the trail and the emigrant-Indian fighting that occurred along the trail in the area to the east. There are also deep trail swales that can be accessed and followed. Camping, hiking and picnicking are all available in the park. Nearby is another trail site, Register Rock, located in a favorite emigrant camping ground.

The park is located ten miles west of American Falls off I-86, exit 28, Register Road on Park Lane, north of the interstate.

CITY OF ROCKS NATIONAL RESERVE, ALMO, IDAHO

Through this geologically unique valley passed the California bound emigrants who had taken the Fort Hall Road and also those on the Hudspeth Cutoff. The cutoff rejoined the main route only a few miles before it entered the valley. The emigrants mentioned various rock formations throughout the valley and named many of them. Perhaps the most frequently commented on is the Twin Sisters or Steeple Rock at the south end of the park. It also marked the junction of the California Trail with the Salt Lake Road. Here you can enjoy the beauty created by the forces of nature, hike, horseback ride, picnic, or camp where the emigrants did. It is also a popular site for rock climbers.

The main visitor center is located in the little town of Almo, Idaho, on the Elba-Almo Road before you enter the valley from the east. Castle Rock State Park is next door.

PILOT PEAK & DONNER SPRINGS, UTAH

The peak was the landmark the Hastings Cutoff emigrants aimed for and the springs were the life giving water after the long dry crossing of the Great Salt Lake Desert and salt flats. From Salt Lake City I-80 is very near the trail in places. It is generally on the south side following along the edges of the hills avoiding the flat wet areas. West of the Grass Mountain Rest Area, Mile 55 the trail crosses the interstate aiming for Pilot Peak which can be seen to the west from the rest area. At the Mile 22 is "Floating Island" on the north. At mile 4 at the Bonneville Salt Flats exit, it is possible to drive to Donner Spring. Most of it is by a local dirt road. Turn north and in a little over a mile the road forks. Take the left fork towards the TL Ranch on Leppy Pass Road. It will go to Pilot Peak and the ranch (about 23 miles). The ranch is on the right. The spring is on private property near the ranch house towards the flats through the cattle pens. It is a short walk from the parking area near the cabin to the spring. Remember that this is private property.

TRAIL OF THE 49'ERS INTERPRETIVE CENTER, WELLS, NEVADA

From City of Rocks and Granite Pass the main trail was heading southwest towards the Mary's or Humboldt River. Its headwaters were from the springs near Wells. There is a small museum dedicated to the California Trail, and it is manned by enthusiastic volunteers with big plans for the future. It is located off I-80, exit 352 on the business loop at #436 6th Street.

ELKO, NEVADA AREA

There are two museums and visitor centers that would appeal to our trail enthusiasts. The **Northeastern Nevada Museum** has displays on the trails, Indians, pioneers, and mining in this area. Outside is part of the restored Ruby Valley Pony Express Station. It is located on 1515 Idaho Street in the heart of town.

The recently constructed **BLM California National Historic Trail Interpretive Center** is located about ten miles west of Elko at exit 292, I-80. This center's many excellent inside and outside displays are devoted to interpret the story on the California Trail, and, especially, its relationship to the "Elephant." The center is located a few miles north of where the Hastings Cutoff finally rejoined the main California Trail and east of where the emigrants either took the dry Greenhorn Cutoff or followed the river through Carlin Canyon.

RYE PATCH RESERVOIR STATE RECREATION AREA, NEVADA
While there is no major museum or center here, the trail was on both sides of the Humboldt River. Travelers today can picnic or camp along the Humboldt and look up at the stars at night much the way the emigrants did in this area more than one hundred seventy years ago. Drive over the dam to the west side of the river and in about one mile west on the somewhat winding road there is an intersection; turn right. Soon a number of parallel trails ruts will appear on the river side.

The recreation area is located on Highway 401 about one mile west off the I-80 Rye Patch Siding exit 129.

CHURCHILL COUNTY MUSEUM, FALLON, NEVADA
This is another of the fine county museums that can be found along the trail. As with others, the focus of this county museum is wider than only the trail period, but that is part of its special appeal. The trail is put in its proper perspective. The displays relate to the California Trail, Pony Express, Indians and the geological features of the region — there are displays for every interest.

The museum is located at 1050 Maine Street in Fallon, Nevada

NEVADA STATE MUSEUM, CARSON CITY, NEVADA
The State Museum is located in the old Carson City Mint which has a history unto itself. It houses the artifacts that tell the story of Nevada – "A Walk through Time." For those interested in the native Americans, it has extensive exhibits. The mining industry is also emphasized. There are changing exhibits including the present one on Charles Fremont, who was an important person in Nevada's history.

The museum is located at 600 North Carson Street, a few blocks from the State Capitol.

Fort Churchill State Historic Monument, Nevada

This fort was built in 1860 on an alternate river route of the Carson Trail and Pony Express Trail. It was constructed in response to the Pyramid Lake/Paiute War to protect the emigrants and pioneers in the Carson Valley. The fort was abandoned in 1869 and sold by 1870. There is a visitor center with interpretive displays related to its military role in the region. The fort's ruins have been stabilized and one can walk around the large main parade and imagine what it must have been like. Camping, picnicking and hiking are available on the grounds.

The fort is located about ten miles south of Silver Springs off U.S. Highway 95 on Fort Churchill Road, CR 2B, U.S. Alternate Route 50.

Mormon Station Historic State Monument, Genoa, Nevada

Here is a replica of the Mormon Station which was first constructed in 1850. It includes a stockade and trading post. Many emigrants stopped here on the Carson Route. They were able to rest briefly and if lucky, obtain some needed supplies before their hard pull over the Sierra Nevada. The small town that grew up around the station was named by Orson Hyde, an early emigrant because the area reminded him of the mountains behind Genoa, Italy.

Mormon Station is locate at 2295 Main Street in Genoa about four miles west, off U.S. Highway 395 on Genoa Lane/SR 57. Inside are displays about the history of Genoa and the station. Across the street is the Genoa Courthouse Museum. This museum is affiliated with the Carson Valley Museum in Gardnerville, Nevada, which also has exhibits about the history of the Carson Valley, Washoe Indians, the California Trail and the Pony Express Trail. It is on U.S. Highway 395 in Gardnerville and worth a visit.

Carson, Ranger Station, Carson Pass, California

At the top of Carson Pass or the "first summit" on the Carson Route is a small forest service station. Inside this crowded station you may find information about the site, but the real feature is just east of the station and downhill a little in another parking lot. The view from near the lot is of the area the trail just climbed with Red Lake at its base. A short walk brings you to the trail itself, and if you want to, you can hike down and up to experience just how steep the climb up "Devil's Ladder" was for the emigrants.

The station is at Carson Pass on California Highway 88.

State Historical Society Museum, Reno, Nevada

The Truckee Meadows was a great emigrant camping and recruiting area, and today it is the site of an expanding Reno. It is also the home of the Nevada State Historical Society's museum, a place to rest and learn about Nevada's history. Within the museum are permanent exhibits on "Living from the Land" focused on the native peoples of the Great Basin, including the Washoe, Northern and Southern Paiutes, and Western Shoshone and the impact of trapping and ranching. Another section focuses on the concept of "Passing Through" and the emigrants and trails. "Riches from the Earth" deals with the Comstock Era and mining. Others deal with "Neon Lights," the gaming and tourist activities, and the federal government's role in Nevada.

The museum is located at 1650 North Virginia Street, University of Nevada campus.

Donner Memorial State Park, California

The park and Emigrant Trail Museum is dedicated to all those emigrants who risked their lives in the attempt to get to California, but the area is especially known for the ordeal endured by the Donner Party during the harsh winter of 1846.

Near the park's entrance are the monument and a fine expanded visitor center/museum. Some members of the Donner Party camped in the present park while others, including the Donner family, camped nearby on Alder Creek off Highway 89. The party had been traveling on the Truckee Route. In the vicinity of Truckee Lake they decided to camp before they attempted their final climb over Truckee (Donner) Pass. Then the snows came. As noted in the history section, it appears that many members of the party finally resorted to cannibalism in order to survive that dreadful winter. Donner Pass is not located on I-80, but off old U.S. Highway 40, Donner Pass Road which generally follows the old wagon route. The drive is worth it. The recently

315

identified Stephens Pass is to its north closer to I-80. For hikers in the family, the Pacific Coast Trail from Donner Pass connects with Roller Pass and the later Cold Stream Pass. They were higher, but the climb, perhaps, easier. A variety of activities are available in the park including, swimming, hiking, picnicking and camping.

The park is located off I-80 on U.S. Highway 10 on Donner pass Road at the east end of (Truckee) Donner Lake.

LASSEN VOLCANIC NATIONAL PARK, CALIFORNIA

Within the park are the remnants of the Nobles' Road and the Lassen Trail. They are located in the northern portion of the park. Information can be obtained at the visitor center at the northwest park entrance station near the junction of California Highway 44 and 89. It is about 55 miles east of Redding.

The Lassen Peak and National Forest was part of the hunting grounds for a number of California Indian tribes including the Yahi. This area is associated with Ishi, the last of the Yahi. Information concerning the local tribes' basketry is in the Loomis Museum in the park.

SACRAMENTO, CALIFORNIA

Two of the major attractions for trail enthusiasts are Sutter's Fort and "Old Town" in Sacramento. **Sutter's Fort**, the center of Sutter's New Helvetia, was the goal of most of the early emigrants and Argonauts. Sutter's Fort has been reconstructed to appear as it did just before the gold rush. The restored central adobe building is the only remaining original structure; the rest of the structures and walls have been reconstructed. There are a variety of displays concerning the fort's functions and role in the early history of California. Unfortunately for Sutter, when gold was discovered, it did not bring him wealth as he thought it might, but instead it resulted in the destruction of his empire. The fort is located on Twentieth and L Street in Sacramento. It has just completed its first major restoration program inside and out in over fifty years. It provides a prefect way for all to learn about and enjoy its history.

Sacramento's **"Old Town"** is well worth a visit. There are a number of interesting museums and sites. Sacramento was subject to flooding during its early years and there are a few places where one can see how the problem was dealt with. The Sacramento History Museum, located at 101 I Street, has extensive sections on Sacramento's early history, the California Trail and gold rush. Just down the block is the California State Railroad Museum, one of the largest and best in the world. Adults or kids, if they love trains, this is the place. Sacramento was also important in the history of the Pony Express and has sites related to it.

MARSHALL GOLD DISCOVERY STATE HISTORIC PARK & MUSEUM, COLOMA, CALIFORNIA

Here, gold was first discovered by James Marshall in 1848. The Gold Discovery Museum, with its various displays and programs, the Marshall statue, and a replica of the mill that was being constructed when gold was discovered are on the park's grounds. Marshall is buried in the park. Kids will enjoy the nature center and gold panning. Also, within the town are other restored historic buildings from the gold rush era.

The park is located on Coloma Road, California 49, in the town of Coloma, California, and the visitor center and museum at 310 Back Street of Highway 49.

PLACERVILLE CALIFORNIA – HISTORIC DISTRICT

This was one of the many gold towns that developed in California. It was originally known as "Dry Diggings," but soon became known as "Hang Town" because it was the first gold town to use hanging as a method of dealing with lawbreakers. This was the goal of Betsey and Ike of the folksong. Today there are a number of buildings that date from the gold rush era. One purportedly holds the remains of the old hanging tree. There are also a number of events related to its early history that would be of interest to travelers. One is the annual wagon train celebration held in June. It starts out at Lake Tahoe and follows U.S. Highway 50, which closely approximates the Johnson's Cutoff of the Carson Route into Placerville. The Placerville Museum has displays on the California Trail and its history in the Tallman Building at 524 Main Street (U.S. Highway 50). The El Dorado County Museum has displays on mining and its early history. It is located at 104 Placerville Rd, off U.S. 50.

THE END OF THE TRAIL, CALIFORNIA

For any traveler whose primary interest is the gold rush era, California Highway 49 from Mariposa in the south to Sierraville in the north, traverses the area frequently called the "Mother Lode." Most of the small towns are associated with the gold rush and have buildings from that period. Many have small museums or places of interest that are worthwhile. If time is not a problem, the ride is slow, long, beautiful, and full of interesting places. This larger area was the goal and "El Dorado" that the forty-niners sought. Another approach would be to visit the towns at or near the terminus of the other routes, such as Shasta and Redding at the end of the Nobles Trail.

There are many more places along the trail in addition to those mentioned. There are numerous highway historical markers, waysides and interpretative panels along the highways or in rest areas not mentioned. More are being added by the appropriate federal and state governmental units. Local towns and historical groups have become more active in preserving and interpreting their history. Some have pamphlets describing local sites. It is important to keep one's "eyes peeled." All these will provide the modern "emigrant" with information about the trail. They usually do not require a lot of time to visit, but they add to one's appreciation and understanding of the emigrants' trek to California and should be examined. The "gold" is still there!

Chapter Nine

Additional Reading

It's been more than thirty-five years since I first started my research for this book and thirty years since it was first published. It was republished in 1993 with some additional information. In the ensuing years I have researched and written books on other historic trails. During this time there have also been many additional volumes published about the California Trail. Many of the books I used or recommended are now harder to find or obtain. Some are still in print. Some volumes have revised editions, which are helpful, but, unfortunately, a few other excellent ones are now out of print. However, most of this section will be left basically as first written with minor changes. At the end I will add additional comments and a few recommendations.

As mentioned at the very beginning of this volume one of my goals was to inspire the reader's interest enough so they would want to find out more about the California Trail and the westward movement and would see the value in preserving the trails. Mentioned here are some of the basic books, but there are many others that specialize on specific topics. This is one opportunity to begin your involvement in a quest for information.

There are a variety of books available on emigrant trails. Every year new books both large and small are become available. Since the main California Trail coincided with the Oregon Trail for more than its first half, this gives U.S. a place to begin our investigation into the publications available for your use as a modern emigrant or argonaut traveling the California Trail. There are two very fine books written by Gregory Franzwa about the Oregon Trail. The two books actually supplement each other.

The Oregon Trail Revisited is the first book. It takes the reader mile by mile and turn by turn along the modern highways and farm roads that most closely follow the twists and turns of the old emigrant trail that began in Independence, Missouri. Along with this milepost approach to the trail there are comments from various emigrants who had taken it themselves. When there are places where the modern traveler might not be able to venture in a passenger car, those places are noted. The important historic sites along the way are also mentioned and their significance is explained. Franzwa's later editions also contain additional information. While the book does not include all the routes from the jumping-off places, the modern traveler can use this as a guide from Independence and drive along most of the trail all the way past Fort Hall to the Raft River where the California Trail turns off.

Franzwa's second book is *Maps of the Oregon Trail.* It is perhaps even better for the traveler who reads maps well and can visualize the trip. Again the emphasis is on the main Oregon Trail from Independence, Missouri, so the book is primarily useful for the same section of the California Trail as mentioned above. Most of the maps are drawn having a scale of one-half inch to a mile and include not only the main roads but also the section line and farm roads. The book also indicates many of the important cutoffs, which were not included in his first book. Additionally, his maps are constantly being updated for most of the recent discoveries concerning the trail in his new additions. The locations of large segments of visible trail ruts are also located on the maps as are the related historic sites. Therefore, they are much easier for the present-day traveler to find and see.

Another related book is *Historic Sites along the Oregon Trail* by Aubrey Haines. It contains the specific locations of 394 sites of which 318 also relate to the California Trail section. These same sites are located in Franzwa's book of maps. They include items such as major forts, crossings, landmarks, locations of some graves, and even prominent camping grounds with emigrant comments about each place.

For a historic overview of the development of the trail and the various jumping-off places mentioned earlier in the book, there is Merrill Matte's book, *The Great Platte River Road.* It covers the trails from their various points of origin through the Platte River Valley to

Fort Laramie. The book includes a wealth of information, and the trail is vividly described by the extensive use of primary source materials.

Another book, which also gives the reader a broad overview of the emigrant experience, is John Unruh's *The Plains Across*. Unlike the other books already mentioned it does not take the reader mile by mile along the trail, but instead discusses the development of the Oregon and California trails over time. It examines the forces that impacted the trails and their interrelationships. Various topics, such as improvements in the trail, Indians, Mormons, trading posts, the government, emigrant motivations and opinions, are all discussed. This approach employed in the above book gives the modern traveler an excellent perspective of the trail experienced by the emigrants.

Perhaps one of the best books for describing the overall historical development of the California Trail is George Stewart's *The California Trail: An Epic with Many Heroes*. It is considered one the classics of the California Trail books. It covers the development of the trail starting with the Bartleson-Bidwell party in 1841. From that period until the gold rush, it has a chapter for each year. It mentions the wagon companies for each year and the major ones for the years when travel was heavy. After the gold rush in 1849 additional routes were developed. Stewart spends less time on the developments during the 1850s. His book includes many small maps showing the locations of the trails and the various cutoffs with the years they were established. It gives one a good overview of the whole development of the California Trail.

For locating the California Trail where Franzwa's books left off there are a few suggested books. One of the most recently published works is *Emigrant Trails West* by Devere and Helene Helfrich and Thomas Hunt. It is *A Guide to Trail Markers Placed by Trails West, Inc. Along the California, Applegate, Lassen, and Nobles's Emigrant Trails in Idaho, Nevada, and California*. It includes maps of the trail drawn with a scale of four miles to an inch, the specific locations of 201 trail markers, and excerpts from diaries concerning each of the locations. Using the maps it takes the reader from marker to marker starting at the Raft River where the main California Trail leaves the Oregon Trail. It then continues down the main route of the California Trail to where the Applegate Trail turns off and the Lassen Trail begins. *Emigrant Trails West* also shows where the Nobles' route cuts off from both the Lassen and Applegate trails and follows the California Trail. However, it must be noted that this book does not include the sections for the Truckee and Carson routes that were developed before 1848 nor the Hastings Cutoff.

There is a smaller publication by the Nevada Historical Society called *The Overland Emigrant Trail to California. A Guide to Trail Markers Placed in Western Nevada and the Sierra Nevada Mountains* in California, which is helpful for tracing the Truckee and Carson trails. The historical society has placed fifty-eight markers starting at the point where the Applegate-Lassen trails branch off and then following the trail down the Humboldt to the split in the Carson and Truckee trails. It then follows both up the mountains to the divide, but unfortunately goes no farther. Its two main maps are drawn to a scale of nine miles to an inch and five miles to an inch. However, they do not include excerpts from emigrant diaries for each location.

Charles K. Graydon has written a wonderful short book, *Trail of the First Wagons over the Sierra Nevada*. It covers the Truckee route west from where it entered California until it approaches Dutch Flats. That section of the trail is then shown in ten maps. Each map has the trail marked in red and is full of details about the trail.

Another very practical book for following the trails in Idaho is *Emigrant Trails in Southern Idaho*. The first edition published in 1976 is useful, but the later 1993 edition is even better. The later edition was produced by the BLM-Bureau of Land Management, Department of the Interior, in cooperation with the Idaho State Historical Society. It includes both the Lander Road and the main trail to Fort Hall, the main trail to Goose Creek, the Hudspeth Cutoff, and the section of the Salt Lake Cutoff or Road that cuts through Idaho. It is an excellent resource with detailed maps, diary excerpts, illustrations, and other useful information about the route. If you are interested in the trail to Oregon through Idaho, this book also covers the main route and the various cutoffs that developed.

In addition to the scholarly approach to the study of the California Trail there are numerous narratives and diaries of emigrants along the trail. J. Goldsborough Bruff traveled the trail in 1849. His diary and writings are the source of many of the drawings in the pictorial section of this volume. Unfortunately, his journal published as *Gold Rush: Journals, Drawings, and Other Papers* can be found only in a few libraries. The work was published in 1949 was edited by George Read and Ruth Gaines and is excellent. Bruff was the captain of a company, and he noted almost "everything." His route took him to Fort Hall and down the Lassen or "Greenhorn" route to California. Additional information about Bruff is included in the pictorial section.

One of the journals that has recently been published is *The California Gold Rush Overland Diary of Bryon McKinstry*. This was published in 1975 and is still available. It includes both the diary of Bryon McKinstry and also the comments made by his grandson Bruce McKinstry as he tried to relocate and retrace the specific route taken to California by his Grandfather. McKinstry went to California by way of the Sublette Cutoff, Fort Hall and the Carson route. It should also be noted that McKinstry was also in the company that pioneered the route on the north side of the North Platte west of Fort Laramie and rejoined the main trail west of Deer Creek where many of the other emigrants started crossing over. The book is interesting both for its historical narrative and for the experience of one trying to locate specific sites along the California Trail.

Another of the interesting and recently published books is *Overland to California with the Pioneer Line: The Gold Rush Diary of Bernard J. Reid*, edited by Mary Gordon. The Pioneer Line was the first overland commercial venture to bring emigrants and gold seekers to California. The venture was mentioned a number of times by James Wilkins whose drawings are included in the pictorial section of this book. The book includes not only the diary, but also additional comments made later in life by Bernard Reid. Gordon also includes many comments from the diaries of other members of the train, and thus affords the reader a variety of perspectives on this first commercial and problem filled venture.

These are but a few of the many works that a student of the trail would enjoy. There is also a ten volume series called *Covered Wagon Women: Diaries and Letters from the Western Trails 1840-1860* by Arthur H. Clark Publishers. Other publishers, such as Ye Galleon Press, offer reprints of earlier published works on a limited scale. They have a number of fine reprints available for order. Two older books, which are considered classics, are Irene Paden's *The Wake of the Prairie Schooner* and *Prairie Schooner Detours*. She traveled over the old trails in the 1930s and describes both her experiences and the trails as they existed then.

Additionally, the journals of various state and local historical societies are fine sources for diaries and should not be overlooked. The publication of the Oregon-California Trails Association, *The Overland Journal*, published quarterly is another excellent source of material. It even includes information about the present condition of the trail and efforts aimed at preserving it. There are also many books available that focus on specific topics such as the Donner Party, John Sutter and the gold rush.

One other area which must be mentioned is the bibliographies of all the books mentioned. They are full of outstanding source materials, which you may find of interest.

Happy Reading! Happy Traveling!

Since the 1993 reprint of this book Greg Franzwa had published another book, *Maps of the California Trail* in 1999. It is best used with his *Maps of the Oregon Trail* since if refers back to some of its maps. It uses the same format, only the trail is marked in gray which is sometimes harder to distinguish from other lines on the maps. The segments where the trail is still visible are not identified as they are in his other map book. It includes the main route out of the Council Bluffs and also the one out of St Joseph, but not those from some of the other jumping-off towns unless portions of those routes are parallel or near the two of them. For those interested in the Mormon Trail, it does include the main Mormon route in Iowa, but not that of the handcart route. For the western section of the California Trail the main portion follows the Truckee route, and, importantly, it contains maps of the Lander, Hastings, Hensley (or Salt Lake Road or Cutoff,) Hudspeth, Applegate-Lassen, Nobles, and Carson routes. The Sublette Cutoff is in the Oregon book.

These maps are very good for anyone wishing to follow the trails using local roads and the modern highways. However, Gregory Franzwa passed away and his books are now out of print. One will have to search the net and bookstores for copies. Even though some roads have changed and additional information about the trails and the specific locations of portions have changed and new traces identified, his books are still worth searching for and using. Haines' book is also out of print but can also be found online. Mckinstry's book is also available on the net. Edwin Bryant's *What I Saw in California* was referenced in the diary section and should be reviewed and can be obtained. Irene Paden's books are also still available.

The old Trails West's *Emigrant Trails West* guide has been replaced with a new series of guides that focused on the individual segments and cutoffs. The guides start where the main California Trail turned off the Oregon Trail at the Raft River. It continues down to the Humboldt River and Wells, Nevada. For the section along the Humboldt to the sink there is another guide. Guides are then available for the Truckee, Carson, Applegate, Nobles, Beckwourth, Yreka, and Hastings routes. These with their accompanying maps and guides have more information and routes than the first printing, including the GPS coordinates for the trail markers placed by Trails West. They could also be referred to in place of the old Nevada Historical Society's book. For those wishing to follow the trail and variants, these are excellent resources. The books by Mattes, Unruh, and Stewart are still available and are highly recommended. The *Covered Wagon Women* series is also available and presents eye witness accounts over a twenty year period.

One of the most recent works, *Overland West, the Story of the Oregon and California Trails* by Will Bagley is slated to be a four volume series. Volume I, *So Rugged and Mountainous: Blazing the Trails to Oregon and California, 1812-1848*, and Volume II, *With Golden Visions Bright before Them, Trails to the Mining West, 1849-1852*, are published and available. Their focus is also about the northern routes discussed in this volume. They cover the development of the early and main routes and then most of the cutoffs that developed during the gold rush period. These are scholarly works that will provide the reader with all the details to better understand the various forces involved, the experiences of those who blazed the trails and the emigrants—men, women, and children whose use developed the trails and the Indians whose lands they passed through. Much of the material and descriptions are in these folks' own words. The two additional volumes will focus on the later years and also the vast changes and the conflicts that ensued with the American Indians through the 1860s. Taken together they will allow for a broader and more complete understanding of the westward movement. This series is highly recommended.

As mentioned earlier in this volume the National Parks Service's *Auto Tour Route Interpretive Guide* books for the trail states are also highly recommended for those driving the trail. Hopefully by the time this book is published all the state booklets will be available. The various trail related organizations and their websites should also be examined and used.

Once again, Happy Reading! Happy Traveling! And Happy Trails!

BIBLIOGRAPHY

Books, Booklets, Articles

Barry, Louise. *The Beginning of the West.* Topeka: Kansas State Historical Society, 1972.

Brock, Richard K., and Don Buck. *A Guide to the Applegate Trail from Lassen Meadow to Goose Lake.* Reno,NV: Trails West, 2010.

_____. *A Guide to the California Trails Along the Humboldt River.* Reno, NV: Trails West, 2012.

Byrant, William Cullen, *Picturesque America.* Vol. II. NY: D. Appleton & Co., 1874.

Driggs, Howard R. *Westward America.* NY:JB Lippincott, 1942.

Estergreen, M. Morgan. *Kit Carson: A Portrait in Courage.* Norman: University of Oklahoma Press, 1962.

Franzwa, Gregory. *Maps of the Oregon Trail.* Gerald, MO: Patrice Press,1982.

_____. *Maps of the California Trail.* Tucson: Patrice Press, 1999.

_____. *The Oregon trails Revisited.* Gerald, MO: Patrice Press, 1972.

Froncek, Thomas. "Winterkill, 1846. The Tragic Journey of the Donner Party." *American Heritage.* December, 1976, Vol. XXVIII, No. 1. Pp .29-42.

Ghent, WJ. *The Road to Oregon, A Chronicle of the Great Emigrant Trail.* NY: Tudor, 1934.

Gilbert, William, et. Al. *The Trail Blazers.* NY: Time/Life Books, 1973.

Graydon, Charles K. *Trail of the First Wagons Over the Sierra Nevada.* St. Louis, MO: Patrice Press, 1981.

Grebenkemper, John, Kristin Johnson, and Adela Morris. "Locating the Grave of John Synder, Field Research of a Donner Party Death." *Overland Journal.* Fall 2012, Vol. 30, No.3.pp.92-108.

Grebenkemper, John and Kristin Johnson. "Forensic Canine Search for the Donner Family Winter Camp at Alder Creek," *Overland Journal.* Summer 2015, Vol. 33, No.2. pp.64 -89.

Haines, Aubrey. *Historic Sites along the Oregon Trail.* Gerald, MO: Patrice Press, 1981.

Harris, Earl R. *Courthouse and Jail Rocks.* Nebraska State Historical Society, 1962.

Helfrich, Devere and Helene, and Thomas Hunt. *Emigrant Trails West.* Klamath Falls, OR: Craft Printers, Trails West, Inc. 1974.

Hill, William E. *The Oregon Trail, Yesterday and Today*. Caldwell, ID: The Caxton Printers, Ltd., 1986.

_____. *The Pony Express Trail, Yesterday and Today*. Caldwell, ID: Caxton Press, 2010.

_____. *The Mormon Trail, Yesterday and Today*, Logan: UT, Utah State University Press, 1996.

Hollecker, David. "A Report: The First Wagons over Donner Summit," *Oregon-California Trails Association Convention Book*, 2015, pp. 10-14.

Horn, Huston. *The Pioneers*. NY: Time/Life Books, 1974.

Jackson, Clarence S. *Pageant of the Pioneers. The Veritable Art of William H. Jackson*. Minden, NE: Harold Warp Pioneer Village, 1958.

_____. *Picture Maker of the Old West*, William H. Jackson. NY: Bonanza Books, 1947.

Jackson, Donald Dale. *Gold Dust*. NY: Alfred A. Knopf, Inc., 1980.

Jackson, Joseph Henry, ed. *Gold Rush Album*. NY: Bonanza Books, 1949.

Jackson, William Henry. *Time Exposure*. NY: GP Putnam's Sons, 1940.

Johnson, Paul C. *Pictorial History of California*. NY: Bonanza Books, 1970.

Jonson, William W. *The Forty-Niners*. NY: Time/Life Books, 1974.

Lavender, David. *California: A Bicentennial History*. WW Norton & Company, Inc., 1976.

_____. *The American Heritage History of the Great West*. NY: Bonanza Books, 1982.

Laxalt, Robert, and others. *Trails West*. Washington, DC: National Geographic Society, 1979.

Lewis, Oscar. *Sutter's Fort: Gateway to the Gold Fields*. Engelwood Cliffs, NJ: Prentice Hall, Inc., 1966.

Mattes, Merrill J. *Chimney Rock Nebraska*. Nebraska State Historical Society. 1978.

_____. *The Great Platte River Road*. Nebraska State Historical Society. 1969.

_____. *Scott's Bluff*. Washington, DC: National Parks Service, 1975.

_____. "The Council Bluffs Road: The Northern Branch of the Great Platte River Road," *Nebraska History*, Vol. 65: (1984), pp. 179-194.

Mokler, Alfred James. *Fort Casper*. Casper, WY: Prairie Publishing Co., 1939. Reprint: Mountain States Lithographing Co., 1982.

Moody, Ralph. *The Old Trails West*. NY: Crowell Co., 1982.

Murphy, David Royce. *Scenery, Curiosities, and Stupendous Rocks: William Quesenbury's Overland Sketches, 1850-1851*. Norman, OK: University of Oklahoma Press, 2011.

Paden, Irene D. *The Wake of the Prairie Schooner*. NY: The Macmillan Company, 1947.

_____. *Prairie Schooner Detours*. The Macmillan Company, 1949.

BIBLIOGRAPHY

Petersen, Jesse G. *A Route for the Overland Stage, James H. Simpson's 1859 Trail Across the Great Basin.* Logan, UT: Utah State University Press, 2008.

Place, Marian T. *Westward on the Oregon Trail.* NY: American Heritage Publishing Co., Inc., 1962.

Ross, Marvin C. *The West of Alfred J. Miller.* Norman: University of Oklahoma Press, 1968.

Schlissel Lillian. *Women's Diaries of the Westward Journey.* NY: Schocken Books, 1982.

Stewart, George R. *The California Trail: An Epic with Many Heroes.* NY McGraw-Hill Book Co., Inc., 1962.

Troner, Ellen Lloyd, ed. *California: A Chronicle and Documentary Handbook.* Dobbs Ferry, NY: Oceana Publications, Inc., 1972.

Unruh, John. *The Plains Across, The Overland Emigrants and the Trans-Mississippi West, 1840-1860.* Chicago: University of Illinois Press, 1979.

Wagner, Henry R. *The Plains and the Rockies: A Bibliography of Original Narratives of Travel and Adventure 1800-1865.* Columbus: Long's College Book, Co., 1953.

Watkins, T.H. *California, An Illustrated History.* New York: Weathervane Books, 1973.

Wheat, Carl I. *Mapping the Trans-Mississippi West.* Vol. III. San Francisco: Institute of Historical Cartography, 1957.

Emigrant Trails of Southeastern Idaho, Bureau of Land Management. U.S. Department of the Interior. Idaho, 1979,

"The Raft River in Idaho History." *Pacific Northwestern Qu*arterly. July 1941. Vol.32, pp. 289-305.

Story of the Great American West. Pleasantville, NY: The Reader's Digest Association, Inc., 1977.

Oregon Trail, National Historic Trail: Comprehensive Management and Use Plan. Appendix II & III. National Park Service. August, 1981.

The Overland Emigrant Trail to California. Nevada Historical Society.

Diaries, Journals, and Guidebooks

Applegate, Jesse. "A Day with the Cow Column in 1843." *Oregon Historical Quarterly.* Vol. I. December 1900, pp. 371-383.

Baker, William. *Diary of William B. Baker—California 1852.* Ventura Historical Museum.

Borthwick, JD. *Three Years in California.* William Blackwood and Sons, 1857.

Bruff, J. Goldsborough. *Gold Rush: Journals, Drawings, and Other Papers.* Edited by George Willis Read and Ruth Gaines. NY: Columbia Press, 1949.

329

Bryant, Edwin. *What I Saw in California.* NY: D. Appleton and Co. 1849.

Bryarly, Wakeman and Vincent Geiger. *Trail to California. The Overland Journal of Vincent Geiger and Wakeman Bryarly.* Edited by David Potter. New Haven: Yale University Press, 1945.

Burnett, Peter H. "Recollections and Opinions of an Old Pioneer." *Oregon Historical Quarterly.* Vol. V, 1904, pp. 64-99.

Carleton, Phebe A. "Phebe Abbot Carleton, 1864." *West from Salt Lake: Diaries from the Central Overland Trail.* Norman: The Arthur H. Clark Company. Ed. Jesse Petersen, 2012. pp.195-211.

Carpenter, Helen. "A Trip Across the Plains in an Ox Wagon, 1857," *Ho, for California: Women's Oveland Diaries.* Ed. and annotated by Sandra I. Miles. San Marino, CA: Huntington Library, 1980.

Casler, Mel. *A Journal Giving the Incidents of a Journey to California in the Summer of 1859, by the Overland Route.* Fairfield, WA: Ye Galleon Press, 1969.

Child, Andrew. *Overland Route to California.* Milwaukee: Daily Sentinel Steam Power Press, 1852.

Clayton, William. *The Latter-Day Saints' Emigrants" Guide.* St. Louis: Chambers & Knapp, 1848. Reprint:Fairfield, WA: Ye Galleon Press, 1981.

Clyman, James. *Journal of a Mountain Man.* Edited by Linda M. Hasselstrom, Missoula: Mountain Press Publishing, 1984.

Conyers, Enoch W. "Diary of E. W. Conyers, A Pioneer of 1852." *Transactions.* O.P.A. 1905: 423-512.

Cooke, Lucy Rutledge. *Crossing the Plains in 1852.* Fairfield, WA: Ye Galleon Press, 1987.

Cummings, Mariett Foster, "A Trip Across the Continent," *Covered Wagon Women: Diaries and Letters from the Western Trails, 1840-1890. Vol IV 1852,* pp. 117-208. Ed. Kenneth L. Holmes. Glendale, CA: The Arthur H. Clark Company, 1985.

Davis, Sarah, "Diary from Missouri to California, 1850," *Covered Wagon Women: Diaries and Letters from the Western Trails, 1840-1890. Vol. II, 1850,* pp. 171-206. Ed. Kenneth L. Holmes. Glendale, CA: The Arthur H. Clark Company, 1983.

Dundass, Samuel Rutherford and George Keller. *The Journals of Samuel Rutherford Dundass & George Keller. Crossing the Plains to California in 1849-1850.* Fairfiled, WA: Ye Galleon Press, 1863.

Farnham, Elijah Bryan. "From Ohio to California: The Gold Rush Diary of -----." Edited by Merriall J. Mattes. *Indiana Magazine of History*, XLVI (1950), pp.297-318, 403-420.

Fremont, John Charles. *The Exploring Expedition of the Rocky Mountains, Oregon and California.* Buffalo: Geo. H. Derby & Co. Publishers, 1849.

_____. *The Expeditions of J.C. Fremont.* 1 and 2, maps. Editied by Donald Jackson and Mary Lee Spence. Urbana: University of Illinois Press, 1970.

Frink, Margaret, "Adventures of a Party of Gold Seekers," *Covered Wagon Women: Diaries and Letters from the Western Trails, 1840-1890. Vol.II, 1850,* pp. 55-169. Ed. Kenneth L. Holmes. Glendale, CA: The Arthur H. Clark Company, 1983.

Gibson, John McTurk. *Journal of Western Travel.* Ed. Weldon Hoppe.: Colon, NE: Duck Creek Publishing, 2009.

Gray, Charles Glass. *Off at Sunrise: The Overland Journal of Charles Glass Gray.* Ed. Thomas D. Clark, San Marino: The Huntington Library, 1976.

Gordon, Mary. Ed. *Overland to California with the Pioneer Line: The Gold Rush Diary of Bernard J. Reid.* Stanford: Stanford University Press, 1983.

Hale, Israel. "Diary of Trip to California." *Society of California Pioneers Quarterly.* Vol. 2, 1925, pp.61-130.

Harvey, Charles H. *California Gold Rush: Diary of Charles H. Harvey,* February 12-November 12, 1852. Annotated by Edmund F. Ball. Indianapolis: Indiana Historical Society, 1983.

Hastings, Landsford. *The Emigrants' Guide to Oregon and California. 1845.* Reprint Princeton University Press, 1932.

Hittle, Jonas. "Diary, 1849." Original (Illinois State Historical Library).

Holmes, Kenneth L. ed. *Covered Wagon Women: Diaries and Letters from the Western trails 1840-1890.* Glendale, CA: Arthur H. Clark. Vol. I, II, III & IV, 1985.

Horn, Hosea. *Horn's Overland Guide.* NY: JH Colton, 1853.

Howell, Elijah P. *The 1849 California Trail Diaries of Elijah Preston Howell.* Ed. Susan Badger Doyle & Donald E Buck. Independence: Oregon-California Trails Association, 1995.

Hulin, Lester. *Day Book or Journal of Lester Hulin 1847.* Eugene,OR: Lane County Historical Society, 1960.

Ingalss, Eleazr Stillman. *Journal of a Trip to California by Overland Route Across the Plains in 1850-1.* Fairfield, WA: Ye Galleon Press, 1979.

Ingersoll, Chester. *Overland to California in 1847.* Fairfield, WA: Ye Galleon Press, 1970.

Karchner, Mary. "Mary Karchner, 1862," *West from Salt Lake: Diaries from the Central Overland Trail,* Norman: The Arthur H. Clark Company. Ed. Jesse Petersen, 2012, pp. 137-146.

Kerns, John T. *"Journal of Crossing the Plains to Oregon in 1852."* Transactions, OPA, 1914, pp. 148-193.

Leinhard, Heinrich. *From St.Louis to Sutter's Fort, 1846.* Edited by Erwin & Elizabeth Gudde. Norman: university of Oklahoma Press, 1961.

Leeper, David R. *The Argonauts of 'Forty-Nine, Some Recollections of the Plains and the Diggings,* Columbus, OH: Long's College Book Co., 1950. [Reprint of 1894 book]

Mathews, Edward J. "Edward James Mathews, 1859," *West from Salt Lake: Diaries from the Central Overland Trail.* Norman: The Arthur H. Clark Company. Ed. Jesse Petersen. 2012. pp. 65-77.

McAuley, Eliza Ann. "Iowa to the Land of Gold," *Covered Wagon Women: Diaries and Letters from the*

Western Trails, 1840-1890. Vol.IV, 1852, pp. 33-81.-Ed. Kenneth L. Holmes. Glendale, CA: The Arthur H. Clark Company, 1985.

McKinstry, Byron N. *The California Gold Rush Diary of Byron N. McKinstry.* Edited by Bruce L. McKinstry. Glendale, CA: The Arthur H. Clark Co, 1975.

Marcy, Randolph B. *The Prairie Traveler. A Handbook for Overland Expeditons.* NY: Harper & Bros., 1859.

Mumford, Violet Coe & The Royal Family Association, Inc. *The Royal Way West, Vol. II, Crossing the Plains, 1853.* Baltimore: Gateway Press, Inc. 1988.

Murphy, Virginia Reed. *Across the Plains in the Donner Party: a personal narrative of the overland trip to California, 1846-47.* Golden, CO: Outbooks. 1980 [re-print of 1891 article in *Century.*]

Paden, Irene. "The Ira J. Willis guide to the Gold Mines." *California Historical Society Quarterly,* XXXII. 1953, pp. 193-207.

Page, Elizabeth. *Wagons West.* NY: Farra & Reinhart, Inc. 1930. (Diary & Letters of Henry Page, 1849.)

Parkman, Francis, Jr. *The California and Oregon Trail.* NY: William L. Allison Co. 18—(1849).

Parsons, Lucena, "An Overland Honeymoon," *Covered Wagon Women: Diaries and Letters from the Western Trails, 1840-1890. Vol.II, 1850,* pp. 237-94.-Ed. Kenneth L. Holmes. Glendale, CA: The Arthur H. Clark Company, 1983.

Petersen, Jesse G. *West from Salt Lake: Diaries from the Central Overland Trail.* Norman: The Arthur H. Clark Company. 2012.

Piercy, Frederick. *Route from Liverpool to Great Salt Lake Valley,* Edited by Fawn M. Brodie. Cambridge: The Belknap Press of Harvard University Press, 1962.

Pleasants, William. *Twice Across the Plains—1849 & 1856.* Fairfield, WA: Ye Galleon Press, 1981.

Reading, P.B. "Journal of Pierson Barton Reading." *Society of California Pioneers Quarterly.* Vol. 6, 1930, pp. 148-198.

Sawyer, Francis. "Kentucky to California by Carriage and a Feather Bed," *Covered Wagon Women: Diaries and Letters from the Western Trails,*

1840-1890. Vol.IV 1852, pp. 83-115 .-Ed. Kenneth L. Holmes. Glendale, CA: The Arthur H. Clark Company, 1985.

Shively, JM. *Route and Distances to Oregon and California*. WA: W. Greer, Printer 1846.

Smith, Azariah. *The Gold Discovery Journal of Azariah Smith*. Edited by David L. Bigler. Salt Lake City: University of Utah Press, 1990.

Smith CW. *Journal of a Trip to California—Across the Continent from Weston, Missouri to Weber Creek, California in the Summer of 1850*. Edited by RWG Vail. Fairfield, WA: Ye Galleon Press, 1974.

Snyder, Jacob R. "The Diary of Jacob R. Synder —1845." *Society of California Pioneers Quarterly*. Vol. 8, 1931, pp. 224-260.

Stansbury, Howard. *An Expedition to the Valley of the Great Salt Lake*. Philadelphia: Lippincott, Grambo, and Co., 1852.

Street, Frank. *Concise Description of the Overland Route*. Cincinnati: RF Edwards & Co., 1851.

Tracy, Albert. "Journal of Captain Albert Tracy." *Utah State Historical Society Quarterly*. Vol.XIII, Nos. 1, 2, 3, 4. 1945. pp. 84-117.

Ware, Joseph. *The Emigrants' Guide to California*. St Louis: J. Halsall, 1849.

Wilkins, James F. *An Artist on the Overland Trail. The Diary of James F. Wilkins, 1849*. Edited by James McDermott. San Marino: The Huntington Library, 1968.

Velina A. Williams. "Diary of a Trip Across the Plains in 1853." Transactions, O.P.A. 1919, 178-226.

Willis, Ira J. "Best Guide to the Gold Mines, 816 Miles." Great Salt Lake City, 1849.

Woodworth, James. *Diary of James Woodworth across the Plains to California in 1853*. Eugene, OR Lane County Historical Society, 1972.

Pamphlets

"California National Historic Trail," National Park Service, Washington, DC.

"Chimney Rock," National Park Service, Washington, DC, 1974.

'The Donner Party," Donner Memorial State Park, Department of Parks & Recreation, Sacramento, 1977.

"Fort Bridger," Wyoming Recreation Department, State Archives & Historical Department.

"Fort Caspar Museum," Casper, WY.

"Fort Churchill," Nevada Division of State Parks, Nevada Magazine.

"Fort Kearny," Nebraska State Historical Society, Ed. Leaflet No. 7.

"Fort Laramie," National Park Service, Washington, DC.

"Hollenberg Pony Express Station," Kansas State Historical Society, Topeka, KS.

"Marshall Gold Discovery State Historic Park," Department of Parks and Recreation, Sacramento, CA.

"Mormon Station," Nevada Division of State Parks, Nevada Magazine, 1979.

"The Oregon Trail," National Park Service, Washington, DC.

"The Oregon Trail," Nebraska Game and Parks Commission.

"Rock Creek Station," Nebraska Game and Parks Commission.

"Route of the Oregon Trail in Idaho," Idaho Historical Society Bicentennial Commission and the Idaho Transportation Department, 1974.

"Salt Lake Sites," Salt Lake Convention & Visitors Bureau, Salt Lake City, UT.

"Scotts Bluff," National Park Service, Washington, DC, 1978.

"Self-guided Tour of Fort Leavenworth, the Gateway to the West." Fort Leavenworth Historical Society, Fort Leavenworth, KS, 1982.

"Weston, Queen of the Steamboat Days, Old Homes Tour." The Weston Historical Museum, 1972.

The Author

His address may be in the East, but his heart is in the West.

William E. Hill has been traveling west during the summers for most of his life. Part of his family roots took hold in Kansas after the Civil War. His family frequently visited and vacationed in the West when Bill was young. He never got it out of his system.

Bill received his BA in History from the University of Minnesota, his MS in Education and a CAS in Administration from Hofstra University. He is a charter life member and former director of the Oregon–California Trails Association, a life member of the Santa Fe Trail Association, a member of the Lewis and Clark Trail Heritage Foundation, the National Pony Express Association and a life member of the Kansas, Nebraska and Wyoming historical societies. He is a retired teacher and lives in Centereach, New York, with his wife Jan.

Index

339

For a free catalog of Caxton titles write to:

CAXTON PRESS
312 Main Street
Caldwell, Idaho 83605-3299

or

Visit our Internet web site:

www.caxtonpress.com

Caxton Press is a division of THE CAXTON PRINTERS, Ltd.

CPSIA information can be obtained
at www.ICGtesting.com
Printed in the USA
BVOW11s0927080517
483295BV00003B/3/P